Dangerous Ambition

Dangerous Ambition

THE MAKING OF ÉAMON DE VALERA

COLUM KENNY

EASTWOOD BOOKS

First published 2024 by Eastwood Books

Dublin, Ireland
www.eastwoodbooks.com
www.wordwellbooks.com

First edition

Eastwood Books is an imprint of the Wordwell Group

Eastwood Books
The Wordwell Group
Unit 9, 78 Furze Road
Sandyford
Dublin, Ireland

ISBN: 978-1-916742-60-4 (Paperback)
ISBN:978-1-916742-72-7 (epub)

British Library Cataloguing in Publication Data.
A catalogue record for this book is available from the National
Library of Ireland and the British Library.

Copyediting by Heidi Houlihan
Layout and design by Wordwell
Printed in Ireland by Sprint Books

Front cover illustration: Éamon de Valera, by John Lavery, July 1921.
Exhibited at the Autumn Salon, Paris, 1921.
By kind permission Collection & Image © Hugh Lane Gallery.

*Praise is our most terrible enemy. It excites in us ambition,
a thing not sinful in itself but highly dangerous to one
that wishes to be a man of God.*

Éamon de Valera (aged nineteen) to his half-brother
Tom Wheelwright (aged eleven), 1902

———————————————————————

*I am in blood
Stepped in so far that, should I wade no more,
Returning were as tedious as go o'er:*

Macbeth (William Shakespeare),
quoted in a private notebook of Éamon de Valera

CONTENTS

– 1 –

'HERE GOES'

'A' IS FOR AMBITION

'A is for APE who has four clever hands, he lives in the woods in the tropical lands.' It was nearly eighty years since Éamon de Valera (1882–1975) had received an alphabet book from his mother who lived in New York. Yet, when president of Ireland in 1966, he could still recall much of its text and he recited some of it aloud from memory.[1]

'A' is for 'ambition' too. Eddie de Valera – as he was called for almost thirty years before he adopted an Irish form of his first name – developed his earliest ambitions in one of those dwelling houses in the Irish countryside known as 'labourers' cottages'. He lived there with an unmarried uncle, and with a grandmother who died when he was thirteen. Eddie long wished to return to his mother in America; to know who his father and his father's father had been; to escape from rural Limerick as soon as possible; to rise above his social station in life. He later wanted to win rugby matches, to keep open the option of becoming a priest, to become an inspector of schools or an engineer or an assistant examiner of patents and then, above all, to be a university professor of mathematics. Until he reached his fourth decade of life he had no evident political ambitions, although he shared a general nationalist desire for Ireland to be more independent of Britain.

Nobody could have guessed what fate held in store for him. There was to be, in his thirties, a dramatic transfiguration – a metamorphosis from aspiring academic to audacious rebel, and then from survivor and symbol of a revolution to peripheral participant in a civil war that he

1

helped to provoke. Finally, somehow, from 1926 he mustered his 'soldiers of destiny' (or '*fianna fáil*') and led them into a promised land of political power as a potent party of that Irish name. How it got to that point and who he was before 1926 are the themes of this book. The account is based on facts as we know them, rather than on amateur psychoanalysis or on speculation about his manipulative skills. In the end destiny did for de Valera quite kindly when compared to how some others fared who were part of the 'Irish revolution'. Too many fell by the wayside or died bitter.

In 1917 de Valera described his appearance on the political stage that year as 'a monument to the brave dead' of the 1916 Rising.[2] But monuments do not erect themselves, and his own reshaping from maths teacher to republican hero had been the work of militants. He was to side with them in the coming civil war, surviving many who died while regretting his decision to repudiate the new Irish parliament as 'foolish'. Only afterwards did de Valera break away and create his own political party, coming to enjoy a long and highly successful constitutional career. If one were to describe his earlier decades in the near blasphemous way that the Easter Rising of 1916 is sometimes depicted – as a kind of blood-sacrifice or death and resurrection comparable to that of Christ, one could say that Eddie, like Jesus, had a hidden life of thirty years before emerging to embrace his destiny. It might seem to some that he got ahead 'as if by magic' – in the words of a contemporary admirer– but he actually did so by design and determination.[3]

Eddie's mother in Manhattan dispatched him to her family's home in Ireland when he was just two and a half years old. Without a partner, she could not cope with both rearing a child and working outside her home at the same time. Her son, when later prime minister of an independent state, ensured that the Irish constitution he shepherded into law in 1937 declared in Article 41.2 that 'by her life within the home, woman gives to the State a support without which the common good cannot be achieved'; and further that 'the State shall, therefore, endeavour to ensure that mothers shall not be obliged by economic necessity to engage in labour to the neglect of their duties in the home'. De Valera clearly had personal reasons for thinking such provisions desirable. In 2024 Irish voters heavily rejected a proposal to delete them from the constitution, notwithstanding persistent suspicions that Dev himself was fundamentally sexist.[4]

Eddie's life might have been very different had paths he first wished to walk opened to him. But destiny, or chance, intervened. He stumbled out of his private life into a very public rebellion, from which he emerged later to become the symbol of an absolute republican ideal. What brought him to a point where he chose to die in 1916, confident that he would not see his wife and young children again? Nothing in the first three decades of his life before then indicated that such a wild course of action was likely. He played hurling and rugby, pursued a middle-class career as a teacher and academic, married an older woman and learnt to speak the Irish language moderately well. He might have lived all his days quietly with his family. Even by his own reckoning Éamon de Valera's active political life did not begin until 1913 when, aged thirty-one, he joined the nationalist militia known as the Irish Volunteers.

Had Eddie/Éamon had his own way he would not even have been in Ireland at the time of the 1916 Rising. Into his teenage years he longed to go back to America, to live in the land of his birth. He even contemplated the possibility of taking a job in a bank there. His mother, who resided in New York State, did not facilitate his return. She hoped that he would become a priest one day. He himself repeatedly expressed an interest in doing so, as did many other young Irish Catholics then – at least vaguely. Such an ambition could serve as a career path or psychologically as a cushion, a notional alternative in case one did not find a satisfactory secular job or enter into a long-term sexual relationship for example. However, while his mother pressed him to realise his idea of a vocation, the priests to whom he spoke appear not to have done so. Why they did not do so is unknown, although his social class and the absence of documentary evidence that his father married his mother before dying or deserting her may have been factors. In his early twenties Eddie finally abandoned the idea of becoming a priest, although he was to remain firmly committed to the dogma and institution of the Catholic Church and to be buried in the robes of a religious order.

He might have stayed a life-long labourer in Co. Limerick, where his uncle had him from early youth shouldering the burden of agricultural work. Uncle Pat conceded that Eddie should be employed part-time as a teaching assistant ('monitor') in the local national school but he was not eager for him to pursue further education. Eddie had other ideas. He felt trapped in Bruree and was determined to get out. Already a citizen of the United States by birth, he even daydreamed of being a Native American. Remarkably, as will be seen, he fulfilled that ambition in a way.

Eddie displayed ability and determination by winning 'exhibitions' (scholarships) that allowed him, thanks also to a chance meeting, first to attend Blackrock College in Dublin and then to pass examinations for the Royal University of Ireland. He ultimately graduated from the latter and went on to enrol as a student at Trinity College Dublin. Very few boys from the labouring class made it that far in those days.

Eddie thought about going to England to become an engineer. Instead, he remained in Ireland and built on his abilities as a mathematician. He became a teacher, mainly working at a teacher-training college in Co. Dublin as its 'professor of mathematics', but also attending post-graduate courses in the hope of advancing to a job in a university. He saw the teaching of mathematics as open to him whether or not he was to become a priest, for the Catholic Church in Ireland was then actively expanding its educational infrastructure in order to create greater opportunities for the majority of the Irish population that was Catholic. Many of its priests were to teach in new schools and colleges acceptable to Church authorities. At one point he applied for the position of state schools' inspector but was unsuccessful. He was no wild revolutionary.

Eddie undoubtedly had a bent for mathematics, and solicited favourable references from some leading mathematicians in Ireland whose courses he attended. But he was no outstanding mathematical genius as is sometimes thought. His applications for a professorship in the university colleges of Galway and Cork ended in disappointment. Those who got the jobs were better qualified. Ironically, within a decade he himself was to become lifelong chancellor of the National University of Ireland (NUI), due to his rapid political rise in the interim. Three of his children (Máirín, Ruaidhrí and Éamon) and his son-in-law, Brian Ó Cuív, became full professors at NUI colleges while he was chancellor there.

By the time he turned thirty in 1912 it looked likely that he would have to settle permanently for the less exalted status of 'professor' at a teacher-training establishment in the Dublin suburbs rather than become a full professor at a university. He was also rebuffed when he tried to play a leading role in the Gaelic League, and he blamed Sinn Féin for this when in fact he had fallen victim to a conspiracy of the Irish Republican Brotherhood (IRB) which wished to control the Gaelic League. De Valera had never displayed any great interest in Sinn Féin before 1917, and he was slow to join the IRB itself even when it was urged on him by those preparing the rebellion of 1916. If and insofar as he was a nationalist before the age of thirty he was so in the casual way of many Irish Catholics who supported the Irish parliamentary party at Westminster and who were growing frustrated by the failure of the United Kingdom government to deliver some level of 'Home Rule' to all Ireland, as long promised. Whilst Eddie set his heart on learning to speak Irish fluently – encouraged by his new wife who was an enthusiast for it – this was principally a cultural rather than a political pursuit. His membership of the Gaelic League also enhanced his career prospects in a changing Ireland. However, from 1913 he devoted most of his part-time energies to the Irish Volunteers.

Consideration of the lost careers of Eddie de Valera – as an American bank official, farm labourer, priest, engineer, schools' inspector, examiner of patents or university professor of mathematics – throws into sharp relief his decision in late 1913 to play an enthusiastic role in the new Irish Volunteers. Even as his younger half-brother Thomas, a child of Eddie's mother and her English-born husband, became a priest in America in 1916, Eddie chose that same year to sacrifice himself and his family on the very weekend that commemorates Christ's death on the cross and resurrection. Not a prominent leader of the Easter Rising, de Valera was nonetheless one of its senior commandants and his survival when others were then executed was by no means predictable – notwithstanding his US citizenship. From that survival flowed new ambitions that were successful, first to be president of Sinn Féin and later to be prime minister and president of Ireland. From it flowed too his ambition to force a newly elected Irish government to abandon the Anglo-Irish Treaty or be defeated in a civil war in 1922. Ultimately his side lost the war and this might have spelt the end of his career. But he was to reinvent himself again, this time as a constitutional politician who in 1926 founded the Fianna Fáil Party that was to sustain his prominence in Irish life for half a century.

A cousin of Eddie – a daughter of Uncle Ed who brought him to Ireland in 1885 – much later wrote of de Valera that 'He seems utterly without personal ambition. For many years he was in a sense a dictator of Ireland – a dictator with a little "d" who has avoided the folly of personal power.' However, he was clearly driven by personal ambition both before and after 1916.[5] And ambition, as he himself warned his younger half-brother in 1902, might not be sinful in itself but it could be 'highly dangerous'.

IF DEV HAD DIED IN 1916

Writing on 4 May 1916 to Michael Ryan, an Irish international rugby player and personal friend since his own days playing rugby at Blackrock and Rockwell colleges, Éamon de Valera bid the man farewell:

> Just a line to say I played my last match last week and lost. Tomorrow I am to be shot so pray for me, an old sport who unselfishly played the game.[6]

Had de Valera been executed after the Easter Rising that year, who would have remembered him? Certainly his pregnant wife and children whom he left in the lurch by quitting his job to join a minority of the Irish Volunteers in rebellion, while other men joined the British Army to fight Germany. He believed armed revolt was desirable or necessary in 1916. The public soon forgot the names of many who died then, whether combatants or civilian casualties – and many were indeed civilians, the usual 'collateral damage' of warfare.

De Valera was surely playing no 'game' – his curious metaphor has a ring of the playing fields of imperial Eton about it rather than the accent of rural Limerick. Nor was he being purely 'unselfish'. He had 'sacrificed' his family and not just himself, as he would explicitly admit a year later. Sinéad's family was in no state financially or physically to take care of his 'poor wife' and their 'little' children, whom 'I leave unprovided for behind' – as he appears to have written in a farewell letter to Mother Gonzaga of Carysfort College when he expected to be executed in 1916.[7]

As it turned out he was not among the rebels executed that year. He was the most senior commandant to survive, but the British deemed him relatively insignificant. Before joining the Volunteers, he had played virtually no role in any political movement – and had at least once publicly voiced his approval of constitutional monarchy relative to republicanism.[8] He was also not a leading light in the cultural revival and cut an odd figure as a soldier. In his battalion area in 1916 he was absent from the main engagement at Mount Street Bridge. He was unknown to the general public before the Easter Rising that year, and first known afterwards because of it. He came to serve as a figurehead or symbol of militant republicanism – as much its creature as its creator.

A FABLE AGREED UPON

When asked in 1966 to name the books that he liked reading as a youth, de Valera recalled just a few titles. They included a popular account of the life of Napoleon Bonaparte, written by John S.C. Abbott, an American historian and pastor who was said to 'revere' and 'love' the former French emperor.[9] De Valera remarked that it was a very big book but that he eventually got through it as a boy while minding cattle on a hillside near Bruree.[10] The influence of Napoleon on those who supported the 1916 Rising generally has been considered elsewhere.[11]

De Valera shared a sceptical view of history that has been explicitly attributed to Napoleon. In the course of a memorandum he dictated on 11 September 1922, he stated that he had been 'asked by several recently to write my memoirs [sic]'. During the previous month Arthur Griffith had collapsed and died under the pressure of civil war, and Michael Collins had been among those killed in fighting. On notepaper of the Irish Republican Army, De Valera's views were typed out under the heading 'MEMOIRS':

I suppose it is because sudden death is around that they are so anxious about the matter. It does look indeed as if most of the actors who occupied the stage in the political life of the country for the past five or six years are likely to go down in this struggle. Few who can speak with intimate knowledge and with authority may be left. So in order that the history of the 'four glorious years' may not come to be a 'fable agreed upon' here goes. But where shall I begin?[12]

'Here goes'. Under this declaration de Valera set out a schedule of principle events or moments in his life, as he saw them. He did not identify the source of the definition of history as 'a fable agreed upon'. But the count de Las Casas (also given as 'Las Cases'), who accompanied Napoleon in exile to the remote island of St Helena in 1816, had attributed it to the former emperor. The original French phrase has also been translated as 'a concerted fable'. The word 'concerted' may insinuate a higher degree of deliberate or even dishonest intent than the word 'agreed', but neither necessarily denotes objectivity.[13] De Valera used the same expression once again in a draft of a preface he was invited to write for Dorothy Macardle's *History of the Irish Republic*, published in 1937. Macardle prepared her book with his encouragement and cooperation. In his preface and her foreword each stated that they were not in agreement on all points in the book but yet he praised it and promoted new editions. Appointed director of publicity for Fianna Fáil in the 1920s, Macardle saw him as a friend whom she addressed in correspondence as 'Dear Chief', being described later by the historian Joe Lee as his 'hagiographer royal'. For some reason De Valera's reference to 'the proverbial fable agreed upon' was omitted from his preface as printed when her book was published in 1937.[14] Was it feared that he might be thought to lack due democratic humility by bracketing his own views with those of a French emperor, an emperor whom – as shall be seen – Eddie lauded in a debate when at Blackrock College? He supported there the motion that 'the rule of the first Napoleon [Bonaparte] was beneficial to France' and in doing so 'dwelt on the horrors of the revolution and showed how necessary a Napoleon was to save France from scenes of Anarchy'.[15]

It is worth laying out Napoleon's reported opinion on history, as evidently known to de Valera. Particular actions and words of the latter, not least during the Irish war of independence and civil war, have been understood in various ways that are difficult to reconcile:

'It must be admitted, my dear Las Casas,' said the Emperor, 'it is most difficult to obtain certainties for the purposes of history. Fortunately, it is, in general, more a matter of mere curiosity than of real importance. There are so many kinds of truths! The truth which [Joseph] Fouché, or other intriguers of his stamp, will tell, for instance – even that which many very honest people may tell, will, in some cases, differ essentially from the truth which I may relate. The truth of history, so much sought for, to which everybody eagerly appeals, is too often but an idle tale. At the time of the events, during the heat of conflicting passions, it cannot exist; and if, at a later period, all parties are agreed respecting it, it is because those persons who were interested in the events, those who might be able to contradict what is asserted, are no more … I have given an order, but who was able to read my thoughts, my real intentions? Yet everyone will take up that order, and measure it according to his own scale, or adapt it to his own plans or system … And then, memoirs are digested, memoranda are written, witticisms and anecdotes are circulated, and of such materials is history composed!'

'I have seen the plan of my own battle, the intention of my own orders disputed with me, and opinion decide against me! Is not that the creature giving the lie to its creator? Nevertheless, my opponent, who contradicts me, will have his adherents. This it is which has prevented me from writing my own private memoirs, from disclosing my individual feelings, which would naturally have exhibited the shades of my private character. I could not condescend to write confessions after the manner of Jean Jacques Rousseau, which everybody might have attacked, and, therefore, I have thought proper to confine the subjects of my dictations here to public acts. I am aware that even these relations may be contested, for where is the man in this world, whatever be his right, and the strength and power of that right, who may not be attacked and contradicted by an adverse party?'[16]

De Valera likewise never wrote his 'own private memoirs'. He has left us among his papers a sprinkling of recollections that are lacking in range and depth. Much of what we read about him comes from accounts which – like that of Napoleon by Las Casas – were written by admirers with whom he collaborated to varying degrees years after the events described. These included Frank Gallagher, Dorothy Macardle, the earl of Longford, T.P. O'Neill and Mannix Joyce. Longford co-wrote with O'Neill what was in effect an authorised biography of de Valera.[17] Decades earlier, as plain Frank Pakenham, Longford had also produced with de Valera's assistance a significantly flawed and yet even today highly influential account of the vital Anglo-Irish Treaty negotiations of 1921, sympathetic to de Valera. I have analysed this in detail elsewhere.[18]

When de Valera did sometimes speak of his youth in public, he did so most notably in anecdotes that highlighted his ostensible cleverness and humanity. This, as shall be seen, involved a kind of 'humble boasting' or self-serving modesty. De Valera's memorandum of September 1922, quoted above, indicates that he wished to see his own side of a story told and his careful cultivation of his reputation was a life-long habit. He did not wish himself to be the public storyteller.[19] That he outlived so many of his contemporaries gave him an advantage over them in terms of shaping the dominant narrative or 'fable agreed upon'.

Napoleon explained how the nature of the fable that is history deterred the former emperor from 'disclosing my individual feelings, which would naturally have exhibited the shades of my private character'. De Valera's own reluctance to speak much in interviews about personal matters may have an even more subjective root, given his uncertain ancestry, but it is frustrating for a modern biographer who wishes to understand him. Frank Gallagher, who was very close to him and who accompanied him on his trips to America in 1927–28 noted an exceptional occasion when de Valera 'in one of those few moments when he has spoken of his younger days – for in personal affairs he is the least communicative of men – has told of a running race…'[20] Gallagher

St Helena, 1816: *Napoleon Dictating to Count Las Cases the Account of His Campaigns*, by William Quiller Orchardson (1832–1910). Courtesy Lady Lever Art Gallery, Wirral.

'Dear Chief': Her friend Éamon de Valera receives from Dorothy Macardle a copy of a new edition of her *Irish Republic*. Courtesy UCD Archives P150/3663.

also referred to 'de Valera's abhorrence to [*sic*] any publicity on the religious side', which was an aspect of his identity that mattered very much to him.[21] In 1936 Desmond Ryan thought that de Valera had 'always frowned on or politely discouraged any attempt to write him up authoritatively'.[22] In 1955 the makers of a planned television interview with de Valera, for the US network NBC, noted that he would not talk about himself or his ideas.[23]

His ambitions were bound not only by conservative cultural and social norms but by a personal reserve that earned him the respect of many people. The tale of his life as he told it might have occasional picaresque moments that gave it some colour but was essentially that of a virtuous Celtic hero who did not need to explain himself, a Cú Chulainn persevering in the face of adversity to fulfil his destiny.

THE TINKER AND THE FAIRY

She swept him off his feet, and in little more than a year they were married. Within another twelve months she bore him the first of seven children. She cared for their offspring when he abandoned them to join a doomed rebellion. She believed she saved him from execution in 1916 by furnishing evidence that he was an American citizen. He emerged from jail in 1917, along with other interned rebels, while she was despatched with their children to a large house in the Burnaby – an exclusive housing development in the largely unionist village of Greystones about thirty miles (48km) from Dublin. This was her home until late 1922, after the Irish Civil War broke out. He spent much of his time elsewhere, in 'safe' houses in Dublin or, for eighteen months during the Irish War of Independence headquartered at the luxurious Waldorf-Astoria Hotel in Manhattan, the borough of his birth. When Michael Collins arranged for her to visit him in America it did not go as happily as she had hoped, and she regarded the trip as a mistake. There were unsubstantiated claims that her husband was having an affair. According to the *Dictionary of Irish Biography* she herself was 'rumoured to be pro-treaty' but 'made no public comment on politics'. In 1921 she gave what was said to be her first ever newspaper interview. This was to an American feminist, Doris Stevens, for the *Chicago Tribune*. Doris reported that Mrs de Valera 'launched into earnest praise' of Arthur Griffith and said 'I date my interest in Irish freedom from the time I was a very young girl and read the little Gaelic paper published by Mr. Griffith in Dublin. He it was also who inspired me to learn Gaelic.'[24] Members of the public commonly gossiped that she held the killing of Michael Collins against her husband.

Jane Flanagan was older than Eddie, as Josephine was older than Napoleon. For years before she met her labouring lad made good as a Blackrock past-pupil, Jane herself had a full life as a national school-teacher and amateur actor. One of her roles was as 'Red Hugh', in a play by the writer and political activist Alice Milligan, who also wrote a poem about her. An enthusiastic Celtic revivalist, Jane joined the Gaelic League in 1899 – almost a decade before de Valera did so – and adopted an Irish form of her name, Sinéad Ní Fhlannagáin. In 1900, with Arthur Griffith's sister and twenty-seven other women, she was one of the inau-gural members of *Inghinidhe na h–Éireann*, a pioneering movement of advanced nationalist Irish women.[25] She won medals for oratory at the Gaelic League's annual Oireachtas festival, and took to teaching Irish at the Gaelic League's Leinster College. One of her students there in 1908 was de Valera, newly interested in the Irish language which was then gaining importance as a qualification for those who wished to advance as a teacher or academic. Eddie started using an Irish form of his name, and also emulated her by attending and then running Irish language summer courses in the west of Ireland. They were soon married. Some of more than twenty certain letters that he wrote to her, long kept pri-vate, then stolen and recovered and now located somewhere unknown, indicated (as will be seen) the warmth of his erotic attachment to and fondness for her.

She was self-effacing when her acting attracted praise, notably in 1902 when she appeared in a well-attended private performance of *The Tinker and The Fairy* at the home of George Moore, novelist and cultural activ-ist. She and the play's author Douglas Hyde, a future president of Ireland, were the leading actors. It was the second time they appeared together

in one of his plays. On this occasion the select audience included lumi-
naries such as Kuno Meyer, Michael Davitt and W.B. Yeats. The weather
behaved very well and a puff of wind blew just at the time when she as
an old hag was to change into a fairy. She said Yeats told her 'You and
the wind were the success of the day'. The writer Mary Butler penned
a glowing review of her performance. With masses of 'long Titian hair'
that was the colour of gold, Jane was also said to be a dainty dancer. But
she was the daughter of a carpenter too and lacked the class confidence of
some fellow members of *Inghinidhe na h–Éireann*, not least its president
Maud Gonne. Sinéad later told one of her children that she was invited
by William Fay to join the Abbey Theatre company, but 'I didn't for I
would not feel at home in such high society.' George Moore also offered
to get her work on the stage.[26]

Sinéad passed up such opportunities that might have changed her life,
quitting her paid job and other activities when she married de Valera. It
was not easy to be his wife, especially in 1916 when he might have been
killed and was jailed. Yet her personal effacement was quite usual for
women of her day, and she seemed happy to support him emotionally.
She was no dupe or 'innocent' but, as Máirtín MacDhomhnáil described
her in late 1916, a 'co-partner' in her husband's 'patriotic designs'. At
least one of her sons did not doubt that she changed Eddie's life: 'after
all she could justly claim to have first awakened his interest in Ireland, its
language and its nationhood'.[27]

Two women defined de Valera. One was his mother Kate in America
who had sent him to Ireland and visited him there only twice, but kept in
touch by mail – many of their letters now lost too – and had wanted him
to be a priest. The other was Sinéad, who is not known to have dissented
strongly from any of his decisions (if she did so). Kate had been an ocean
away from him for nearly all his life. Sinéad was now always there, for
procreation and housework, personifying the ideal wife and mother of
de Valera's Ireland that he would enshrine in his 1937 Constitution. She
wrote loyally of missing him when he was away and was grateful that he
appreciated her domestic role. Around 1913, for example, she told his
mother Kate, whom she had never met:

Ed never makes any complaints about my housekeeping and he is ever so good at coming punctually to his meals and giving me as little trouble as possible. I only hope the children will be as good as he.[28]

At Christmas 1921, when de Valera, as president of Dáil Éireann, was embroiled in bitter debates about the proposed Anglo-Irish Treaty, Sinéad, at their home in Greystones, fretted about the fact that 'the maid here had and has a very sore finger and I had everything to see to. The rush of the Xmas was awful and for the once that Dev was at home with us the place was filthy and not too comfortable.'[29]

We do not know to what extent Sinéad influenced de Valera's decision to join the Irish Volunteers in 1913 or to pursue a political career from 1917, but by her clear dedication to and care for their children she facilitated his dangerous decisions to join both the rebels in 1916 and the anti-Treaty insurgents in 1922. Like that of other republicans, their home was subjected to periodic armed raids by forces of the Crown and later of the new Irish Free State.

De Valera's public life during this period was made possible by the fact that Sinéad abandoned her teaching career and acting to take care of their children. Later, as a writer of children's stories, she was to carve out a respected new career. The fact that her husband's lost letters to her were never part of the papers that he donated for public archiving raises the question of what other records of Sinéad herself may have been lost that could inform us of the extent of her influence on him. She supported him until her death in 1975, in the same year as his own, a century after she had been born. If he seemed to some citizens to be severe or miserable in public, she exuded by his side a certain benign warmth. Whatever about how different Irish history might have been had de Valera not 'gone out' in 1916, it may be only due to Sinéad's influence and support in the first place that he took the path to armed rebellion and later into politics. There is just one dedicated biography of this important woman, but her role should be borne in mind throughout.[30]

ACTS OF OBLIVION

The public career of Eddie de Valera did not begin until he was in his thirties. Before then he pursued no political ambitions – simply wishing to escape the life of a labourer in Co. Limerick, imagining himself first as a priest but then as a leading academic. He hunted with his rifle, played hurling and rugby, and studied mathematics. And he did a little charity work while attending Blackrock College.

At about the age of seventeen, de Valera himself wrote that 'In reading the biography of a celebrated man, there is no part in which we take such interest, as in the account of his youth. Some men's childhood [*sic*] are full of acts which foreshadow his future greatness; others in oblivion spend their first years.'[31] Did he believe that his early years were spent 'in oblivion', or did he regard some of the little stories that he repeated about his youthful self as 'acts which foreshadowed his future greatness'?

Although a first biography published in Dublin and London in 1922 was expressly entitled *Early Life of Eamonn* [sic] *de Valera*, it did not in fact dwell long on his three earliest decades. The author, a local Limerick man David Dwane, devoted just forty-five of his 236 pages to the period before 1916. That biography is, in any event, unsatisfactory – due to both its bias and its absence of clearly identified sources.[32] Wordsworth thought 'the child is father of the man', and the first three decades of Éamon de Valera's life are surely significant in trying to understand the most complex political figure of the twentieth century in Ireland.

The present book makes de Valera's early decades the main focus of attention. In 1962, aged eighty, he remarked 'I have often been asked to write the story of my life, or at least some memories. To do this with any thoroughness would require volumes, for it covers an active political life of practically fifty years. It may be said to have begun when I joined the Volunteers … on the day on which they were formed at a meeting at the Rotunda on November 25th 1913. This was the casting of the die.'[33] De Valera more than once 'cast the die' before he founded in 1926 his own political party Fianna Fáil (usually translated as 'Soldiers of Destiny'). The first occasion may indeed have been when he joined the Irish Volunteers, although many peaceful nationalists did that. Then in 1916 he and some other Volunteers challenged the British Empire by armed rebellion. In 1922 he fanned the flames of a civil war in Ireland for which many blamed him. In 1950 he recalled how, as he put it then, he had when younger 'crossed the Rubicon' (Chapter 6).[34] The well-known Rubicon idiom refers to Caesar sparking a civil war by traversing a stream of that name to approach Rome from Gaul without permission. Any account of de Valera's youth and destiny is pregnant with the question of what might have been – for himself and Ireland – had he realised his early ambitions instead of opting in his thirties to become a rebel.

There is scarcely a more divisive figure in recent Irish history. Many Irish families in the twentieth century had grandparents or parents who differed heatedly and radically from each other about him. In the *Dictionary of Irish Biography* he is described as 'the most controversial figure in the history of modern Ireland', whilst another respected authority has him as 'the most significant figure' in the political history of modern Ireland.[35] Yet, for the most part, when it comes to his youth the principal sources of information for historians are himself writing in his later life and people who were close to him.

As a boy myself, when I lived with my family on the North Circular Road in Dublin, I frequently saw Éamon de Valera pass by in the presidential state car, flanked by a few outriders on motorbikes. He was going to or from what was, between 1959 and 1973, his official residence in the Phoenix Park nearby. He cut a solitary figure as he sat bolt upright in the dark Rolls Royce. I occasionally waved. He sometimes seemed to respond by raising an arm, although by then his weak eyesight restricted his ability to see clearly. My mother respected him, in a way that she certainly did not respect some subsequent leaders of Fianna Fáil. Partly because of his personal history, his conventional Catholic devotion and his personal dignity, he established a link with many citizens that was as much a matter of empathy or identification as it was of politics. I have never shared the politics of his party but, not least due to my mother's influence on me, I would not wish to disrespect de Valera. In saying so, I am conscious that I am by no means the first author to have felt it advisable or necessary to make such a declaration. This fact itself says something about his unique character and status.

A MAN FROM MANHATTAN

START IN LIFE

Eddie was born in the year 1882, in the city of New York, though not of that country, his father reputedly being a foreigner of Spanish descent and of good family. His mother Kate said that his father had got a living first as an artist and sculptor, but a stone chip flew into his eye. So, leaving off that trade, his father lived afterwards by playing and teaching music in Manhattan. There he met Eddie's mother, whose family in Ireland was named Coll.

Eddie's father is said to have left Kate and their baby and gone west, reportedly dying soon afterwards. Unable to cope on her own with caring for the boy while at the same time having to make a living as a single mother, Kate sent Eddie to Ireland in 1885. There he lived with Kate's brother Pat and her widowed mother, near the village of Bruree in Co. Limerick. This was his destiny, although in truth one cannot say that he embraced it happily.

Eddie's grandmother and his Uncle Pat dwelt in a small rural cottage. Pat himself was a labourer as Pat's own father had also been, and he now reared Eddie to work hard. There was scarcely an operation on the land that the youngster had not to perform.

Eddie later said that what he liked best when a boy was to go and play in the stream: 'I had an island in it. I could get away from everybody. I used to play Robinson Crusoe there … What I liked best was playing Robinson Crusoe.'[1]

Robinson Crusoe, first published in 1719 and often republished, was one of the earliest novels in the English language. It is the tale of the only survivor of a shipwreck who is washed up alone on an uninhabited island, and of the dangers he encounters there for years. An adventure story, it is also a 'wide-ranging reflection on ambition, self-reliance, civilization and power'.[2] Ironically, given Eddie's enjoyment of the novel, its author Daniel Defoe was no friend of Ireland or of the Irish.[3]

Eddie's mother married Charles Wheelwright in 1888 in America. Eddie's 'Uncle Charlie' was an English Protestant immigrant there and made his living as a coachman and servant. Kate and Charlie had two children, a daughter and her second son. The family settled in Rochester, New York. She never yielded to Eddie's pleas as a child or boy to allow him to rejoin her in America. She returned to Ireland only twice, on short visits in 1888 and 1907.[4] He once wrote to her that 'Every time I hear others talking of their mothers I feel more or less an orphan.'[5]

Eddie's friend Frank Gallagher met Kate in the 1920s and told his own wife that Kate used to end stories of what she and Wheelwright did in the past with the declaration 'Charlie was a real sport always.'[6] Yet what Charles did in America before 1888 and how he met Kate are unknown.

In his thirties, Eddie said that when he was a boy he had also read about and understood the slavery of Native Americans and longed to become one of them (Chapter 7 below). 'And yet, though I dreamed a great deal, I had no ambitions or expectations. I had nothing but the spade,' he added.[7] Not at first anyway.

PREGNANT IN NEW YORK

On 9 January 1882 Oscar Wilde stepped onto a stage at the corner of Fifth Avenue and 18th Street, and blushed. The Irish writer's fashionable audience filled every seat in Chickering Hall.[8]

Elsewhere in New York, early that same year, Kate Coll conceived a baby. A 'corrected certificate and record' of birth, issued in 1916 for that child, would give Kate's address in October 1882 as 61 East 41st Street. It 'corrected' the child's father's name to 'Vivion de Valera' (below).

Down on the corner of Fifth Avenue Wilde got into his stride. The *New York Times* described him next day as 'the young English versifier and aesthete'. It reported that 'many representatives of families conspicuous in the fashionable world' had come to hear him talk. It was, the journalist noted, Wilde's first appearance on any stage and his blushes when making his entrance were news. He reddened again ('like a schoolgirl') when exiting to vigorous applause. Wilde had arrived in New York harbour from Europe just one week earlier. People would later say that he had told customs' officials as he disembarked that he had nothing to declare but his genius. His tour of America was managed by the D'Oyly Carte company and during it he would also be promoting *Patience*, a new light opera by Gilbert and Sullivan; they too were clients of D'Oyly Carte.[9]

If Kate Coll from Bruree had gone to Chickering Hall, if she could have afforded even a standing-room ticket, she might have felt very out of place: a housemaid among patrons arriving in horse-drawn coaches to see Oscar Wilde. Many fine ladies were present 'in rich costumes'. They levelled their opera glasses at Wilde. Several Protestant clergymen and a Catholic priest 'had choice seats'. There was much giggling and tittering among the audience before it settled down. Wilde rattled off a litany of writers and designers whose work he thought constituted an 'artistic renaissance in England'. He told his audience that 'a noble national life' was the prerequisite of great national theatre and that 'there can be no great sculpture without a beautiful national life'. It is not known if Vivion de Valera, who would soon be registered as Eddie's father, had strong views on aesthetics. Vivion's own career as a sculptor was said have ended earlier, not because of the want of 'a beautiful national life' in America but due to an eye injury. Kate once told Eddie that his father thereupon 'took to bookkeeping [keeping records of the financial dealings of a trader etc.] and later taught music after he married'.[10]

The *New York Times* had made a mistake by calling the Anglo-Irish Wilde 'English'. In St Paul, Minnesota, two months later – when Wilde spoke there impromptu on St Patrick's Day – nobody would have made

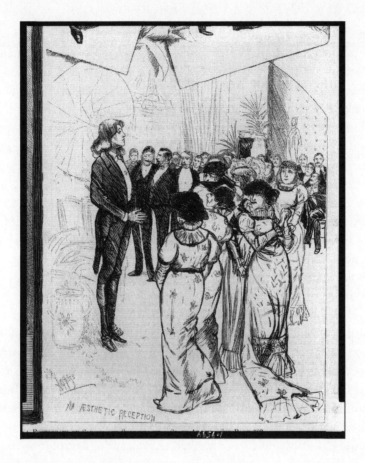

Oscar Wilde, 'An aesthetic reception in New York', from *Frank Leslie's Illustrated Newspaper*, 21 January 1882. Courtesy Library of Congress.

such an error. Wilde was then in the audience at a gathering of Irish immigrants, at the Opera House. That night on stage Fr John Shanley praised Lady Jane Wilde (alias 'Speranza'), who was Oscar's mother. The priest, a future bishop of Fargo, spoke highly of her writings on Irish folklore and other topics. These, he said, 'did much to keep the fire of patriotism burning brightly in the hearts of Ireland's sons'. Wilde's mother had used her art powerfully to condemn as 'murderers' those who reduced Ireland to the point at which, in the 1840s, the Great Famine ravaged her country's population, driving a million people to an early grave and over a million more to emigrate.[11] Ireland thereafter remained blighted by emigration, as Kate Coll knew well from her personal experience. Oscar Wilde, invited by Fr Shanley to address the Minnesota audience, condemned in particular the damage done to Ireland's cultural development by the English. The *Daily Globe* reported him saying 'When Ireland gains her independence, its schools of art and other educational branches will be revived and Ireland will regain the proud position she once held among the nations of Europe.'[12]

By September 1882 Wilde was back in New York. His tour of the United States and Canada had already taken him to scores of venues. By the time it ended later that year he would have addressed more than 140 audiences. And Kate Coll would have a newborn son.

In September 1882 Kate was surely concerned. She was just another pregnant immigrant maid, a 'Bridget' or 'Biddy' as they were known. The baby's father had already left her once. He said the city was bad for his health. Would he go again? She felt the baby kick. Like Oscar Wilde, her son too would one day embark on a great tour of the United States, his speeches as Éamon de Valera applauded by large and admiring audiences. His theme would be Irish politics, not English aesthetics. But in the autumn of 1882 the future of that child in her womb was uncertain.

Kate made her way ten blocks north and two west from where she lived on 41st Street, until she reached the corner of Lexington Avenue and 51st Street. There stood the Nursery and Child's Hospital. By the standards of Manhattan, it was not a particularly large building. But to a girl reared in rural Ireland it may have seemed daunting. Four storeys high and eight windows wide, with a range of annexes behind it, the hospital was a refuge for poor pregnant women and for abandoned children. Perhaps it reminded her of the four-storey corn mill in the village of Bruree, near where she grew up in the Irish countryside. The Irish Catholic woman had decided to apply for admission to the American Protestant institution in Manhattan. She wanted herself and her baby to survive.

As its contemporary annual reports indicate, a prerequisite for entry then to the Nursery and Child's Hospital in Manhattan was a 'certificate

De Valera's birthplace in 1882: the Nursery and Child's Hospital on Lexington Avenue, Manhattan. From its *Annual Report.*

Broadway at Morris Street, Manhatten, in 1882. Includes poles erected to carry lines of the recently invented telephone network. Courtesy Irma and Paul Milstein Division of US History, The New York Public Library Digital Collections.

Kate and Eddie's New York: Fifth Avenue at 42nd Street, Manhattan, 1885. The boundary of the Croton Distributing Reservoir is visible left. Courtesy Library of Congress.

of former good character'. One 'Mrs Abraham [*sic*]' provided a reference for Kate. A patient on entry must also be clean and free from all contagious diseases. Every woman must bring sufficient clothing for her own use, and provide for her infant twelve diapers. If a pregnant woman could afford to pay $25 for her board at the hospital while she stayed there then she could leave the place as soon after the birth of her own child as the physician deemed prudent. But if she was unable to pay then she must give her service there for three months, nursing and feeding two infants unless medically unfit to do so.

If Kate ever gave a detailed account of her experiences and feelings in New York it does not appear to survive. What little is recorded of what she said about her life then, by her son and others, is sparse and even contradictory. We do not have reliable details of her employment or whereabouts, let alone more personal matters. Éamon de Valera later stated that his mother had told him that she was born in 1858 and before emigrating had worked for local farmers near her home in Co. Limerick when she was aged sixteen – 'first at Pat Herlihy's, later at Will Walsh's (Terret) and also Regan's, Ballinaught [Bruree]', and also at Horgan's of Mount Russell. De Valera said later that big farmers might have two boys and two girls employed. The Mortells, close neighbours of the Colls, had one boy and two girls usually, with extra help at harvest and sowing time: 'The home help [maids] generally were Kerry girls. They left for home for Christmas and did not come back until about the end of January. The nearest hire fair was Charleville (Rathluirc), but people around Bruree did not usually get their help at the fair.' Kate stopped working for local farmers and later told her son Eddie that she sailed for America on 21 September 1879, arriving there on 2 October. There is a record of an Irish woman named Kate Coll, aged twenty-two, disembarking at New York on 2 October. The US census of 1900 gives 1876 as the date of her arrival in the United States, although that of 1910 gives 1879. In either case, her father was dead before she sailed. If Kate was not in Ireland between 1879 and 1882 then later assertions that she may have been pregnant with Eddie in Limerick before emigrating were false. She is said to have brought with her to America the address of an aunt who lived at 145 Tillary Street in Brooklyn. This 'aunt' may have been married to 'Uncle Ned', a brother of Kate's mother said to have emigrated to the United States and about whom no more is known. Kate's first work was said to have been at Bennett's near Park Avenue, Brooklyn. There she got diphtheria. She is said to have worked subsequently at Giraud's on 'Gold St' and 'Myrtle Avenue' (both Brooklyn street-names). Thereafter, it appears, she was employed by people named Fisher at New Jersey, and later with the Armstrongs at Greenville, New Jersey.[13]

The US Census of 1880 does indeed record Kate, aged twenty-two, living in Brooklyn as a servant of the actor Francis Giraud (stage-name 'Frank Girard') and his family, at 98 Lawrence Street – just five minutes on foot from the junction of Gold Street and Myrtle Avenue. The Giraud household was closely connected to the world of entertainment.

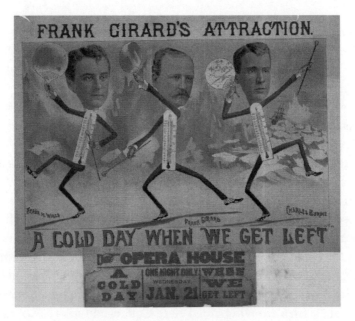

A poster from the 1880s showing Francis 'Girard' (centre), for whom de Valera's mother worked. Courtesy The Huntington Library.

Although perhaps French by descent, the US census does not support Éamon de Valera's statement that this was 'a French family' – for not only were the couple and all their children born in New York but so too, according to that census, were the parents of Francis and his wife.[14]

Giraud/Girard was a well-known player and stage presenter who began his career with Hooley's Minstrels in Brooklyn, but then enlisted in the navy during the American Civil War. In 1866, not long after that war ended, he was one of 500 passengers bound for New Orleans on a steamer wrecked about 300 miles (480km) off the coast of Florida. He is said to have been the only man who survived, and to have been on the water for five days before being rescued. He returned to New York, and became identified with some of the principal minstrel companies there. He subsequently acted as a stage manager and played in farces and other performances. In 1880 the census records him living with his wife Martha, their servant Catherine Coll, their son 'Edgar', their daughter Ella and Frank's sister Lilie who was aged twenty-four.[15] Their son was then seventeen and worked with a 'dry goods broker', but was later to manage the Gotham Theatre in Brooklyn. While working with this family or a little later Kate became pregnant.

Did Kate go directly by Lexington Avenue from where she lived on East 41st Street to admit herself to the Nursery and Child's Hospital? Or, wrapped in thought, did she perhaps first wander two blocks west to come to busy Fifth Avenue and 42nd Street, where Croton Distributing Reservoir rose behind its massive walls – the whole structure like some stunted Egyptian pyramid? That reservoir, like the Nursery and Child's Hospital itself, is long gone. One could take it easy ascending to the elevated walk on top of the walls, and get a view of the great volume of water that fed so much of the city. One could sit and have a rest there. Her bag no doubt felt heavier the further she walked, and her great size probably made her uncomfortable. From the vantage point of a quiet seat Kate could have gazed across the calm expanse of water and wondered if she was doing the right thing? What was the point of having this baby anyway? Why was she admitting herself to the care of Protestant ladies very different from herself and from the other Irish women she knew? She might slip into the reservoir when nobody was looking – hold her case tight, sink to the bottom, never emerge. If she was tempted to do so, she did not yield to that temptation.

The walk to the hospital was north from 41st or 42nd Street. There was a strong smell from many horses pulling carriages and carts through the great city. In her mind perhaps she longed for the green fields of County Limerick. In her ears she would have heard the rumbling of elevated railways, with their braking screech of metal wheels on tracks: 'You can scarcely form any idea of this last place unless you saw it, and even then it baffles description', one woman had written to a relative shortly after arriving from Ireland.[16] New York was booming, its grid of new streets pushing up and across the island as public and private enterprise rushed to supply services to central Manhattan. There was already electric street lighting on Broadway, and the Edison Illuminating Company had begun to provide electricity to private customers at a price competitive with that of gas suppliers. However, crime and alcoholism and prostitution were found in neighbourhoods all over the island. There was a book of advice for Irish women in America, a book published in 1872 and written by a nun who lived in Kenmare, Co. Kerry. Many tenants had emigrated from around Kenmare to Five Points in Manhattan. 'Mind I say,' the good nun warned, 'any girl who marries a man given to drink, deserves the life of misery which is certain to be hers afterwards ... No girl should ever meet young men at drinking-saloons, or go to such places. If you do not respect yourself, no one else will respect you. Take care on this. No good man will care to marry a girl whom he sees going to such places.'[17]

On admission as a patient, Kate informed the hospital authorities that they should register her baby's first name as 'George'.

DEV'S MOTHER AND CHILD HOME

In some years there was a high mortality rate at the Nursery and Child's Hospital, Manhattan. But Kate did not die giving birth there.

In 1854 a group of philanthropic Protestant ladies had set up in Manhattan the 'Nursery for the Children of Poor Women', –later the 'Nursery and Child's Hospital'. It was intended as a place where the children of wet nurses could be taken charge of, for no place was then provided to care for them 'and statistics showed fearful infant mortality'– as its secretary Adeline Townsend wrote in its published report for 1883. The institution also began to take in 'foundlings', babies or very young children whose own parents could not or would not care for them adequately. By 1859 it was providing basic paediatric and lying-in facilities for some poor pregnant women generally.[18]

The hospital's printed annual reports provide many insights into the place. Townsend wrote in her report for 1881 that 'It is a matter of statistics that children brought up with maternal nourishment thrive better and resist disease quicker than others; next [healthiest are those brought up] by a wet nurse, and those brought up by hand are feeblest.' The following year she noted claims that pauperism and crime were on the increase: 'The work of the "Nursery" stands unique in itself, as it cares for children of such a tender age, and for mothers, in most cases, so young and so unhappy.' She added, 'The cases are many and sad that are presented to the ladies on duty, to whom the cases for admission are referred, and too many are the times where admission has to be refused for want of a room.' She told the hospital board about instances of children brought from a home 'where the father had murdered the mother and the rest of the little ones. Babies found in a cellar wretched and hungry, crying for warmth and food over a dead mother's body. Then a father brings his infants to us worse than motherless, as the mother was a raving maniac.'[19]

Many of the foundlings were ill and weak. Of 275 children admitted to the Nursery and Child's Hospital in the year of de Valera's birth almost a quarter died. 'We have had babies just beginning to talk, call for whiskey', the directress wrote in 1883 for the hospital's Annual Report, adding that some destitute women made their children drink beer or liquor to stop the cries of hunger. Of 219 babies delivered to mothers in the Nursery and Child's Hospital that year, sixteen were still-born and forty-three died. Eleven women also died in childbirth. The hospital medical board's list of the causes of death was long and detailed. Not only were measles and whooping cough rampant, but the number of cases of septicaemia was rising again. There were also illnesses that were not fatal but that caused misery. In 1885 the founding directress Mary Du Bois looked back over her thirty years of work and remarked in the *Annual Report* on one peculiarity that plagued that institution:

> Wherever children are congregated, there is always danger of inflammation of the eyes. It was long before it was understood that it was caused not only by overcrowding, but that dampness from newly-scrubbed floors almost inevitably produced sore eyes among infants and children. Wherever the greatest cleanliness was observed, and spotless floors were seen, the more ophthalmic disease was manifested. A manager stopped on her way to the Nursery and ordered several rolls of carpeting to be sent, and no scrubbing to be done in that ward till further orders. The change was remarkable. No new cases appeared; and although carpeted floors are not desirable, our experience showed that damp floors, fumes of soap, and particles of wood loosened by scrubbing, however minute, were some of the causes of inflammation of the eyes. No child should be allowed to remain in a room damp from scrubbing.[20]

Yet this did not rid them of eye diseases, for in the following year it was reported that ophthalmia had been very prevalent at the hospital, although 'owing to close attention, it has caused a slight amount of injury to sight in one case only'. As a sanitary measure, sand was substituted for tan bark that had long been used on the grounds. The Medical Board decided that tan bark was a medium for the retention of compostable materials, 'besides being thought by some to intensify ophthalmic difficulty, with which so many of this class of children are afflicted'. Neonatal ophthalmia alone, contracted from a mother in the course of birth or otherwise, can have severe effects and even cause blindness. In many cases it is associated with a mother who has been infected with a sexually transmitted disease.

During his life Kate's son suffered from severe eye problems, for which he underwent specialist operations in Zurich and Utrecht.[21] One wonders if de Valera had eye troubles even at the outset of his life in Manhattan.

There were no distinctly Irish names among the many officers and managers of the Nursery and Child's Hospital listed in its annual reports then, but prosperous New York families were represented. Mrs Cornelius Vanderbilt was on the list, for example, as well as Mrs J.C. Fargo, wife of the president of American Express and sister-in-law of the founder of Wells Fargo. Its assistant secretary was Miss M.D. Van Winkle. On its advisory committee was Erasmus Brooks, editor and politician, who was no friend of the Irish or of Catholics. He backed the 'Know-Nothing' movement, hostile to immigrants from Ireland. One critic had publicly damned the hospital as a 'proselytising nursery trap'. Its founding directress, Mary Du Bois, a friend of Brooks, was still working there in 1882. An Evangelical religious reformer, she worried about poor working girls tempted by the flattery of 'fast' young men. Du Bois explained in an annual report how 'an idle word and a slight pleasantry at first amuses, then is expected, and the result of flattered vanity is ruin. They are turned out, disgraced, and driven by the horrors of remorse often to suicide.'

In 1882, the year de Valera was born there, the hospital cared for 483 adults and 653 children. The death rate among immigrant mothers and their impoverished children in Manhattan was alarming. Irish women formed a great band of such mothers, having poured into Manhattan in large numbers during the previous few decades. They sought regular work but in too many cases felt obliged to resort to prostitution to survive.[22]

The Manhattan ladies held gala charity balls to raise funds for what was the first infant asylum of its type in the USA. This stream of income, along with bequests, had been used not long before de Valera's birth to construct a new annex– 'so sadly needed' and completed in 1881. Donations of goods seem to have been sparse. In the autumn of 1882, when Kate's baby was born, the only gifts recorded were a crate of tomatoes and flowers from one woman, seventy new children's garments from a sewing circle in Connecticut, and reading materials and papers from four donors – including *The Story of the Bible* and twenty-four hymn books.

A rule had been introduced at one point requiring any woman to present a marriage certificate on admission, even if her husband had deserted her. How strictly that rule was enforced each year is unclear, but the ladies wished it to be known that they did not approve of unmarried women having babies and could not be relied upon to support repeat offenders. This was an incentive to applicants to declare that they were married.

Did Kate take another child to wet-nurse for three months along with her own? This might explain why de Valera was not baptised in a church for seven weeks after his birth, as his mother would have been very busy. As observed earlier, if a pregnant woman could not afford to pay $25 for her board at the Nursery and Child's Hospital she must agree to give her service for three months, nursing and feeding another infant as well as her own unless medically unfit to do so (two others if her own baby died).[23] Not long after the hospital opened, it had reported 'One great difficulty we labor under is the want of wet nurses. We keep twenty-five constantly. But women in the station they occupy are seldom found with the maternal instinct strong enough to induce them to remain and nurse their own infants, when they can obtain high wages and enjoy the luxurious life of a wet nurse in a private family.' Compared to London, there were comparatively few women in New York City's hinterland who were poor enough to need to nurse foundlings in order to earn an income. In the hospital's annual report for 1876 its secretary A.W. Van Rensselaer had explained that every year they found too few mothers available as good wet-nurses: 'We take women who, by their appearance, give good promise, but whether English, Irish, German, Swedes, or Americans, the fact remains, that there are very few good wet-nurses to be found in the class which our Institution seeks to benefit. Even with our extra diet and nourishing food we find it difficult to provide adequate nurses for the infants who are brought to us. But we do all that is possible.'

Provided that the conduct of any woman admitted was good during her stay at the hospital, the ladies of the institution might assist her to find work afterwards in 'a desirable situation as wet-nurse or otherwise'. In 1883 they found places and homes for sixty-nine women, and in some cases the women were able to take their children with them to their new homes. One American notice of Kate's death in 1932 stated that she had 'entered a training school for nurses in New York City' after she came to the USA. Éamon de Valera wrote that she worked as a nurse for a doctor in Manhattan at one point. In the 1910 US census she is described as a 'nurse'.[24]

Was Kate tempted at any point to leave little Eddie in the long-term care of the Nursery and Child's Hospital? Its annual reports indicate that such care involved much more than just minding children through illnesses and other conditions incidental to the first years: 'As soon as the little ones can understand, we vary their playtime by Kindergarten exercises. It's astonishing to see the progress made by their little minds awakening to new ideas. After four years, we find that country life is far more beneficial, with outdoor exercise combined with somewhat closer application to study.'[25] The hospital had a facility for this purpose outside the city. Kate might also have been urged to consider the possibility of adoption.

An ironic twist to the birth of Éamon de Valera, at first named 'George de Valero', in a Protestant charitable institution in New York, is that he later became the politician who dominated the evolution of the Irish nation state in the twentieth century – with its paraphernalia of Magdalene laundries, mother and baby homes and dubious birth records. He might have ensured a better environment for those like himself who longed for knowledge of their fathers and whose mothers found themselves at the mercy of others. The falsification of certain Irish birth records has left people unaware that they were adopted and has meant that some are unable to trace their family histories even if they discover the fact of their adoption. Indeed, one of de Valera's own sons, who was also named Éamon and who became a leading gynaecologist, facilitated unlawful Irish adoption schemes that involved putting pressure on single mothers to give up their babies.[26]

GOODBYE TO A GILDED AGE

Eddie de Valera spent the first two and a half years of his life in America. The growing prosperity of New York City encouraged a level of competitive philanthropy among the rich. They funded many charitable institutions, including the Nursery and Child's Hospital. The last decades of the nineteenth century were known as New York's 'gilded age', and the city boomed. It had already grown rapidly, pushing its grid of streets ever further north on the central island of Manhattan.

New York was lively and noisy, full of the sounds and smells of many nations. Its harbour was crowded, with vessels full of cargo bound for destinations across the expanding United States, and with ships of immigrants bound for Ellis Island to meet immigration officials. Rail tracks were elevated above Manhattan's busy avenues and streets. They carried train engines belching black clouds of smoke, the subways not yet having been dug. The boom brought great wealth for some people, and this was another magnet for immigrants who poured into New York. When in 2022 the American Home Box Office network made a television series about this era, its historical drama was premised on an incident in the very year of de Valera's birth, 1882, and it included a maid named Bridget – 'a decent and hard-working immigrant girl from Ireland who has come to America to build a new future, though she has low expectations of life because of a troubled and abusive past'.[27] However, the boom was interrupted by a significant downturn or depression from 1882 to 1885. The year 1884 was particularly fraught, with a panic on Wall Street in May. Within a year Kate had decided to send her son Eddie to be raised in Ireland. It is not known if she or her mother back in Ireland took the initiative. One writer thought that Grandmother Coll 'begged' Kate to send Eddie to Limerick.[28]

Among the de Valera papers in University College Dublin (UCD) Archives are three photos of Eddie as a baby in New York in 1882–83. He is lying alone in a featureless space of what was presumably a photographic studio, like an offering laid out on an altar. In two other photos he is old enough to sit alone on a chair. How the photos survived is unknown but Kate may have sent them back to her family in Co. Limerick. These only images of him before he left for Ireland in 1885 are singularly uninformative. Why did at least one of them not include his mother if not also his father, or even Mrs Doyle who is said to have cared for him in New York?[29]

It is usual for people not to have conscious memories of particular places or events with which they were associated before the age of three, but they sometimes do so. In 1934 de Valera told the author Dorothy Macardle 'The first thing I remember was my mother coming to see me. It was in America, so I was not two and a half years old. An old woman from the same part of Ireland had the care of me, because, after my father died my mother went to work. I remember her coming to see me there.'[30] In 1954 this became,

The first scene imprinted in my memory is that of a visit from my mother. She came to see me to the house of Mrs Doyle, to whom she had given me to nurse when my father died. I was at the time, I suppose, about two years of age. My father had died about a year previously, and my mother had to surrender me in order to earn her living. She went to work I think, to a Doctor Dawson, in Fifth Avenue, as a nursemaid. My recollection is that of a rather large room; I suppose it was the sitting room of the house. I think I must have been lying on the floor, or kneeling, as I looked up at this woman in black who was looking down at me. I think of the figure always as that of a rather slim woman, pale face, with a handbag – a woman's bag, in her hand. I think also of the fireplace at the other end of the room, and of a man sitting by the fire. He was I suppose the man I had been accustomed to call Papa Doyle. The house was in Grand Street, New York. I must have been with the family for about a year at this time. One of my playmates there was a girl that I called Maggie Doyle. I met her later in New York, about 1920, for the first time since my childhood. I met her again some five or six years later. She presented me with a little white kid [young goat's skin] child's shoe. She said it had been mine. I have not seen her since.[31]

Notable in these accounts are that his mother was 'coming to see' him on a 'visit', and that decades after he left New York as a baby he had not one but two conversations with someone who had known him there. It seems that his was no mere daycare arrangement, and that Eddie may have been living away from his mother's home in Manhattan for up to a year or more ('given' to Mrs Doyle 'to nurse', in his words above). The reference to Maggie Doyle is quite uninformative. How did they meet? Why the qualifying words 'a girl that I called'? Why and how had Maggie still got a shoe that she believed once belonged to him? Was she not able to provide considerably more information about Mrs Doyle and the man he then called 'papa', and about their set-up? In a letter to his mother in 1900 (Chapter 5 below) he once made a passing reference to hearing that Mrs Doyle had died but 'the old man is still living'. These are not the only times when reading documents about de Valera in the UCD Archives that one is struck by the unsaid or absent, by the fact that his autobiographical notes are not as frank or full as they might have been.

His authorised biography by Longford and O'Neill, published more than three decades after Macardle wrote, opens with a more anodyne version of de Valera's 'one vivid memory of his earliest childhood'. It is the same apartment room: 'Beside the fireplace sits a man. On the floor lies a small, fair-haired boy. A slim, pale-faced young woman is bending over him, dressed in black. The child's eyes are fixed wonderingly on the shiny metal fittings which ornament her handbag.'[32] And again, in another note looking back 'over seventy years of conscious life', de Valera revisited the scene:

My first recollection has no definite emotion associated with it. It is of a child sitting or lying on the floor of a room and gazing up at a woman in black; it was in the home of a Mrs Doyle in Grand Street, New York. The woman on whom I was gazing was my mother; but what attracted me was a bag she had in her hand, with its bright metal furnishings.[33]

Perhaps this was his mother's farewell, before her brother took Eddie to Ireland. Did she not walk with them to the boat? Kate had arrived into New York harbour just a few short years earlier. Now her son was leaving from it for Ireland. Bromage thought that Kate 'watched from the pier of the Inman Line' as her brother carried Eddie on board. If Eddie saw her on the quay then, he seems to have forgotten her presence.[34]

He also appears to have entirely forgotten an incident – if it ever really happened – that a Limerick man David Dwane included in his fawning 1922 biography of de Valera. De Valera himself told Dwane, who grew up near Bruree village, that there were errors in this book. The very fact that such an unlikely scenario was taken seriously at all by Dwane is indicative of the need for caution in respect to sources of information concerning de Valera's private life generally:

Long before he commenced to notice passing events, and while still a child, it is remarked that he had a soldierly gait and that he bore himself in a manner befitting a citizen of the great Republic. Born of Spanish-Irish parents he inherited the indomitable fighting spirit of both races. This characteristic was not very apparent in his early boyhood, but an incident which occurred shortly before his transfer to Ireland, and when he was not yet two and a half years of age, is significant. It is related that one day he toddled across the street to where a wealthy Englishman dwelt. We are not aware whether this Englishman was a professional gentleman or a large storekeeper, but at any rate he approached young de Valera and proffered him the choice of two flags. One was the Union Jack and the other had emblazoned upon it the Stars and Stripes. After a short pause de Valera accepted the American flag. 'Come, now', said the Englishman in merry mood, 'give me back that flag and take this one.' 'No, no', muttered de Valera, tightening his grasp of the one he had. 'Well, then, you will take both', replied the Englishman, at the same time giving effect to the statement by sticking the Union Jack in the pocket of his tunic. He had no sooner done so, than young de Valera plucked it out, and throwing it on the ground, folded his arms, and faced his would-be benefactor with an air of stubborn independence. This was, perhaps, only a childish fancy, but it had the effect of arousing the innate patriotic feelings of an exiled Irishman who had been watching the incident from near by. Uttering such words as 'maith an páiste', 'maith an buachaill', 'maith an fear' [Irish: 'Good child, good boy, good man'] he rushed up and taking the little lad in his arms in a wild embrace hugged and kissed him as if he were a long lost child. The Irishman was an old Fenian. To him one flag stood for freedom and advancement; the other for slavery and bondage.[35]

Later, two of Eddie's cousins in America were to write accounts of his departure from the United States based largely on what they had heard when young from their father Edward Coll, the uncle who brought Eddie de Valera to Ireland in 1885. One cousin was Edward Coll junior, born in Connecticut in 1890, who met de Valera for the first time in 1919 at New Rochelle, New York, during the latter's first return visit to America since he had left it on the SS *City* in Chicago thirty-four years earlier.[36] According to US census returns, Edward Coll senior had been born Ireland in the late 1850s and emigrated to the United States in 1882. Those returns give him as 'Edward', although Dwane in his book calls him 'Edmund'. He died in 1946.[37]

It had not been easy at first for Edward Coll senior to get work in America. His son later wrote:

As the result of the tremendous influx of his countrymen, my father found jobs surprisingly scarce in the New York of that day, so he went to New Jersey and hired out to a farmer. In spite of long hours and low wages, to the young Irishman the work seemed easy and quite remunerative ... New Jersey in those days was a land of swamps that now have been drained and filled in. Mosquitoes bred and multiplied there unmolested. Malaria was rampant ... Not more than a year after his arrival in America, my father not only came down with malaria but the disease also so weakened him that he was forced to seek lighter work in the city. Soon he got a job as janitor in a large office building and there he met a young architect, Ehrick Rossiter, who later invited my father to work for him on his estate in Washington, Connecticut. For over fifty years my father was caretaker on the Rossiter place.[38]

Malaria developed to a climax in the United States between 1850 and the end of the century, with the lowlands of New Jersey being a centre of infection.[39] Ehrick Rossiter was a highly respected architect in New York City, but he played a special role in the township of Washington in Litchfield county, Connecticut, where he lived for part of the year and which he helped to shape.[40] Uncle Ed was to marry and raise a large family there.[41] When Kate provided her brother's name as next-of-kin on admission to the Nursery and Child's Hospital for the birth of her son in 1882, she gave his address as still being in New Jersey, at Rahway care of one A.F. Shotwell. Abram Shotwell was a farmer and leading citizen, whose ancestors were among the founders of Rahway, a town about thirty miles (48km) from Manhattan. This evidence of Uncle Ed's presence in New Jersey, coupled with his son's belief that it was not more than a year after his arrival in America that Uncle Ed was forced by his health to quit that state, lends support to his uncle's US census returns of 1900 and 1910 which give his year of immigration as 1882.[42]

In 1960 Edward Coll junior wrote that his father frequently went up from Rahway at weekends to accompany Kate to Mass. He described Kate as working as 'a governess', conferring a higher social status on her than that of servant or nursemaid found elsewhere. Coll stated that when his father came to say goodbye to Kate in Manhattan before leaving for Ireland with his nephew Eddie in 1885 he found her 'again working all day for her living and forced to leave her child in the care of others. In fact she described to my father how the baby would be asleep in the early morning when she had to leave for work and, upon her return in late evening, the little fellow would again be in bed. In spite of the heart-ache that would follow such a separation, she felt that her son would be far better off and get much better care, were he in the family home in

Ireland.' Coll's account implies that at that time Kate may have collected or at least seen her baby each evening.

In 1938 Elizabeth Coll Millson, another child of de Valera's Uncle Ed, also wrote of the separation of mother and child:

So it was late one afternoon in April of 1884 [*sic*] a trio acted a little private drama on the pier of the Inman Line in New York, as the *City of Chicago* was leaving for Great Britain and Ireland. They stood apart from the hurrying crowd – a man, a woman and a little boy of about two and a half years. The man was in his early twenties, very tall and dark and decidedly serious. The woman was a pretty, slender widow who wiped her eyes constantly as she bade the other two good-bye.

'Be sure and give him porridge every morning,' she admonished, 'and the day you land in Queenstown [in Ireland], put on his little velvet suit. I want him to be his prettiest for mother.'

A whistle blew. There followed a shouted order. The woman picked the boy up quickly and hugged him for one tense moment. Then she handed

The SS *City of Chicago*, on board which Eddie de Valera first arrived in Ireland, in 1885. It later sank at the Old Head of Kinsale in 1892. Photo: Caledonian Maritime Research Trust.

him hurriedly to the man who went quickly up the gangplank, pausing behind the crowded rail to hold the child up for a last farewell.[43]

As the SS *City of Chicago* steamed out of New York harbour for Europe, did little Eddie hold his uncle's hand tightly? Perhaps Uncle Ed pointed out Bedloe's Island, where they were already making preparations for the erection of the Statue of Liberty, a gift from the people of France.

Forty years earlier, during the Great Famine that devastated the population of rural Ireland, people had spent on average eight or nine weeks crossing the Atlantic Ocean by sailing ship. Now, due to the addition of steam power, the crossing usually took eight to ten days.[44] The SS *City of Chicago*, with its iron hull, was the Inman company's newest and largest passenger vessel. It had been launched in Glasgow in 1883 and weighed 5,202 tons, sporting two funnels and four masts. There was keen competition between shipping lines for passengers. Conditions on board were better than they had been during the Great Famine, but for poorer passengers in the 1880s they were still far from luxurious.[45]

Uncle Ed's daughter Elizabeth would write later that her father often told them about the journey, and that it took ten days. There was a price war on among the steamship lines. By 1886 Inman would be offering a reduced rate of £3 for a single crossing in steerage. This was still equivalent to what an Irish agricultural labourer might earn in nine weeks. Elizabeth added,

> The first night out, the child cried uncontrollably for hours. Nothing seemed to pacify him, not even the toy violin to which he clung so desperately ... There must have been unusual anguish in that sobbing, for fifty-two years later my father described its bitterness thus: 'Half the night I was kept awake with his crying that tore at the very heart of me.'[46]

According to Edward Coll this toy violin amused others on board, for 'the ship passengers loved to watch the boy as he tucked the small instrument under his chin and pretended to play'. He wrote too that his father undertook the voyage because his malaria had not cleared up when he went to work in Connecticut and 'Doctor Ford' had advised him that seasickness was a cure for the illness:

> My father found himself too good a sailor to be sick in the prescribed form, although still suffering from malaria. One day he told a sailor how he would give much to be really seasick. The latter immediately pulled a knife and a plug of tobacco from a pocket, shaved off bits and ordered my father to chew and swallow the tobacco. For days he was the sickest man on the ship. Suffice it to say that, at the end of six months, my father came back to the United States, and although he lived to enjoy eighty-six years of life, never once was he again troubled with malaria.[47]

In the same month that uncle and nephew crossed the Atlantic to Ireland in 1885 there were recurrent gales and frequent dense fog. The captain of the SS *Nürnberg* reported that on the evening of 5 April 1885, to the south-west of Ireland, 'the mast-head and yard-arms were tipped with Saint Elmo's fire, and vivid lightning came out of the heavy black clouds; a ball of fire exploded with a loud noise resembling the report of a gun; after this phenomenon the gale increased to hurricane force.' Eddie and his uncle could count themselves lucky, because their crossing took place in a space between two severe April storms.[48] The first had forced back to Queenstown the White Star Line's SS *Germanic*. It also seriously damaged a steamer 500 miles (800km) west of Cape Clear on its way to New York. The vessel was carrying 700 people in steerage and 150 in saloon class. It reportedly shipped a tremendous sea that stove in an iron bulkhead – breaking furniture, injuring passengers and flooding the saloon. Another great wave rose on the port bow and broke right over the vessel, dashing with full force against the wheelhouse and smashing it to pieces. This wave took seven lifeboats overboard. The rush of water caught a seaman and he drowned. The storm blew all day and the ship lurched out of control for a while. Passengers feared that the vessel would sink, but the crew eventually got it under control and turned back.[49]

On the evening of Friday, 17 April 1885, Eddie's ship approached the coast of Ireland. Rounding the Old Head of Kinsale, the SS *City of*

Chicago disembarked passengers at Queenstown soon after dawn. The vessel then resumed its journey to Liverpool. Seven years later, it ran aground in fog at the Old Head of Kinsale. All on board were rescued then but it was lost, and its captain blamed for reckless speeding.[50]

On 6 January 1922, nearly four decades after he left New York, de Valera rose in Dáil Éireann (the Irish parliament) during a heated debate on the proposed Anglo-Irish Treaty and declared memorably 'Whenever I wanted to know what the Irish people wanted I had only to examine my own heart and it told me straight off what the Irish people wanted'. This was – as he put it then – because 'The first fifteen years of my life that formed my character were lived amongst the Irish people down in Limerick; therefore, I know what I am talking about.' The evident fact that all or almost all other deputies in the Dáil had themselves spent the first fifteen years of their lives 'amongst the Irish people' made this a relatively unremarkable assertion. But what is remarkable is the fact that his declaration elided or erased the first two and a half years of his life, spent in Manhattan. Between his arrival in Bruree from America in April 1885, aged two and a half, and his departure to Dublin in October 1898 just twelve and a half of his 'first fifteen years' were lived in Limerick. Psychologists regard the very first years of life as significant.

Little or nothing is known about the immediate formative circumstances of those first two and a half years that de Valera spent in the teeming and multicultural milieu of Manhattan. What sights did he see? What people did he meet? What excitements and tensions? Where exactly did he live? How did the Doyles help to look after him? If his father was in New York after Eddie's birth, where was he working? Why is Eddie alone in the only surviving photographs of him from that period? Who was his father?

HIS UNKNOWN FATHER

Éamon De Valera had no memory of his father, if he ever met him. Because of the lifelong significance of his absent father to him, this section considers in detail what is known.

There survive three contemporary records relating to de Valera's birth and parentage.[51] In addition, there is an officially 'corrected' version of a contemporary record. The first surviving contemporary record is the register of the Nursery and Child's Hospital for 1878–83. This shows that his mother 'Mrs Kate de Valero [*sic*]' was admitted on 13 October 1882. Her religion was 'Romanist', her 'nation' Irish and her age '24 years'. The register required neither the name of her baby's father nor of the baby about to be born. It requested 'Residence of Parents' rather than residence of the mother and/or father. Kate gave the address of no parent but of her fellow immigrant, 'Brother, Edward Coll, Rahway N.J. [New Jersey] c/o A.J. Shotmill Esq.' She also gave as required a reference: 'Mrs. Abraham, 61 East 41st St, 3rd bell'. No other detail was registered.[52]

The second surviving contemporary record is an official New York State 'Birth Return' document dated 10 November 1882, signed by Dr Charles Murray of the Nursery and Child's Hospital. This gives 'George de Valero' as the only child of 'Kate de Valero (maiden name Kate Coll), age 24, of Ireland'. It gave the baby's date of birth as 14 October 1882 and returned as his father 'Vivion [*sic*] de Valero [*sic*], birthplace Spain, age 28', by occupation an 'artist'. The form required neither the signature nor home address of a child's parent. It is not known why Kate first called her child George. Her father's name was Patrick.

This 'birth return' appears to have constituted or served as what is usually commonly referred to as a 'birth certificate', for in the New York City Municipal Archives it alone is attached to a 'corrected certificate' obtained thirty-four years later (below). On 30 June 1916 the New York Commissioner of Health approved this 'corrected certificate' of birth, on the basis of a submission by de Valera's mother (by then 'Catherine Wheelwright' of Rochester in upstate New York).[53] She and her second son (Thomas Wheelwright) were that summer asking the US State Department and others to lobby the British, on the basis of de Valera's US birth and citizenship, to reduce the prison sentence imposed on him for participating in the Easter Rising 1916. The new 'corrected certificate' now recorded her first child's name officially as 'Edward' instead

Above: 'Birth Return' by the Nursery and Child's Hospital, Manhattan, for 'George de Valero', the future President Éamon de Valera of Ireland, born 14 October 1882. Courtesy NYC Department of Records.
Below: Original baptismal record for 'Edward De Valeros', 3 December 1882, with later 'corrections'. Courtesy Church of St Agnes, Manhattan.

of 'George' and 'de Valera' instead of 'de Valero', and was thus clearer evidence of Éamon de Valera's birth in the USA. Kate had explained (according to a copy or draft of an affidavit of 1916 in her name) that in 1882 she had 'instructed Doctor Murray, the physician who attended during her illness, that the child was to be called "George" and that in pursuance of such instruction the said Doctor Murray had the name recorded as such, but deponent [Kate] at the Baptism of the child gave it the name of "Edward", by which name he has always been called ...'.

Did the 'deponent' Kate alone drop the name 'George' or had both of his parents agreed to do so? This is unknown. The amended certificate of 1916 also adds addresses for Kate and for 'Vivion de Valera [*sic*]' in 1882 – each being 61 East 41st Street. According to the 1882 register of the Nursery and Child's Hospital this too was the address of Mrs Abraham who provided Kate with a reference as required before her admission to the hospital. In 1916 Éamon de Valera's father's birthplace was again given as Spain.[54]

Trow's *New York City Directory* for the year ending May 1883 includes neither Mrs Abraham nor Kate (nor any de Valera) among the seven people listed as separate occupants of 61 East 41st Street. However, a Solomon Abrahams [*sic*] is given as having his home there, and a cigar business nearby on 42nd Street. If he was related to Kate's referee, was Kate their maid? Trow shows Abrahams still there in 1886. The house appears to have been divided into at least six apartments throughout the 1880s. Trow's *Directory* for the year ending May 1881 shows apartments there being occupied then by a clerk, a policeman, an agent, a builder, a man for whom no occupation is given, a janitor and a widow.

The third surviving contemporary record shows that Kate's son was not christened until 3 December 1882, almost two months after his birth. The baptismal register of the Church of St Agnes in Manhattan recorded the boy as Edward de Valeros [*sic*], his father as Vevian [*sic*] de Valeros [*sic*] and his mother as Kate Coll (not de Valeros/Valera). It gave no addresses or other personal details. John Hennessy and Mary Shine were recorded as witnesses.[55] The entry was later defaced by someone writing on it 'Valera' and 'Eamon [no accent, one letter n]' and crossing out the letter 's' in de Valera's father's registered family name 'Valeros'. It is said that Éamon de Valera's son Vivion was given permission to make the changes. The legal scholar Geoffrey Hand, himself a past pupil of Blackrock College, chided the college's Fr Seán Farragher for dismissing what seemed to be 'quite substantial tampering with the baptismal entry as "notable misspellings … corrected"' Hand added 'Historians aren't very happy with the "correction" of authentic records.'[56]

Noting that Kate's second and third children were born at home – as evidenced by the fact that Charles Wheelwright's address in Trow's

Directory is recorded on their birth certificates as the location of their births – one American genealogical researcher has asked 'If 61 East 41st Street was the de Valera residence [as indicated on the 1916 "corrected certificate" for "Edward de Valera"], why wasn't Éamon born in the house, as were most children at that time?'[57] There are a number of possible answers to that question and one should avoid making assumptions, including that Eddie's father had left Kate by the time Eddie was born.

St Agnes' Church in Manhattan came to use a standard printed certificate on which to give people details of their baptisms there if later requested to do so. It included in each case after the father's name the printed words 'his lawful wife' before the mother's name. One such certificate dated 1897 is among de Valera's personal papers in UCD. He seems to have taken consolation in this when rumours that he was 'illegitimate' circulated in 1917. He was standing for election to parliament and reportedly wrote to his wife, 'By the way isn't "lawful wife" in Baptism certificate. I think it is – that would be sufficient to prove the lie …'[58] However, only the parents' names 'Vevian De Valeros' and 'Kate Coll' – and no such indication of Kate's marital status – appear in the original hand-written register entry. The Church of St Agnes later adopted a more exact form of printed certificate, dropping the words 'lawful wife' – as can be seen on later copies of Eddie's baptismal details made in 1927, 1931, 1956 and 1961 that are also among the de Valera papers in UCD.[59]

De Valera, as a child in Limerick and later as a boy at Blackrock College in Dublin, was known only as Eddie and never as George or indeed Éamon – the latter being a form that he adopted later. When Kate changed the name George to Edward she may have done so to honour her brother named Edward who was living in America. However, her mother too had a brother 'Ned' who went to America, and de Valera's close colleague Frank Gallagher appears to have been told that the child was named after this Edward Carroll.[60] It may also be noted that at that time in the Roman Catholic calendar the feast day nearest to the date of Eddie's birth was that of Edward the Confessor, on 13 October.

The three contemporary records above concur in giving the last letter in his surname as 'o' where a second letter 'a' was subsequently used instead.

No other officially recorded information relating to Éamon De Valera's birth and paternity has been found for the period. As regards any references by de Valera or his biographers or by other authors to his father and his father's ancestors, a frank statement at the head of a memorandum on the matter prepared by his personal secretary in 1961 is worth bearing in mind: 'The only information President de Valera has of his father and his father's family is that derived from conversations with his mother who, of course, had to rely on what she recollected of conversations with her husband.'[61] The fullest surviving account written by Kate herself appears to be that in a letter from her on which he commented when in an English jail in 1916 (Chapter 7 below), and even in that letter she conceded that her account of de Valera's father might contradict what she had previously told him. Researchers have been singularly unsuccessful in trying to add to or confirm what little information she passed on.

His wife Sinéad told one of their sons that 'before the Rising, I gave Dev's birth certificate to my people [family] in Munster Street'. She said she did so because she had not wanted it found by the British in any search of her and her husband's own home.[62] It is not known when or why such a certificate was obtained, but if it was so obtained Eddie does not appear to have tried to have any details on his New York State birth return 'corrected' before his mother did so after Easter 1916 in the manner explained above. However, Sinéad may have meant to say 'baptismal certificate', for she wrote in July 1916 that she then made use of his baptismal certificate to save him from execution. As mentioned above, the de Valera papers in UCD include a certificate of 1897 from St Agnes' Church in Manhattan confirming his baptism there in 1882.

The couple may not in fact have had a copy of de Valera's actual birth return certificate before 1916. For De Valera gave 'Vivian' as his father's first name when registering their marriage in January 1910 – closer to the 'Vevian' given as Eddie's father's name on the register of St Agnes' Church than to 'Vivion' as given on the New York State birth return. When their first son was born on 13 December 1910, the registrar of Irish births recorded his name as ending in 'an'. Éamon de Valera also returned his son's name as Vivian in the 1911 census. Later, however, the name of their son born in 1910 was to be spelt 'Vivion'.

*

On his visit to the United States with de Valera in 1927, his friend and assistant Frank Gallagher got Kate talking of her youth in Co. Limerick and of her coming to New York – a city in which as she appears then to have told him, contrary to other sources, she 'knew nobody' when she arrived. It was on Christmas Day that they spoke and Gallagher was a guest with de Valera at the home of Kate and her English husband Charles Wheelwright – in what Gallagher called a 'very Anglophile' Rochester, New York. He wrote that the couple lived in 'a pretty wooden bungalow (they call them frame houses) in a long avenue of wooden houses':

> The Chief [de Valera] went off to see his aunt [Annie] at about 4 o'clock … I sat in the kitchen with [his] mother and Charlie and went down once to stoke the furnace. Dev's mother is nearly eighty and I saw her go down and heard shovelling. I followed and discovered her piling in coal into the furnace – does it all as in the day's work. I asked her about the conditions when she left Ireland [in] 1879. She was full of clear-cut memories: of the quietness of that time, [Isaac] Butt just beginning to make a stir but absolute peace nationally. The biggest sensation she remembered was the local baker being arrested for singing a Fenian song. She knew nobody in New York and had no relatives there but she was a pioneer for her family and there are now many families of Colls all over the eastern states.

But Gallagher's attempt to get her talking about de Valera's father failed:

> I tried to get her on to her first marriage – being very careful not to mention it merely leading up to it chronologically – but she talked of other things first and when I might have succeeded back came Tom and the Chief. Then more eats and presents [gifts]. [63]

Éamon de Valera said that his mother told him that she first met his father at Frank Giraud's when he came to see Frank's sister Lilie there in 1880: 'When mother went to Armstrong's [at Greenville, NJ] the acquaintanceship [with de Valera's future father] was continued. His friend Hamilton was with him.' She added that his father went to Denver in the autumn of 1880, but later returned to New York.[64]

On 9 April 1931, almost half a century after her first son's birth, Kate swore an affidavit in Rochester, New York, stating that she 'was the widow of Vivion de Valera now deceased' and that she had been married to Vivion de Valera on 19 September 1881, by a Fr Hennessy, 'pastor of the Roman Catholic Church of St. Patrick, situated at Greenville, Jersey City, State of New Jersey' and that the sole issue of the said marriage was 'Edward de Valera who was born in New York City on the 14th day of October, 1882' and that the said Edward 'is the legitimate son' of herself and Vivion. A month later two supporting affidavits were sworn, one by Catherine Daly and the other by Patrick Hennessy. They are word-for-word identical, and were clearly drafted for them. Daly and Hennessy each swore they were 'well acquainted' with Kate and 'knew her in the year 1882, at which time she introduced her husband, Vivion De Valera, to your deponent's family' (not explicitly to the deponents themselves). They each 'had various other friends who knew the said Catherine de Valera and the said Vivion de Valera to be wife and husband'.[65]

However, at least once, Kate reportedly stated – in 1924 – that she was not, after all, married in New Jersey but in New York.[66] In fact no record of her marriage in either state has ever been found. In the 1950s Monsignor J.A. Hamilton of St Patrick's Church, New Jersey made 'extensive searches' of both Jersey City and New York church records for any certificate of a marriage between de Valera's parents and found none.[67] Others too, on behalf of de Valera or independently, have tried to find any reliable evidence or record of his father or paternal grandfather but have drawn a blank – as have biographers including the present author.

An anonymous document found in the de Valera archives states that Kate said that 'Juan Vivion de Valera' and herself 'called each other always Jack and Kitty' but that 'he only used Vivion on cheques, etc.'[68] Yet a statement ostensibly made by Kate in 1924 says that Eddie's father's name was 'Juan Vivian [*sic*]'. In this statement Kate also denied that Eddie's father was Portuguese or a Jew.[69] De Valera's authorised biographers (O'Neill and Pakenham earl of Longford) wrote in 1970 that Eddie's father's name was Vivion Juan (not 'Juan Vivion') de Valera and his grandfather's was Juan de Valera. They give no source for this but appear to depend on de Valera's private papers. For their account seems to draw on his records now in the UCD Archives, some made for him and some by himself – his own in this case said by him to rely on what his mother told him.[70] None of the three official documents relating to Eddie's birth, considered above, include any reference to a man named 'Juan'.

Kate told her first son that his father's father 'frequently visited New York' and stayed at a place in Brooklyn, this being certain 'Spanish houses on 26th or 27th Street West'. In a memorandum said to be of 'the President's mother's recollections' made in 1961, long after her death, Éamon de Valera's secretary wrote that Eddie's grandfather appeared to have traded between Spain, Cuba and New York. When he came to New York he used to call to see his son Vivion and Kate, according to Kate.[71]

Over the years there have been various iterations of de Valera's paternal ancestry, none substantiated in their details beyond what has been set out above. De Valera wrote one version on a blank page in an edition of the Douay Bible that he had won as a prize when a college student at the Castle in Blackrock at Christmas 1902. Its details have never been independently verified. At the top of the page he set out four lines of descent. On the first line is 'Juan (Ricardo?) m[arried] Amelia (A?)costa', and on the next line are offspring of this couple – namely Leon, Vivion Juan [&] Kate Coll, Charlotte ('Lotti'). On the following line appear 'Eamon [and] Sinéad Ni Flannagáin' and after these the latter couple's seven children. The last of these children, given by de Valera in the Bible as 'Toirdhealbach' (known as Terry), was born in 1922. This indicates that the entry on this page was made later – and possibly much later – than that birth. Below these lines are added:

Note. Mother said Leon and Charlotte died before my father. Grandfather
Juan dd [blank in place of date of death here]. He used travel back and
forth to Europe and Cuba trading in sugar?

Used stop at place 26 or 27th Street and Broadway.

Father. Born in Spain, educated abroad, knew fluently English, German,
Spanish and French. He was trained as a sculptor but chip injured his
sight. He gave music lessons after his marriage.

Met mother in 1880 (at Greenville, village near NY Bay cemetery),
went to Denver in Fall 1880[72] and married mother in Sept. 1881.

Died in Nov. '84 (Minneapolis?). [Added here in a different ink and
ostensibly different hand is the word 'Denver']73

He was 5'7" or 5'8" [five feet and eight inches] in height and could wear
mother's shoes.74 Said he was 28 at time of marriage.

Dr Hagan [Hogan?], Henry St. visited by father – he should be over 80.
Also Dr Dawson on 5th Ave.

Hamilton Frederick bachelor friend of father's – last place mother
knew he lived was Brooklyn. He took wagon-photos.

Mother put things in old storage place – Reilly's (?) in Lex Ave., in
Dec. 1884.75

Éamon de Valera stated elsewhere that his mother told him that his
'father's health gave way in 1884' and that Eddie's father's father sent
Eddie's father out west: 'He said goodbye to Mother June 30th 1884.
She was informed by Hamilton (whom Grandfather sent to her) of
father's death six or eight months later of some lung affection.' Kate
is said to have told Eddie too that Pat Regan, whom she described as a
brother of her own godmother and 'most constant friend from Ireland',
Mrs Johanna Hennessy, 'was in the police force and verified father's
death'.76 No reason is given why Kate and Eddie did not go west with
his father. Terry de Valera much later stressed that 'Vivion Juan' (Terry's
version of Eddie's father's name) 'never enjoyed good health' and was
'often' ill, but this is unsubstantiated and not necessarily a reason for his
leaving Kate in New York with a baby.77 After Kate died, her son Tom

sent Dev a 'Turkish ring' that 'your father gave to her'. Much later it was claimed that Eddie's father had earlier given her an engagement ring of gold, emeralds and diamonds and that she donated this to be part of a new chalice being fashioned as a tribute to a priest who had died.[78] If Eddie's father ever wrote to his mother after leaving her, no such letter survives; nor was any other object said to have been his.

In 1963 Edward Coll, cousin of Éamon de Valera and son of the latter's 'Uncle Ed', went to New Mexico and tried to find details of the burial of Éamon's father. It is clear from his correspondence that the entire state of New Mexico had been added to Denver and Minneapolis as a place where Eddie's father might have died. He found nothing.[79]

If Uncle Ed ever wrote down or otherwise recorded his own account of his sister's circumstances in New York from 1882 to 1885, or of his journey to Bruree with his nephew in 1885, that direct account remains unpublished. It seems likely that he would have met de Valera's father in Manhattan if anyone did so. In 1943, during the Second World War, Éamon de Valera told his half-brother Tom 'I would like also to write to Uncle Ed' – for information about the Coll and Carroll sides of the family, but also about his own father. Why did he not do so? Or, if he did, has his letter and any reply been lost? He told Fr Tom Wheelwright in the letter,

> He [Uncle Ed] will also know something about my father. Mother didn't speak to me very much about my father, and I am anxious to find out what branch of the Valera [*sic*] family he belonged to, as well as the circumstances of his coming to America and his death. The best clue would be my father's mother's name. Mother mentioned 'Costa' or 'd'Acosta'. It would be interesting to find out if Uncle Ed knew anything about this.
>
> By the way, Mother told me that she thought that my father went out west in 1883 or 1884 on account of his health and that he died either in Denver or Minneapolis. I am not sure which. Uncle Ed may know something about this.[80]

Had Eddie/Éamon de Valera himself never pursued his uncle Ed for further information such as he now sought via his half-brother? Why did he delay doing so even in 1943? Had he found that his uncle did not wish to be quizzed about the matter? His uncle had sent a warm note when de Valera returned to America for the first time since 1885, writing on 25 June 1919, 'My dear Eddie, Congratulations and a hearty welcome to you back to the land of your birth. You have made a good deal of history since the day I took you home to your grandmother.'[81] Fr Tom Wheelwright did not reply to de Valera for over two months, saying when he did so that he had hoped to be able to unearth some of the information his brother wanted. However, he could add little about de Valera's father. He did say 'mother mentioned Denver as the place of your father's death'. And he corroborated one aspect: 'I have a distinct recollection of mother mentioning Acosta'.[82] The fact that both Éamon de Valera and his half-brother wrote that Kate said that his paternal grandmother's family name was 'Costa' or 'Acosta' or 'd'Acosta', and gave 'Amelia' as her first name, has not led to the discovery of definite information about her identity or that of his father or grandfather.[83]

In a typed note de Valera claimed that his father's father 'called to see Mother after my father's death and he was disappointed when he found that I had been sent away. The exact date of this I could not get, but he [grandfather] died after Mother had come to Rochester – that was September 1895.'[84] Another version of this reported visit claimed that Eddie's paternal grandfather 'was angry to learn that his grandson had been sent to Ireland; he never gave any sign of life after that'. Yet Kate reportedly said too she refused his offer of help for herself and her son.[85]

The resources of both Church and state were later utilised by de Valera in a futile search for precise details of his father and grandfather, about both of whom his mother's responses never satisfied him.[86]

In his handwritten account of his second trip with de Valera to the USA in 1927–28, Frank Gallagher included what may be a telling observation. He mentioned in passing de Valera's reaction to a film that they saw on board the SS *Leviathan* on their way to New York. This was a melodrama from Tiffany-Stahl Productions: 'A magnificent film was shown tonight in the social hall: *Wild Geese* ... It was a tragedy quite unsuited to a liner's audience but a little gem all the same. The Chief didn't enjoy it at all. He likes the simple joyous sentimental film. *Wild Geese* is the

A photograph that de Valera kept in his office when taoiseach and president, said to be of his father. Courtesy UCD Archives P150/167–9.

story of a father who made a home miserable.'[87] As de Valera long sought certainty about his paternity, he may have harboured doubts about his father's commitment to his mother and himself.

Among De Valera's papers in UCD are two photographs said to be of his father, one that he framed and kept on his desk when taoiseach (premier) and president and the other a miniature of poor quality in a locket. Presumably he received both from his mother.[88]

Eddie's father is said to have left New York in 1884. So, 'Mother having to go to work put me to nurse with a friend of hers, Mrs Doyle of Brooklyn'. Mrs Doyle 'would appear to have come from Limerick'. Éamon de Valera thought that Mrs Doyle cared for him until he left for Ireland in 1885, six months after his second birthday. He thought Kate was then at work at 'Dr Dawson's', on Fifth Avenue, 'as a nursemaid'.[89]

In 1900, at the end of a letter to his mother written when he was a pupil at Blackrock College, Eddie tells her that he has heard 'poor Mrs Doyle has lately died but that the old man is still living'. He does not say where he heard this and has left us no definite information about the Doyles or about the circumstances in which he was kept as an infant. Does the fact that he did not ask his mother about the Doyles in that letter of 1900 indicate that he already knew well enough the circumstances in which he was first reared?[90] It would be wrong to assume that the accounts he left us of his childhood give all of the details that he might have included.

*

There is evidence of Kate having married, but not to a man named de Valera in 1881. She married Charles Wheelwright in 1888. They wed that year at the Catholic church of St Francis Xavier in Manhattan. Charles was an English Protestant immigrant working in the USA as a coachman or driver. Correlating UK and US family records (births, baptisms, marriages and censuses), it appears that Kate's husband Charles was born in Shropshire, England, in 1857, one of a large family on a seventy-seven-acre farm in the small parish of Clee St Margaret, in which parish there was just one Wheelwright family. In the census of 1881 a Charles Wheelwright of Clee St Margaret, Salop (i.e. Shropshire) is employed as a coachman and domestic servant for a coachman in London, one Edward Devall of St George's parish. There is no other Charles Wheelwright from Shropshire (or indeed in the whole of England) in any other UK census whose birth date comes close to matching that of Kate Coll's husband. From immigration and census records, Kate's future Wheelwright husband appears to have gone to America in August 1882 (and no matching or nearly matching Charles Wheelwright is found in the next UK census). It is unknown when he first met Kate.[91]

It cannot be said with absolute certainty that the coachman Charles Wheelwright who worked in London for Edward Devall of the parish of St George was the same man who went to America and married Kate, but from the available data it appears highly probable. What is striking is the coincidence of identical and similar names in 'Edward Devall of St George's parish' and baby 'George/Edward de Valero/s' of Manhattan.

Having married Wheelwright in 1888, Kate gave birth on 13 July 1889 to their daughter Annie (thus on her birth certificate) and on 18 December 1890 to their son Thomas. These names were also those of the Wheelwright parents in Shropshire –Kate's parents being Elizabeth and Patrick and her sister also Annie. Both babies were born at home, at 18 West 18th Street, Manhattan – where Trow's *New York City Directory*

Top left: Kate Coll (Éamon de Valera's mother), about the time she married Charles Wheelwright in 1888. Courtesy UCD Archives UCD P150/189.
Top right: Charles Wheelright in later years. Courtesy UCD Archives P150/195.
Bottom left: The Wheelwright children Tom and Annie, before Annie's death in 1897. Courtesy UCD Archives P150/195.

has Charles down as a 'cutler' and 'driver'. The new family later moved within Manhattan, before leaving New York City.[92]

When Eddie was a child in Limerick, Kate rejected his pleas to bring him back to America, but she did not forget him. The birth certificates of her later children Annie (1889) and Tom (1890) recorded her as having given birth to another child before Annie. However, US census records of 1900 and 1910 give her as the mother of just two children living or dead. It is not known if by then Kate or her husband Charlie wished to conceal the fact she had had a child before she married him. In any event, Kate and Eddie kept in touch by mail, he writing to her in his twenties 'Mother you will think it strange but many times I hear others talking of their mother I feel more or less an orphan. Fate has been rather hard on us'.[93]

The status of illegitimacy was abolished in Irish law only in the 1980s. For much of the twentieth century it was both a legal and social stigma. De Valera's life-long eagerness to find evidence that his parents married, as well as other details about his father, may be viewed in that context. The way in which the possibility of his becoming a priest was deflected when he raised it may indicate doubts about the status of his mother's relationship with his father in light of the absence of a marriage certificate. In canon law illegitimacy was an impediment to ordination. Moreover, his background and physical appearance inspired rumours about him at election time, and even antisemitic suggestions, such as that by John Devoy in New York that de Valera was a 'half-breed Jew'. There was also a racist innuendo by Ernest Blythe that de Valera was 'some class of a mulatto called Demerara [a light-brown sugar]'.[94]

De Valera's personal history mattered greatly to him, like it has to so many people in the last and present centuries who have asked questions about their own uncertain origins or about their background in Irish mother and child homes – or about irregularly recorded adoptions that the state tolerated and that have left them lost for answers. Éamon de Valera might have done more than he did when in a position to protect those who, like himself and his mother, found themselves dependant on strangers. De Valera as taoiseach and president of Ireland was well positioned to mitigate the stigma of illegitimacy had he chosen to do so.

*

De Valera's papers in UCD include various statements concerning his father's family that are unverifiable and sometimes contradictory. Éamon de Valera himself said in the 1950s 'I have not been able to ascertain from what branch of the de Valeras I have sprung. My only information is from what my mother told me.'[95] His mother gave colourful accounts. Mary C. Bromage remarked in her biography of 1956, 'Those who heard about Vivion through Kate were to recall him variously as a sculptor, a professor, an actor, a linguist, a doctor, a singer, a raconteur …' The Irish marriage register entry for Eddie and his wife gives his father's 'rank or profession' as 'professor'. If this was the registrar's error, it was not corrected. In 1933 the author Seán Ó Faoláin decided that 'Vivian [*sic*] de Valera, said to have been a political refugee, was a Spanish doctor.'[96]

Searches of US census, church and other records have not yielded evidence of anyone with the first name Vivion or Vivian or Vevian and a family name de Valero or de Veleros or de Valerio who could be the father of Éamon de Valera, or of any such person's birth, marriage or death before 1888. The name de Valero/de Valerio is seldom found in the US census then, although some variants turn up – mainly in US states adjoining Mexico. In 1880 a Cuban waiter James Davalero [*sic*] lived with his Irish wife Julie in New York City. The name de Valera is even rarer in US records.

There is perhaps just one de Valera in US records who might entice an historical researcher into flights of fancy. Joseph (not Vivian or Vivion or Juan) de Valera was born in Spain in 1855 and came to the United States in 1880. By 1885 he appears to have fathered with a German woman two daughters, Nita born in Mexico in July 1882 – brought into the United States in 1883 – and Fina born in Louisiana in 1884 or 1885. In the latter year Joseph is recorded as living in New Orleans, working as a bookkeeper (a person who keeps records of the financial dealings of a trader etc.). However, in February 1891 he is found marrying a Maria or Mary Furst/Fuerst in Newark, New Jersey. She herself had been born in 1871 in the USA to a German couple. By 1895 Joseph and Maria were living in Jersey City, New Jersey with his first two daughters Nita and Fina as well as three young children of their own. The same census gives the family as having dropped the prefix 'de' before Valera by 1900, and shows Joseph again as a 'bookkeeper' (which was the trade – as seen earlier – that Éamon de Valera said his mother told him his father followed after his eye was injured).[97] Might this de Valera have spent time in the south-western US in 1880–81 but then come up to seek work in New Jersey and had a brief relationship with Kate Coll? Éamon de Valera believed that his mother and father had met in Greenville, Jersey City, where she worked for a while. Might Joseph have left to return south-west even before knowing that Kate was pregnant, or soon after Kate's baby was born? Éamon de Valera did think that for some reason his father had gone away in 1882 (albeit he thought west to Denver, Colorado, rather than south to Louisiana) and that he went west again in June 1884 never to return. The Joseph de Valera in the census, as seen above, was back in New Jersey by the 1890s, settled there in a relationship.[98] It is a flimsy basis for speculation and there is none better.

A suggestion that Éamon de Valera was a grandnephew of Juan Valera, a well-known Spanish author and diplomat who represented Spain in Washington in the 1880s, was in 1936 lent some support by the Marqués de Aunón – a grandson of that diplomat. The Irish ambassador in Madrid, Leopold Kerney, met the marquess specifically to discuss the possibility of the two families being connected. The marquess reportedly said that his grandfather used to call himself 'de Valera' in his younger days, but subsequently discarded the particle 'de':

He [Juan Valera] had a brother who married into a wealthy family in Cuba; there was a '*drame de famille*', due, so it is said, to a lack of fidelity on the part of the lady, from whom her husband therefore parted, taking with him his son; they left Cuba and were never seen there again. The marqués thought there was only one child, but was not too sure on this point. The family learned subsequently (I do not know at what time) that this son had married an Irish girl employed as domestic or cook in a boarding house in New York, and that, subsequently his widow and son had gone to Ireland ... The Marqués de Aunón was somewhat puzzled by the Christian name of Éamon de Valera's father, Vivian [*sic*] not being a Spanish name.⁹⁹

Kerney also met a daughter of Juan Valera who gave him a similar account about this brother of Juan Valera, who seems to have been named Antonio. He also noted there were at least two known sculptors in that Spanish family. Kerney had been appointed ambassador by de Valera, who was then head of the Irish government ('president of the executive'), and had furnished the Spaniards with such details as Éamon de Valera gathered from his mother, which may have rendered the query somewhat leading. In any event, a note on one copy of the memo indicates that De Valera in Dublin was 'very doubtful however of the correctness of this story or that he is descended from the Antonio de Valera in question' and he wished to 'see the matter examined carefully'. For one thing, certain handwritten and typed 'extracts' and 'notes' of what Éamon de Valera later said his mother told him give his grandfather's first name not as Antonio but as 'Juan (Ricardo?) [*sic*]' and also indicate that this 'Don Juan' had with 'Amelia Acosta' three children, not 'only one child'. She told de Valera 'your grandfather as young man was a decorator', but said that he traded sugar between Cuba and Spain and whenever he came to New York City he stayed on 26th or 27th Street between Fifth Avenue and Broadway.¹⁰⁰ Kate 'recalled' her son's grandfather as a Spanish gentleman of rank, very aristocratic in manner and distinguished in appearance, and solidly built, whose wife had died 'many years' before 1880: 'Before the latest uprising of Cuban patriots he and his family enjoyed a large revenue from sugar plantations (destroyed in the insurrection).'¹⁰¹

There is nothing in the UCD Archives that suggests Éamon de Valera believed that Kerney, on his behalf, or anyone else had discovered who his father really was. However, de Valera's son Terry 'vigorously pursued the Spanish connection', furnishing the Irish family with a family tree that he convinced himself proved it was descended from Spanish nobility through one Antonio Valera, and even had a connection to the French court of Napoleon III. Terry claimed that Éamon de Valera had learned 'very much later' that his father was actually known as Antonio, not Juan or Ricardo as Kate had long told her son. According to Terry 'the Spanish are very fond of having a string of names and so Juan almost certainly was one of Antonio's Christian names. Another of Antonio's Christian names is believed to be Ricardo.' 'Almost certainly'? 'Believed to be'?[102]

In his 2015 book, *Éamon de Valera: A Will to Power*, the historian Ronan Fanning wrote of his subject's father that 'Vivion de Valera had been born in 1853 in Spain's Basque country, where his father was an army officer who later brought his family to Cuba…' He gave no source for this assertion and it is unreliable.

A certain Fr Edward Harnett was one of a number of priests who made investigations in America on foot of Éamon de Valera's lasting wish to know more about his family. Harnett, according to de Valera, 'seemed to trace a Juan Valera and a Costa family in New Orleans'.[103] This was the city with which Joseph de Valera also appears to have had a connection, as shown above. However, to the end of his life, Éamon De Valera remained uncertain and concerned about his father's identity and origins. A curious manifestation of this related to a written query from a man called Lawson which he received when he was a teenager. Lawson claimed to be descended from Cipriano de Valera – a sixteenth-century Spanish monk who converted to Protestantism – and asked Eddie if he was too. Eddie did not reply at the time. In 1917 Lawson's mother noticed Éamon de Valera in the news and wrote to give him an account of her family's ostensible connection to Cipriano. De Valera did not at that time pursue the matter, but decades later decided to contact Lawson – only to find that he had died in the Great War of 1914–18.[104]

There were various other individuals who also wrote to Éamon de Valera – including some Spanish de Valeras – suggesting a family relationship/kinship with him on his father's side, seeking assistance and/or offering genealogical information on his family. A number of these letters survive among the de Valera papers in UCD.[105]

- 3 -

NO RURAL PARADISE

IRELAND THEN

On 15 April 1885 inhabitants of Queenstown (known also as Cobh or Cove) saw Edward, Prince of Wales – Queen Victoria's son – step ashore there during a brief visit to Co. Cork. The prince reportedly 'met with an enthusiastic welcome'. Celebratory 'loyal' bunting had been put out for his visit, and this may still have been flying when Uncle Ed and his little nephew disembarked in Queenstown from the SS *City of Chicago*. Just three days after Prince Edward – future king of England –had passed through the port, Edward de Valera –future president of Ireland – arrived in his mother's homeland for the first time.[1]

De Valera used to say that he had only one memory from his early years in America – that of his mother leaning over him. His second earliest memory, he said, was of the vessel on which he crossed the Atlantic in 1885. He recalled 'the gunwale of a ship and the blue sea. That was when my uncle was bringing me to Ireland and we were coming into Cobh'. Or again it was of 'gazing out on a blue-green expanse of water, and in the foreground the rail of a ship; the latter attracted me because of its texture and grain. Was it teak? I was told, apparently in answer to my question, that I was at Queenstown.'[2] Recent research confirms that people may indeed recollect events that happened when they were aged just two and a half.[3] Given these references to what de Valera described as his earliest two memories – his mother bending over him and his being on the ship – it is surprising to find among the papers of Frank Gallagher, who accompanied him when he went back to America in the

1920s, a note that de Valera told him that his earliest memory was, in fact, of Bruree.[4]

His home from the age of two and a half was the countryside of Knockmore and Knockfenora near the village of Bruree. The rural Ireland in which Eddie de Valera found himself was no idyllic garden of paradise. It was less than fifty years since the Great Famine had devastated its population, killing hundreds of thousands of people and tearing families apart. Many sons and daughters had felt forced to emigrate then or subsequently. There had been further economic and political upheavals in the intervening years. The population of what is now the Republic of Ireland would continue to decline until 1961.

On the day Eddie was born in Manhattan in 1882, one of the main stories at the top of the front page of the *New York Times* was headlined 'The Future of the Irish Land Agitation'. The Irish National Land League had been founded in October 1879 to force landlords to reduce exploitative rents and 'to facilitate the obtaining of the ownership of the soil by the occupiers'. It replaced the Land League, which the British had outlawed. Among many priests who supported its objectives was Eugene Sheehy, whom the young de Valera would come to know and admire. During 1882 Michael Davitt, a prominent campaigner and one of the new league's secretaries, advocated land nationalisation.

In the seventeenth century the English had transferred the ownership of vast areas of land in Ireland from native Catholics to a Protestant minority loyal to London. Many Catholic families remained as tenants or labourers on such lands into the nineteenth century and regarded them as rightly belonging to them. Davitt's slogan, 'The land of Ireland for the people of Ireland', attracted them.

The Coll family was of the labouring class, and the small parcel of land attached to its cottage did not qualify Eddie's Uncle Pat to be thought of even as a small farmer. That there were significant strains between farming and labouring classes is evident from the pages of one of the most popular Irish novels of the late 1800s, Charles Kickham's *Knocknagow* or *The Homes of Tipperary*. This appeared first in 1879, although its commercial success began with an 1887 edition which was printed over and over again. Kickham was from Mullinahone, Co. Tipperary, which was similar in scale to Bruree and had suffered a similar decline after the Great Famine.[5] Set in about 1870, the novel carried on its title page a verse by Thomas Davis that hinted at darker truths for Ireland's poor, truths hidden beneath the ostensibly calm surface of country life:

> You meet him in his cabin rude,
> Or dancing with his dark-haired Mary,
> You'd swear they knew no other mood,
> But mirth and love in Tipperary.

It seems inconceivable that de Valera as a literate boy was unfamiliar with Kickham's best-selling novel, set in a neighbouring county. Comerford and, after him, Dudley Edwards seemed to assume that he was – Comerford writing that de Valera 'virtually' paraphrased it in speeches for an Irish people 'he knew to be imbued with its sentiments'.[6] But De Valera did not mention the novel when asked by an RTÉ interviewer in 1966 to name books that he read as a child.[7] Kickham's novel revealed a painful social reality that became politically inconvenient. The film historian Kevin Rockett observed that a popular film version of *Knocknagow* released in 1918 subtly realigned the balance of classes in the story to emphasise affinities rather than differences. This suited a reinvigorated Sinn Féin, then led by de Valera and seeking the widest electoral mandate for independence: 'The suppression of internal contradictions among the Irish population was, after all, crucial to the form of unity envisaged by nationalist leaders, especially de Valera', writes Rockett. He adds 'It was not just a "Labour Must Wait" view which was to the fore at the 1918 General Election, when Sinn Féin won an overwhelming victory over the Irish Parliamentary Party at Westminster, but a drive to suppress the differences between the various rural classes.'[8] In 1885, when Eddie for the first time arrived at Bruree, Uncle Pat had the status of a labourer, albeit a worthy one, but not that of a 'farmer' in the usual sense of the word then.

The divergent interests of Irish farmers and labourers may be missed when viewing the broader picture of land agitation and nationalist rights in Ireland. There were significant class differences, with some farmers as willing to exploit labourers as landlords were to exploit farmers to whom they rented land.[9]

De Valera's well-known visionary speech of St Patrick's Day 1943, with its references to people 'satisfied with frugal comfort', 'cosy homesteads', 'the romping of sturdy children' and 'the laughter of comely maidens', envisaged a kind of bucolic idyll. But he made it clear this was 'what we dreamed of'. What he called this 'thought of a noble future for our country' was not a nostalgic backward glance to the society in which many Irish people of his class actually lived when he first came among them in 1885. He himself yearned to get away from Bruree.

THE LIMERICK LABOURER

On the day on which Eddie de Valera is believed to have set foot on Irish soil for the first time, Saturday, 18 April 1885, newspapers were forecasting a possible international war between England and Russia – due to circumstances in Afghanistan. For their part, his widowed grandmother Elizabeth Coll (known locally as 'Bess Coll')[10] and her son Pat and her daughter Annie had domestic matters on their mind. They were making final arrangements to move into their new home on the following morning. The Colls were fortunate to have been allocated one of the first four cottages built for Irish labourers under the recent and reforming Labourers (Ireland) Act 1883. This stood near to their existing home in the Kilmallock district of Co. Limerick.

Eddie's grandfather Coll had died in 1874, aged just forty-eight. His widow Elizabeth was left on her own with four children to rear, two girls and two boys, ranging in age from five to eighteen years. She was to live until July 1895, when she died at about the age of fifty-eight. Eddie's mother Kate (born 21 December 1856) was the eldest child. Both Kate and her brother Ed (born 6 June 1858) went to America and lived out their days there. Uncle Pat (born 1 May 1864) was Elizabeth's third child, aged not quite twenty-one when Eddie came to Bruree in 1885. Pat stayed in Co. Limerick and remained unmarried until April 1896 – the year after his mother's death. 'Annie' (also known as 'Hannie', born 1869) was just sixteen when Eddie came. Within two years she was to follow her sister and eldest brother to America.[11]

According to de Valera, his mother Kate returned only once to Ireland during the thirteen and a half years that he lived just outside Bruree. That was in March 1888 when she came for a few weeks before her marriage to Charles Wheelwright in America in May of that year. She was to visit Ireland just once more, in July 1907 when de Valera was twenty-five and living in Dublin. She would bring with her then his sixteen-year-old half-brother Thomas Wheelwright to meet Eddie for the first time. De Valera did not see them again until 1919, when at the age of thirty-seven he returned to the United States for the first time. Aunt Annie came back from America twice while he lived in Limerick, he said, first in 1891 and again in 1895 around the time of his grandmother's death.[12]

The first official effort to classify housing in Ireland had taken place in 1841, when his grandparents were young adults. It was the eve of Ireland's Great Famine, and the survey's findings were stark. In rural Ireland more than two out of every five families lived in the lowest class of housing ('mud cabins having only one room') and another two out of five lived in the second-lowest ('still built of mud, but varying from two to four rooms and windows'). Thus, the authors of the census wrote, 'Nearly half of the families of the rural population, and somewhat more than one-third of the families of the civic population, are living in the lowest state, being possessed of accommodation equivalent to a cabin consisting but of a single room.' The average number of persons in an Irish family then was between five and six, and many families in mud cabins were larger than that.[13] When the famine came, it compounded poverty and devastated tracts of rural Ireland. There was no quick recovery. The Colls struggled to get by. Out of four siblings, Pat alone stayed in Ireland. He worked as a general labourer and carter.[14]

The new cottage to which the Colls moved in April 1885 had been built under a recently established government scheme involving the cooperation of landlords. By 1918 about 48,000 similar two-storey labourers' dwellings had been erected across the island. Local authorities let these (along with the half an acre or so on which each stood) at rents well within the means of their occupants. The scheme was part of a social revolution that had a lasting impact on the lives of many people, and on the landscape. Compared to the thatched mud cabins in which the Colls and other labourers' families had lived, the new slated cottages provided considerable comfort, having a toilet in an outhouse and with drinking water to be drawn from a well or the nearest public pump. While these dwellings for labourers were known as cottages, dwellings of any size built by farmers were usually referred to as houses.[15]

Between 1881 and 1914 the number of labourers in Ireland actually diminished, and wages increased in real terms for regularly employed skilled workers: 'Labourers such as herds, ploughmen and shepherds, could be as well off as occupiers of small holdings.' However, hours were long, with 6 a.m. to 7 p.m. in summer usual and Saturday half-days unknown.[16] De Valera later wrote that his grandfather Coll had worked on the O'Mahony farm, 'which was one of the most substantial in the neighbourhood' around Bruree. The Coll's old cottage was in fact, de Valera said, the workman's house on that farm 'and it was in that house that I slept my first night in Ireland. The rood of land attached to the old cottage was incorporated in the half acre attached to the adjacent new cottage given to my grandmother at that time.' He added that his grandmother often spoke of John O'Mahony 'as the kindest of friends and the best of neighbours'. The O'Mahony house was the 'first I visited as a child', said de Valera. The Mortell family succeeded the O'Mahonys in that house and Tom Mortell, older than de Valera, became his 'closest companion'. Either Tom or a brother of his was to spark envy in de Valera when he told the younger boy that he was leaving Bruree to become a shop assistant. By then De Valera was aching to get away too.[17]

It is not known if the Colls were expecting Ed to arrive back from America at their home on exactly 18 April 1885, with or without his little nephew Eddie. It was to be the last night that Bess Coll would spend in the old thatched cabin where she had reared her four children. Its walls of mud and clay were nearly a metre across at the base.

De Valera told Frank Gallagher in 1945 that when Uncle Ed and Eddie reached Kilmallock station the child was carried – 'probably' by his Uncle Pat – over the hills and by the shortest walking way to Bruree.[18] He told Donncha Ó Dulaing twenty years later that 'we were met at the station by his brother, my uncle Pat. He had, probably, a donkey and cart to take the luggage.'[19] Coming to Bruree, young Eddie would be an extra mouth to feed. But Kate could not cope on her own in New York. The Colls were familiar with poverty. There was lots of it about.

On the morning after his arrival Eddie woke with a start, as he later recalled. At first he did not know where he was. There was 'nobody about'. The front door was ajar and hens might come in. Could they bite him? This was not Manhattan. There were strong smells in the old house, their 'mud cabin'. 'I suppose I was frightened and I shouted and screamed [laughs].'[20] Where was Uncle Ed? Why had his own mother sent Eddie away? He started to cry. 'I made a terrible row ... "They are all up at the new house", somebody said to me.'[21] But they had not in fact forgotten him or left him alone. After all, 'somebody' was there. He told a radio interviewer once that on his first night in Ireland his grandmother and aunt 'probably slept in the old house with me, the men in the new house'. When he awoke in the old house, his mother's sister Annie was still outside completing chores. He recalled that, 'a young girl came in, who was my aunt'. She comforted him.[22]

He would later fashion from that morning a story repeated with relish, about how he woke to find 'everyone' gone but was 'very proud to have been the last occupant of his family home'.[23] This declaration drew attention to his Irish ancestry notwithstanding his Spanish surname, and to the rural roots of the boy from Manhattan. Locating himself at the outset in an old mud cabin was certainly more dramatic that simply telling people that on the day after his arrival he was housed in a brand-new cottage made available to his family before others under recent legislation passed by the United Kingdom parliament in London. In fact, according to Frank Gallagher, de Valera once told him that his 'first memory is of what was called the "new house"' and not the old.[24]

The *Cork Examiner* of 21 April 1885 reported that 'last Saturday the first cottages erected under the Labourers Act in the Kilmallock Union were actually occupied by tenants. One is in the village of Rockhill and the other in Bruree. Possession was handed over by Mr M.A. Bolster, Clerk of the Union. The cottages present a nice pleasant appearance ...'[25] From an early age Eddie was aware that his uncle had been among the very first labourers in Ireland to get one of the new cottages, being told when he was young there was only a couple of such dwellings built in another county before these two in the Kilmallock Union area.[26]

So now the Coll family had housing much superior to its former abode. In 1954 de Valera described the old house they then left: 'There was, as far as I remember, but one window. It was not far from the fire-place. The door was situated about two thirds of the way down the side of the room. It was a one-roomed house. The walls were of mud – a type of mud which had dried into something almost as hard as cement. It was thatched. At the end farthest from the fire were two beds ... I would say it was about fifteen feet wide and about twenty or twenty-five feet long. I was lying in the bed nearest the door when I wakened.'[27] He said that the walls were so hard that it took a crowbar and pickaxe to try and break through them: 'They were very substantial'.[28]

When the family was settled in the new house, the old house was first used as a cowshed, as de Valera later recalled: 'I well remember the swallows who built their nests there. It was delightful in the early spring to watch them sweeping in through the open door under the eves. There were some beautiful old roses at the back of that house facing west, those cottage roses, the perfume of which still haunts me.'[29]

The new cottage to which they moved was a big improvement, with a half-floor upstairs as de Valera also recalled:

When I knew it first the kitchen had no ceiling but the roof. I remember well the appearance of the 'rendered' slates – the laths – the crossbeams; these are now hidden today with an upper floor – the floor of the attic, but in my day there were two small rooms to one end underneath [beside the kitchen/living room] with a room overhead spanning the one below. The upper room was called the loft. This loft was reached by a ladder, about seven or eight feet long, with flat steps, some five or six inches wide – that is in depth. The ladder was put on when anyone wanted to reach the room or come down from it. In the daytime when the room was not used the ladder was hung on a peg on the wall near the door. When I was about four I fell off this loft one morning. I used to sleep in the lower room with my grandmother but when she was leaving to take milk to the village in the mornings I was frequently taken up to the loft to my uncle who was still in bed, I remember falling off the loft very well. I was, apparently, coming down the ladder when my eye caught sight of the wing of a goose which was kept for dusting purposes. This wing caught my eye as I was about to descend and, apparently, the bloody end of it frightened me and I missed my footing. I heard my grandmother say 'Is he dead?' before I fell into unconsciousness. I got all right, however.[30]

De Valera's Uncle Pat admired Charles Stewart Parnell and Michael Davitt, leading figures in the nationalist fight for political power and property rights in Ireland. In 1880, when Pat was not yet twenty, the Bruree branch of the Irish National Land League invited Michael Davitt and the newly elected member of parliament for Tipperary, John Dillon, to address it. The branch asked 'Irishmen' to assemble in their thousands 'to show your undying hostility to landlordism, and your sympathy with Parnell and other traversers ...'[31] During the week of Christmas that year, there was also at Bruree 'a splendid torchlight procession' to celebrate the acquittal of Tim Healy MP and another man who were charged under the Whiteboy Acts with intimidation but whose real offence, claimed Healy, was that they 'ventured to offend some of the omnipotent land-lords and agents of a downtrodden district of the country'.[32] On the night of the procession, it is said, Bruree was 'beautifully illuminated, the band paraded the streets, playing a most select collection of national airs, after which Mr T. Sanders J.P [regarded as a rack-renting landlord] was carried in effigy through the town, followed by an immense crowd groaning, hooting, &c., and burned on the banks of the Maigue, to whose waters his ashes were consigned'.[33]

Efforts had been made to get farmers to provide improved housing accommodation and allotments for their workers, but without much success. Amongst other factors 'it was difficult to place the onus on any particular farmer in the many cases where labourers worked for more than one employer'. The Labourers Act 1883 brought the local author-ity into action and initiated machinery under which cottages and plots could be acquired by these bodies and then provided for rural workers under loans raised on the security of the rates: 'The expenses incurred by local authorities were charged as a rate on the sections of their areas in which the cottages and plots were provided. In other words the expenses were shared by all the farmers for whom the labourers might be available.'[34]

Tensions over land were running high. Seven months after Eddie came from America, some people made 'a daring attack' on a sub-sheriff of Co. Limerick who was conducting a seizure for rent at Bruree.[35] Pat sometimes went out at night to attend meetings, and his mother Elizabeth no doubt hoped he would not get into trouble. Might he join the IRB or some Whiteboy association? Such oath-bound organisations, national and local, worked a rough justice on detested landlords and their agents. This exposed young men to the danger of imprisonment or worse. Violence was in the air.

Both farmers and labourers wanted the system of landholding improved. However, there were divisions between farmers themselves as well as tensions between farmers and labourers. In 1884 Martin Fenton, a small farmer, prevailed on a local curate to write to the *Cork Examiner* to assure people that Fenton had surrendered a farm at Rockhill – not far from the Coll's home – that he had taken over a fortnight before in succession to an evicted tenant farmer: 'Fenton and his relatives are anxious to have this publicly known', reported the paper – anxious not to be assaulted or boycotted, presumably. The evicted tenant was said to have offered to pay a fair rent to his landlord but, according to the curate, 'A terrible rack-rent, beneath which he has been struggling heroically for years, has almost made a pauper of him.'[36] The following month, a correspondent ('J. Holy' on behalf of the organisers of a 'monster labour demonstration' in Bruree) explained that some farmers were putting great pressure on landlords not to support the scheme for labourers' cottages, including pressure on reasonable landlords who invested in development locally and created employment: 'The labourers of this locality … bid me say their chief object in banding themselves together is to resist petty tyranny. The farmer seems to envy us.' Holy added that some farmers 'wrote to their landlords to withhold the landlords' consent to the labourers' cottages scheme' and 'what they [labourers] consider still worse they [the farmers] are trying by most infamous means to drive local gentlemen [of the landlord class] who are no tyrants, but spending their fortunes on trade and labour, from amongst them by hound poisoning, &c, &c.'[37]

Although there was a big demand for labourers' cottages, the scheme itself clearly had its opponents and did not run smoothly. Such was the rural society into which Eddie de Valera arrived in 1885.

Fr Eugene Sheehy (1841–1917) was curate of the parish church at the time Eddie arrived in Bruree in 1885. Something of a firebrand, Sheehy had been on the central committee of the Irish National Land League. In 1881 he was jailed for his activities in support of it. He thus earned national attention, becoming known as 'the Land League Priest'. When chief speaker at a demonstration at Knockaderry, Co. Limerick in September 1884, he supported a declaration that 'Ireland will not rest satisfied with any more instalments of social redress, with any mere measure of political right, short of national independence (cheers).'[38] He believed that he was speaking up for the interests of many Catholic famers and labourers who worked on land confiscated by the English in earlier centuries and now owned by landlords descended from Protestant settlers.

Fr Sheehy appeared at a meeting of the Kilmallock Board of Guardians in January 1886, 'speaking on behalf of ratepayers and labourers from Bruree' – although how many of his parishioners were ratepayers who opposed the labourers' cottages scheme is unknown. Sheehy pressed the board to take matters into its own hands at a time when 'hunger and starvation stared the labourers in the face'. He wanted the board to provide outdoor relief for the poor and, 'if it were not outrageously illegal', to engage men to fence in the plots of land already selected for the erection of labourers' cottages without waiting for the usual formalities to be gone through: 'There was growing steadily in the minds of the labourers and many other persons, a belief that though there was an honest surface current tending in the direction of [erecting] the building of the cottager [a person living in a cottage], there was also a strong undercurrent and side current at work to the contrary.' Sheehy remarked that, 'John Mitchell said that the red tapism [red tape-ism] of official departments had caused more deaths in Ireland than occurred during all the wars of Napoleon.'[39]

During 1886 too Sheehy was promoted from curate to parish priest of Bruree. He led a campaign against a local landlord John Gubbins, whose 'heartless eviction' of three widows from their home on Gubbins's Garrouse property excited local passions. The very wealthy Gubbins had bought Bruree House in 1868, spending £40,000 on building stables and kennels. He was master of the Limerick foxhounds in 1886 and it is said that, as tempers flared that year, a crowd stoned his dogs. On a list of de Valera's early political recollections the boycott of Gubbins came first, and in the 1940s de Valera was still making notes about him.[40]

One of de Valera's memories of a protest at Bruree against Gubbins brings to mind a reference at the beginning of Kickham's *Knocknagow* to the strong impression made by hearing a local fife and drum band for the first time. De Valera had returned from a visit with his grandmother to Croom, Co. Limerick, bearing 'a drum, a fife whistle, a toy hammer and an elegant toy sword with a scabbard'. He later told Frank Gallagher:

> He got a drum, a kettledrum for his birthday: it must have been when he was four – perhaps five. He heard sounds, music, and he was brought up to a gable window to look out. There he saw the Fedamore Fife and Drum Band and he was told they were going to the boycotting of John Gubbins. The great drum with Fedamore in big letters across it entranced him and he had no use at all for the little drum which was his present.[41]

In later life he said that his grandmother actually took him to this boycotting event. He also admitted that the boycott 'wasn't very popular afterwards because Gubbins was regarded as being fairly good' as a landlord. He said that the next time he saw such a drum was when, as an adult, he passed an Orange Order march in Portadown, Co. Armagh.[42]

Half a century later the local memory of events that year was still strong, as Mary Jones of Bruree National School – one of the collectors for the Folklore Commission – discovered in 1937:

> Some fifty years ago there lived in Bruree a very rich man [Gubbins]. He owned a very large tract of land. One day whilst out riding a horse he came upon the bailiff evicting a farmer adjoining his land. Taking compassion on him he immediately went to the nearest town and there

bought out the rights of the landlord of this and a number of other farms near his own. The following day he reinstated this man and giving him a good workhorse he had a chance to start life anew.

Some years later this man and a number of other farmers got well into arrears of rent with their new landlord. Things were becoming so serious that he [Gubbins] had to threaten eviction himself. One day these farmers held a meeting and decided to approach the landlord for an abatement in the rent. They called at his house and he received them kindly and when they asked for 25% off the rent he agreed and they parted on the best of terms. Arriving out to the rest of their comrades who waited outside on the road they related what took place. It was then decided that they did not ask for enough and they returned to the landlord for a further reduction of 25% more.

This time he ordered them from his door and refused to take one penny off the arrears. Eviction followed eviction till three farmers were without a home, one a poor widow with a child in arms. The tenants were not idle either. They called a big meeting for the following Sunday when a large crowd marched through Bruree and called on everyone to boycott the landlord. At this time nearly all the poor of Bruree depended for their livelihood on this landlord who employed everyone who sought for work.

Nearly all stood by him. He owned several packs of hounds and when one of these was poisoned whilst he was out hunting he shot the rest and took all his horses with him out to England. It was then his loss was felt locally. After some time when the boycott had died down – it was never a real success – he returned home. Meeting the tenants one by one he settled with them all and being a good man he gave them more than they expected. Some of the ringleaders he treated very fair by buying out their farms altogether and attaching them to his own. He then bought farms for them many miles from Bruree. Everything settled down peaceably after this and until his death this landlord was respected by all and more especially by the poor people of Bruree.[43]

So peacefully did things settle down that de Valera later recalled being asked by Gubbins to ride a horse (Chapter 4 below). Not only did Eddie not object but he greatly enjoyed the experience. He also remembered Gubbins as the first person he knew to have rubber bicycle tyres, and later also 'he had the first motor car to pass the door'.[44]

But, in the meantime, there was further trouble. In 1887 a Kilmallock Board of Guardians meeting was invaded by a large crowd of labourers armed with blackthorns who subjected those they regarded as unfriendly to the labourers' cause to 'very bad treatment'.[45] This was another example of the febrile social atmosphere in which little Eddie found himself.

During 1887 Fr Sheehy toured Ireland giving speeches. By some accounts his sermons and talks appear to have been quite long, that in Dundalk on 'The Struggle for Irish Liberty' being said by the *Dundalk Democrat* to be 'upwards of two hours'. The paper reported that 400 torchbearers were on hand to marshal an enthusiastic crowd. He delivered the lecture 'to obtain funds for the evicted tenantry' in his parish of Bruree. The meeting was chaired by a Protestant nationalist, Joseph Maxwell and at one point Sheehy seized on this fact 'to refute a calumny as base as it was baseless which had been put upon the Catholics of this country. Mr Chamberlain had stated in effect that if Mr Maxwell came to Bruree, that [he] being a Protestant, existence for him would be made impossible'. Sheehy quoted the last lines of the poem 'Celts and Saxons' by Thomas Davis: 'So start not, Irish-born man, / If you're to Ireland true, / We heed not race nor creed, nor clan, / We've hearts and hands for you.'[46]

Later in 1887 people across Ireland were riled up after police shot at a Land League meeting at Mitchelstown, Co. Cork, about twenty-three miles (37km) from Bruree:

His first recollection of political things was the shootings in Mitchelstown [9 September 1887]. He was in a little room off the kitchen and was about five years old when he heard the papers being read and discussed in the kitchen, excitedly discussed by his uncle and others. It was a startling thing then to hear of people being shot – three, his memory was, were killed. That was his first conscious touching of the political scene. Later came the smuggling of a suit of clothes to William O'Brien [to escape from Tullamore Jail] (and as he spoke of it he still glowed with pride at the stratagem). Together these make his first contact with the national movement.[47]

Gallagher noted de Valera's memory of lying in bed and hearing his Uncle Pat in the kitchen speak of politics, of the Mitchelstown shootings and other matters – including the divisive scandal surrounding the great leader Charles Stewart Parnell's relationship with Katharine O'Shea that led to Parnell's downfall: 'I didn't think our part of the country was the scene of bitter conflict and animosity – but rather of pain and sorrow.' Eddie, then aged fourteen, also heard his uncle say that Dick Pigott –whose forgery of letters to discredit Parnell was uncovered – had yesterday shot himself in Madrid: 'I wanted to know who Pigott was and so on.'[48]

Sheehy's continuing involvement in land campaigns gave rise to tensions between himself and the bishops. On 1 April 1894 he was to leave for New York, ostensibly just to raise money for a new church at Bruree, but he did not return until 1903. De Valera said in 1957, 'I was but a short time serving as an altar boy when he left for the United States ... I remember the evening he left. I was not at the send-off: I was minding the cows on the roadside at Athlacca at the time, and reading *Robinson Crusoe*.'[49]

When Sheehy eventually returned to Ireland he quietly resumed some organising activities in Bruree. Later he lived in Dublin with his brother David, long a member of parliament and whose Georgian house at 2 Belvedere Place was the location of literary gatherings attended by James Joyce before he left Ireland. Joyce mentioned David Sheehy and his wife in *Ulysses*. One of David's daughters, Kathleen, became the mother of Conor Cruise O'Brien, a prominent academic, civil servant and government minister for the Labour Party.[50]

De Valera was to see Sheehy twice after leaving Bruree, but for some reason baulked at approaching him on each occasion. The first was at the foundational meeting of the nationalist Irish Volunteers in the Rotunda, Dublin, on 23 November 1913. As he took his seat he saw in the row in front of him a man he knew named Larry Roche. Beside Roche was Sheehy: 'I did not make bold to speak to them, but I thought it strange that three people from Bruree should be so close together. I saw Fr Sheehy again after my release in 1917. He was at the crossing on Leeson Street, not far from Leeson Park [Dublin]. I was cycling, and again I hesitated to approach. I have regretted it because I never saw him later.'[51] It was 'strange' that de Valera did not address a man for whom he had served Mass and who might be expected to be proud of the boy from Co. Limerick taking an active part in the nationalist struggle. Sheehy had provided him with an inspiring example of the socially activist priest.

Why was the Coll family in particular lucky enough to be assigned one of the very first cottages built for labourers under the government's new scheme? Was it simply because Pat knew the system well and got on a list early? Perhaps Pat used the need for Eddie to return from America to press for a cottage. Or was it because he actively supported the local member of parliament, William Henry O'Sullivan? O'Sullivan had personally tried to give the interests of agricultural labourers priority over those of tenant farmers. O'Sullivan's biographer has noted that 'As vice-chairman of the Kilmallock board of guardians, he achieved notoriety by setting a pioneering example of using meetings of poor law boards (then the only elective local government bodies in the countryside) as a platform for championing radical viewpoints on national questions and getting his speeches reported in the Dublin press.' A leading member of the land league, O'Sullivan is said to have faced strong clerical opposition in 1880 when seeking (successfully) to be re-elected, and again in 1885 when he ultimately stood down before polling day.[52]

On 26 May 1928 the *Irish Press*, founded by de Valera himself, wrote on Patrick Coll's death that Eddie's Uncle Pat had not merely been a supporter of William O'Brien MP but had taken an active part in the Land War: 'he organized and was one of the founders of the Bruree branch of "The Trade and Labour Association", an offshoot of the defunct Land League'. He was chairman of the Bruree branch 'for many years', and 'as its nominee, was elected to Kilmallock District Council and Board of Guardians'. In the census of 1901 he appears as a 'general labourer and district councillor'. Local people are said to have described him, when advocating the cause of Labour in the Kilmallock council, as 'a towering figure, of independent character, and as steadfast as a rock in upholding his views'. The paper reported that he had agitated for years unsuccessfully for the adoption of a scheme to give an additional half-acre to each labourer who got one of the labourers' cottages. Then, 'with the rise of the separatist Sinn Féin movement he sat as a Sinn Féin member' on the local council. He presided over de Valera's first public meeting after the latter's release from jail in 1917, held in Bruree on the eve of the East Clare election that would see de Valera returned as a member of parliament for the first time. Pat was president first of the Bruree Sinn Féin Club and later of the Bruree Fianna Fáil *cumann* [branch], and was said not to have missed a meeting of either in twenty years. A neighbour said 'Mr de Valera as a boy got impregnated with national ideas by his association with him [Uncle Pat].'[53]

The Coll household was by no means the poorest possible. It spent sufficient in a local grocery store to merit in return at Christmas a complimentary cake and sometimes a bottle or two of alcohol. An American interviewer later observed that the Colls seemed enterprising and 'a little better off than most farm labourers'.[54] Yet, as will be seen, when Eddie attended the Christian Brothers school in Charleville (Rathluirc) between 1896 and 1898 – a return journey of fourteen miles (23km) – Pat was either unable or unwilling to buy him a bicycle of any kind.

'A CHILD ENTIRELY APART'

The appearance of an infant from Manhattan in Bruree, adorned with curly locks and wearing a velvet suit, impressed itself on the memory of the local station-master. Schoolboys, unaccustomed to sartorial elegance, were most unlikely to let it pass unnoticed. Kees Van Hoek later wrote in the *Irish Times* that when de Valera's Uncle Ed embarked with the child on the SS *City of Chicago* in 1885:

> his sister admonished him to dress her son (who was hugging his toy violin, a souvenir of his violin-playing father) in his velvet suit on the day he was landing at Queenstown. That is what Uncle Coll most distinctly remembered when I questioned him some years ago; and the father of

Senator Professor [Michael J.] Ryan once described that suit to me – he
never forgot the day of young de Valera's arrival in Bruree (where Mr Ryan
[the senator's father] was station-master at the time) because of that suit –
pure Lord Fauntleroy, complete to lace collar.[55]

Although Eddie reportedly brought with him to Ireland a suit consisting
of jacket and breeches, he was not always clothed in trousers in Bruree.
Many boys and girls then dressed in a similar style of clothing, this being
a dress or petticoat such as later became exclusively associated with girls.
When Eddie's grandmother took him with her into the village of Bruree
in 1886, to see the meeting called to support a boycott of John Gubbins:

> I was in petticoats and I had long hair – my grandmother was rather
> proud, if I might put it that way, of my hair. It was a golden colour, I
> believe! She wanted me to keep on wearing it. My uncle on the other
> hand, had more regard for my feelings in the matter with other boys and
> he wanted to cut it off. On one occasion he did cut it off and my grand-
> mother was very, very angry. I remember before it was cut off I must have
> been rather fat at the time and we had a little straw [-coloured] Irish terrier
> named Jess and she had a habit of putting her paws up to my breast and
> throwing me over, and when she had me down she'd catch me by the hair
> and try to pull me along. I seemed to enjoy it but my uncle didn't like the
> long hair and he was determined that he was going to put an end to it.[56]

A photograph of Eddie wearing his 'pure Lord Fauntleroy' velvet outfit
survives. Before his Aunt Annie followed his mother to New York, he was
brought by train to get his picture taken by Henry O'Shea in George St,
Limerick city. De Valera kept a copy of it into his old age:[57]

> I know I had a suit which came with me from America, of which I was
> very proud. It was a velvet suit, and it was always a treat when I could get
> to wear that suit. I think there is a photograph of me in this suit with long
> hair and my Aunt's button boots. When I was taken to the photographer
> the ordinary boys' boots seemed altogether too inelegant, and my Aunt's
> boots were put on although they were much too big for me.[58]

He added elsewhere that he didn't like the idea of wearing his aunt's boots at all and would have preferred his old ones.

> My long hair was also a matter of annoyance to me. My grandmother liked my long curls and wished me to keep them. I felt I was more or less a bit of a sissy as long as I had long hair. My uncle thought with me.[59]

The character 'Little Lord Fauntleroy' was an invention of Frances Hodgson Burnett, whose immensely popular novel of that name was first serialised from late 1885 – before appearing as a book in 1886 in New York and London. By 1888, a correspondent for one Kerry newspaper wrote, it 'had held spellbound thousands of old as well as young children'.[60] In 1882 Burnett had facilitated Oscar Wilde by introducing him to creative and political figures on his visit to America.[61] Her book included illustrations by Reginald Birch that represented young, long-haired Fauntleroy (from the French *l'enfant du roi* meaning 'son of the king') in aristocratic garments, in which some saw the influence of Wilde's personal aesthetic.[62] The story, which soon also transferred to the stage, tells of a young boy born in America who lives together with his mother 'what might have been thought very lonely lives' in a small house on a quiet New York street. His late father had been a European. The boy becomes heir to a property in Europe to which he then travels. The story fuelled 'an explosion of merchandize', most particularly velvet suits: 'Though his costume would eventually typecast Fauntleroy as a sissy and a fop, Burnett repeatedly describes her character as a sturdy, real, noble-hearted boy ... noble by blood, but more importantly ... noble in virtue'.[63] The story echoed aspects of the life of young de Valera, albeit the estate to which he came was not owned by an aristocrat but occupied by a labourer. Birch may have drawn on existing taste, for Eddie is said to have received his suit when leaving New York months before *Little Lord Fauntleroy* first appeared. Indeed a photo of him in New York before he left shows him wearing what appears to be a similar style of suit, differently cut. If other boys in Bruree needed a reminder that he was an outsider, this suit was it.

Left: Eddie in a suit in Manhattan aged about two and a half, 1884–85. Mackey's Gallery, 418 Grand Street, New York City. Courtesy UCD Archives P150/1.
Right: Eddie in a suit in Ireland, aged about four, by Henry O'Shea, Limerick. Courtesy UCD Archives P150/4.

Uncle Ed was later said by his own son Edward Coll to have stayed six months in Ireland after bringing de Valera to Bruree. But his daughter Elizabeth Coll thought he returned to America just ten weeks after departing. Elizabeth appears to have been correct, for a Limerick-born 'Edward Coll' is known to have disembarked from the *City of Chicago* in New York on 13 June 1885. No other passenger list has been found to include an Edward Coll about this time.[64] De Valera's Uncle Ed never again returned to Ireland, although he lived until 1946. Elizabeth remembered that 'News of his nephew, however, came regularly in letters, first from my grandmother and uncle and later from Éamon himself.' Uncle Ed's son and namesake likewise recalled hearing from his cousin:

All during my boyhood days in Washington, Connecticut, a letter from Ireland in the handwriting of 'Cousin Ed' was an event of importance. No matter how busy he was, my father would drop everything, quietly pull up a chair, and read out to mother and the rest of us the news that young 'de Valera' had written. How proud he was on that day when he received the news that his Irish nephew had won a scholarship to Blackrock College in Dublin. All those letters were treasured and wrapped in a neat package. In later years, when de Valera made his first trip to Washington, Connecticut, to visit my father, those letters were given to him. It is my hope that they were preserved for some future biography, for they will throw interesting light upon his formative years.[65]

Unfortunately, no such parcel of letters is found among de Valera's papers in the UCD archives. It might indeed 'throw interesting light upon his form-ative years' if it still exists. These are not the only letters of de Valera absent from the archives. There does, however, survive a drawing that 'Edward' made for 'Uncle Edd' on 4 March 1896. Entitled 'Pugilistic Encounter', it depicts Bob Fitzsimmons and Peter Maher during their World Heavyweight Championship bout at the border between Mexico and the United States in February that year. The former was English, the latter an Irish champion before emigrating to America. Eddie himself would later try boxing when at Blackrock College, investing in a pair of gloves. After that, 'though he admitted that he was no prize-fighter, he maintained his interest and kept the gloves until his wife, Sinéad, sold them after the Easter Rising to help to fight off starvation for herself and the family'. On the same sheet as he sketched his idea of the big fight of 1896 Eddie also sketched the cottage near Bruree in which he had been reared since coming from America.[66]

As Eddie grew, his grandmother and uncle had to make arrangements for his schooling. The system of 'national schools' set up across Ireland in the mid-nineteenth century afforded an opportunity to labourers and others to have their children educated for free at primary level, while various Catholic religious orders were putting in place schools that offered more advanced education to older children. Eddie de Valera attended Bruree National School from 1888 to 1896, and the Christian Brothers school at Charleville, some seven miles (11km) south of his home, from 1896 to 1898.

Neither his grandmother nor his uncle appears to have thought it necessary to accompany little Eddie to the school door on what was intended to be his first day. They expected Jimmy MacEniry, who lived

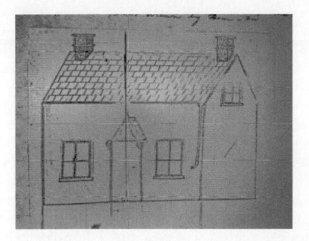

Eddie's home in Knockmore, Co Limerick, one of the new labourers' cottages, sketched by de Valera as a boy. Courtesy UCD Archives P150/207.

along a boreen (Irish *boirín*: little road) near the Colls' house, to take him. But MacEniry went by another route and left Eddie standing with his granny at the top of that boreen: 'I just stood in the road head, waiting for the boy who was to take me. He didn't come.'[67] He later said that he thought he was about five years old at the time: 'I think myself I didn't go to school at all on that occasion and that I was kept back for practically a year. My grandmother then thought it would be a good idea to send me there a few days of the week or two before the [summer] holidays so that I'd get broken in as it were.'[68]

At Bruree National School the boys were taught and examined in reading, writing, arithmetic and spelling, and also (as they got older) in grammar, geography, agriculture, bookkeeping and – in fifth and sixth classes –some algebra and geometry.[69] Irish history and the Irish language were not taught in national schools then as they later would be, and not taught at all in many schools.[70] In Bruree school children practised their handwriting by copying out sentences that included 'Queen Victoria was born 24 May 1819.'[71] At the Christian Brothers school in Charleville from 1896 to 1898 Eddie was to continue with courses in arithmetic, algebra and geometry (also known then as 'euclid') and English, as well as taking new courses in French, Greek and Latin. He would later study

Greek and Latin at Blackrock too, subjects which were earlier part of the curriculum of not only English public schools but also various local Irish 'hedge-schools'. Such classical learning was regarded as part of a rounded education well into the twentieth century.

While Irish history was not formally taught in school, some of the sermons of de Valera's parish priest Fr Sheehy vividly informed him of aspects of it. Sheehy wanted parishioners to have self-respect, to stand up for what was right and just. Eddie particularly liked sermons that the priest gave on 2 January, the annual feast day of the local patron saint, Munchin (also Mainchín): 'his subject was always the ancient glories of Bruree'. Sheehy quoted St Paul (Acts 21:39) to encourage each parishioner to feel like 'a citizen of no mean city'. Where they lived was after all a 'seat of kings' – as the Gaelic name of Bruree (Brugh Ríogh) may be translated into English. Telling them of its connection with Irish royalty, he made them think of the place as second only to Cashel or Tara. He said the Dál gCais came from Bruree and that Brian Boru and his brother Mahon had lived there. They should never forget it. There was royal blood in their veins.[72]

> After hearing him we had a feeling that Bruree was the capital of Ireland, and so, the capital of the world. His ideas may have been exaggerations, but they inspired a love for our parish and our country: love for the locality in which one lives as the natural prelude to the wider patriotism.[73]

Indeed, as de Valera once laughingly confessed, Bruree seemed to be then not just the head of Munster but the centre of the universe! 'Later, when I went to Clare in 1917 [where he was then first elected a member of parliament] I felt very much at home and used to joke some of those who were supporting me there by telling them that the whole of their glories originated in Bruree.' In 1957 Eddie gave a talk from the very spot where Sheehy had delivered his sermons, the former old church having been converted into a local hall. Yet he had been slow to return.[74]

There was another way besides his activism in which Fr Sheehy also impressed young Eddie, who served as one of his altar boys: 'I can still see him as he stood on the altar steps, with his long nose down almost to his lips, and the gold double cased watch, which he consulted from time to time.' De Valera described this as a 'hunter watch', a type kept in the pocket that has a hinged cover or lid to protect its face.[75] He quite literally dreamt when young of having one like it.[76]

Sheehy's sermons touched on aspects of Irish history. In 1952 de Valera told Frank Gallagher that from his formal education 'he knew much more of early Greek history than he did at the beginning of Irish history'. Yet, by the example of Greece, he had 'learned to respect the little nation and its defence of its rights. This, he implied, made it easier to assert the full claim of Ireland'. Sheehy's sermons no doubt helped too.[77]

In later years de Valera was to be closely associated with the Irish language. He did not learn it at school or from his neighbours around Bruree, although in various place names one heard an echo of the old language. He later said that many older people actively discouraged the use of Irish when he was a boy in Co. Limerick. De Valera's early biographer and fellow county man David T. Dwane had a similar experience.[78] For Eddie, the discouragement was not just verbal but physical, with shame and anxiety after the Great Famine sometimes driving Irish speakers to resort to force while committing in little more than two generations what David Greene once called 'linguistic suicide'. 'There were', recalled de Valera in 1957, 'some names I couldn't understand, and when I asked my grandmother for their definition I got a *leadóg faoin gcluais* [a 'clip' on the ear].' The names included 'the best place to swim ... *Poll an Easa*'.[79] Older people thought that they were helping the young to survive in the modern world by getting them to speak English fluently.

In 1901, and again in 1911, the census returns recorded Pat Coll as speaking both Irish and English. A detail the census did not capture clearly was the extent to which people who said they spoke Irish actually spoke it much or well. Late in his life de Valera told an American interviewer 'Neither of my parents, nor my uncle with whom I came to stay when I was [aged] two spoke Irish.'[80] His assertion that neither of his parents spoke Irish is scarcely surprising in the case of his ostensibly Spanish father, but if his mother could not do so it is significant. In any event, English was certainly the daily language of the Coll household by the time Eddie arrived there. Irish was dying out, and Eddie as a boy learnt merely a few words in the old language.

Eddie heard old people around Bruree, including his grandmother, speaking Irish to one another from time to time. Among their immediate neighbours old James Mortell, the nearest, spoke it. And old Tom Sullivan. Going down the road northwards, their next neighbours old James McCarthy and his wife, Joanna Nolan, were also fluent speakers. Then there were Johnnie Bray and his wife on the Howardstown Road:

> What Irish speakers there were in the village of Bruree I did not know, but the older people whom I have just mentioned spoke it habitually among themselves, but they spoke English to the younger people, including their own children who would now [1956] be grown up men and women. I tried to listen and pick up an odd word, but there would be no desire to teach me or to explain. Besides isolated words which were used in English I remember being taught but a few phrases – *Tabhair dom cathaoir* [give me a chair], *Tabhair dom píghe* [give me a pie] and one or two such.[81]

However, there is nothing from de Valera that supports an unreliable reference by Dwane to the 'old shoemaker from Bruree who proved to be a fluent Irish speaker', almost a centenarian no less, who was supposedly responsible for de Valera acquiring much knowledge of Irish and the correct accent and who became 'a frequent caller' at the Coll house.[82]

The Great Famine of the 1840s had killed many of the poorest people in the Irish countryside, or driven them to emigrate, and a higher proportion of these than of the population at large had spoken Irish as their first language. Younger people now saw Irish as a liability rather than as an asset, believing that people would consider you backward or poor or ill-educated if they heard you talking it. The great majority of the people in and around Bruree spoke only English by the time Eddie arrived. In 1851 there had been more than 600 people who spoke *only* Irish in the barony of Connello Upper where Bruree was situated, while at the same time 59% of its inhabitants spoke Irish *and* English (the highest proportion in any Limerick barony). By 1891 in Bruree there were no people who spoke *only* Irish and the proportion speaking both languages had declined to just 16%, these presumably being for the most part the oldest in each house. When de Valera visited Bruree in 1950 'after an absence of thirty-three years', he said that in Bruree 'Irish was spoken in every home sixty years ago … There were people whom he knew as a boy – few of them were alive now – who used the language in their daily lives.' By 1911 only 11 percent spoke Irish as well as English.[83]

At a meeting in Waterford in January 1946, when de Valera received the freedom of that city, he reportedly said that 'some time ago he wanted to know the particular dialect his grandmother spoke and it was something of a revelation for him to learn that the dialect of the Decies extended as far as Co. Limerick where his grandmother lived'. Decies Irish was spoken in Co. Waterford but also in parts of Counties Limerick and Tipperary, being distinct from the Irish dialect spoken elsewhere in the province of Munster. He remembered as a child that when the old people came in for a chat to his home it was Irish they spoke. 'Most of us,' he said, 'who speak English speak it in the Irish medium, and, therefore, there should be no great difficulty in learning the language.' He continued, 'The Irish I learned since [moving to Dublin] has been the dialect of Connacht. I think if I had known it was the Decies dialect my grandmother spoke I would have tried to learn that dialect and would have used it rather than any other.' He also remarked:

> Alas, that it is not the sound of the Decies I have, although these were the first sounds I heard when I was a young lad. Near Bruree, at that time, nearly all the old people were native Irish speakers, and it was the Ring [Co. Waterford] dialect they had [This is the present author's translation of his *Mo bhrón nach iad fuaimeanna na nDéise atá agam, cé gurbh iad sin na chéad fuaimeanna a chuala mé nuair a bhíos I mo bhuachaill óg. In aice le Brú Rí an t-am sin, na sean daoine ar fad, nach mór, ba Ghaeilgeoirí dúchais iad, agus ba í canúint na Rinne a bhí acu*].[84]

In fact the 'first sounds' of all sounds he heard were of course those of New York, and even when he got to Bruree a couple of years later the words he heard spoken were mostly in English.

Ryan in his biography of 1936 wrote that, 'No more feeling and insistent note is ever struck throughout de Valera's speeches but his ingrained love of the Irish language.' De Valera certainly came to encourage its revival and use, as he did at Bruree during his visit in 1950. But he himself had had a very limited grasp of or interest in the language until he joined the Gaelic League in his late twenties and then set about learning the Connacht dialect. By then the revival of Irish was part of a nationalist agenda, and learning it might be good for one's career too.

Frank Gallagher, his friend and admirer, wrote of de Valera's origins that 'the mixture of races produced a child entirely apart'. Eddie might not have stood out as very exceptional in Manhattan but he was certainly notable around Bruree. Another pupil at this primary school, who later became a professor of classics at Fordham University, said that because of Eddie's 'olive complexion' and surname the boys believed that he 'was a descendant of some Spaniard wrecked in the Spanish armada'.[85] Yet while de Valera would recall how a teacher found it difficult to spell his name, if there were any pointed racial insults by other boys these appear to have gone unrecorded. Asked by a radio reporter in 1965 if he was made to feel at home around Bruree, de Valera replied, 'The curious thing when I look back is I seemed to have the entrance to every house in the neighbourhood. I knew them and would walk in ... in any of the houses on my routes, that is around by Howardstown and so on.' Were other young neighbours not likewise welcome? Was his reception 'curious' perhaps precisely because he felt, or indeed was, 'a child entirely apart'?[86]

'A STARK ENOUGH REARING'

The loss of his Aunt Annie to emigration hit Eddie hard. He had become used to her being with him and his Uncle Pat in his grandmother`s house near Bruree, but then she too went to America where his mother and his Uncle Ed were settled:

> I was very fond of my aunt. She had been very kind and apparently understood children well. At last she was going to leave, and I remember the neighbours gathering in the night before to bid her goodbye for her first journey to the United States. Next morning she put on my boots and laced them for the last time, and she said to me, you will henceforth have to put them on yourself. My trouble was to know left from right. I remember

my uncle giving me a few lessons so that I would know. I went with her to the train with my grandmother and my uncle. My grandmother sobbed bitterly as she was saying goodbye and at this stage the train steamed off. I remember saying would I ever see her again. Yes, parting with the emigrants was a sad affair, and that was the lasting memory with me.[87]

De Valera remembered combing his grandmother's hair, 'beautiful and long it was and auburn, reaching down to the seat of the chair she was sitting on'.[88] She brought him with her going on visits around Bruree, and once part of the way to St Colman's Well, near Charleville, when he was aged two or three. It was one of many 'holy wells' or springs that dotted the countryside. Their waters were believed to cure ailments. De Valera later said he was too young to be left at home and too young also to be brought to St Colman's Well itself. So he was brought to a cottage beside the road leading to it. There was a woman in the cottage feeding a baby with 'goody' – bread and warm milk mixed in a cup. She cleaned the spoon in her mouth and, filling the spoon again, offered it to him. He was revolted by this lack of cleanliness but took it, 'and he always remembers that incident for the disgust it created in him'.[89]

Sometimes when she went on her rounds in the village, delivering milk or doing others chores, his grandmother left him alone in the chapel in Bruree. He later told Fr Seán Farragher that he once replied to her when asked how he got on in her absence 'Alright, granny, but I was lonely.' He told Farragher that she said then 'Lonely? How could you be lonely in God's house? Why didn't you talk to him?' Farragher thought that it was the experience of being left thus in the chapel that inculcated in him 'that deep personal devotion to the Lord's presence in the Eucharist, which was at times to amaze even his closest friends'.[90]

In March 1888 Eddie saw his mother for the first time in three years and for the last time for another nineteen. He recalled her having a big black bag, with a pocket in it and a flap over that. There were, his semi-official biographers wrote later, 'a few glorious weeks and a trip to Limerick [city] and then she went back again' – to get married in America. There is no substantial account of what they did together that time she was in Ireland, or how she interacted with him, or with either her mother or her brother Pat.[91]

He was signed into Bruree National School on 7 May 1888, aged five and half years old. Remarkably, this was the very same day on which his mother married Charles Wheelwright in New York.

Bruree national school was one big room, like many such schools then. In it were about sixty pupils of various ages, half of them at any one time standing and being taught directly or examined and the other half sitting in order to write or to do arithmetical exercises. A man called Kelly was teaching in the school. Eddie was to remember seeing him on a penny-farthing bicycle, one wheel like a big penny and the other like a small farthing coin. He was also to say that Kelly 'couldn't write my name on the rolls, and so I had to bring it in written by my uncle on my book'. Kelly gave Eddie's name in the ledger as 'Eddie Develera'. De Valera remembered 'We had two very fine globes, one a terrestrial globe and the other a celestial one.' The room was sometimes 'very, very cold' and each student was expected to bring in one shilling annually, the cost of a hundredweight of coal. During his first full year there seven out of the thirteen contemporaries listed in the surviving roll on the same page as Eddie had a better attendance rate than he did, with each of the best two being present on 209 days and Eddie himself on 167 days.[92]

By the time Eddie went to school Uncle Pat was already working him. He had him out with the cows by the roadside. The Colls had just a half-acre attached to their cottage, but managed to keep three or four cows of their own by feeding them elsewhere on the 'long acre' or 'long farm' – this being the good, broad edges at that time between a road proper and the fences, hedges or walls along it. There was not such an amount of traffic then. The Colls supplied milk to villagers. An owner of cows might be fined for letting cattle stray in public, so Eddie would be sent to stay with the cows and to watch out for police patrols: 'On Saturdays I'd probably spend the whole day with them. I got to know every blade of grass. I certainly knew nearly every bush on the roadside!' If he saw constables coming he would fetch Pat or his grandmother quickly, or else start herding by himself. For some years Pat used to buy a few store cattle too and fatten them on land let out locally to him. He also took meadowland in the autumn sometimes and passed it on to farmers in the springtime when their own supply of grass ran short. The Colls kept some pigs and hens too, as well as an old horse and a donkey.[93]

At one period his uncle used to collect between six and nine cases of eggs locally and take them to Limerick to sell. He would bring home from there a chest of tea, a bag of sugar, flitches of bacon, tobacco and even tins of sweets 'which at this period we used to retail. I was said to be very good at examining the eggs'. Eddie sometimes went with him, the two of them generally seated on top of the load. The long, slow journey to Limerick City began very early in the morning and ended late at night. Eddie tended to fall asleep. He had a lucky escape one night, tumbling from on high to land on the roadway without injury: 'Some good spirits, the neighbours said, had been looking after me.'[94]

At times they had enough money to buy sugar and tea and other items from O'Donoghue's shop in the village if they wished. There was butter too: 'When I was quite young the farmers around all churned.' Some used a horse to drive a butter churn and some churned by hand. Butter was packed in firkins and sent to the markets in Cork and Limerick. Eddie remembered the first pound of creamery butter that he saw in O'Donoghue's, looking nicer than the butter his grandmother herself churned for them he thought. As noted earlier, they bought enough items in that shop for Mrs O'Donoghue to want to give them a big cake each Christmas and with it some alcohol, usually a bottle of whiskey and another of port wine. Uncle Pat made sure that a poor man called Johnny, who used to come by their cottage, had a glass of whiskey going to Mass on Christmas Day. Granny Coll put a white cloth on the table at Christmas and Eddie was let light a candle in the window. On Easter Sunday morning he used to be brought outside to see the sun dancing. But, 'I saw no sun dancing. I was terribly disappointed! [laughs].'[95]

Whenever his grandmother got cross with him about something she told Pat, and left it to Pat to beat Eddie if he saw fit to do so:

My uncle was severe; he was very young – too young, really, to have the responsibility of my upbringing; but he was a wonderfully good parent in his way; he had very high standards. I gave trouble. I remember staying out one day when I knew I shouldn't. All the boys of the school played hurley but I remember saying to myself that I would be beaten in any case so I might as well see what there was to be. Hurley he didn't approve of being played. I had two hurley sticks and I'd leave one standing in the corner so that he would think I was not playing.[96]

Decades later de Valera would remark of his upbringing that 'It was a stark enough rearing.'[97] Corporal punishment was quite common then, with parents physically beating children for bad behaviour. Uncle Pat, for example, punished Eddie when he went 'on the sling' (as the boys called mitching) and when he misused the donkey's best reins to make a swing:

Swinging from a cord or rope attached to a branch of a tree was also a game we played. There was an old elm tree about fifty yards to the south of Mortell's gate. There I remember on one occasion I, having no other rope available, took the reins which my grandmother had specially preserved for the donkey on Sundays – always an unfrayed one – to make the swing. We tied it on the bough and had a glorious time swinging, but unfortunately the reins got frayed and discoloured. When our fun was over I put it back on the peg behind the kitchen door. My grandmother saw it and guessed what had happened, and I was reported for a thrashing. The next time I remember getting a thrashing was when I stayed from school.[98]

He again got a whacking from Pat when he went to see cranes that were being used to lift the wreck of a train at Bruree Station, instead of coming home at the time expected.[99] One of his contemporaries at school also said that her brother saw Eddie stripped, beaten and put into a basin to wash at his home after he took part in local games – where he had won races and jumping events.[100]

The games that boys played as they got older sometimes had a very rough edge to them. There were set battles on the sloping schoolyard. A lad might use as a weapon the big sow thistle (*geosadán*), swinging it by its good healthy roots. Sometimes away from school they used stones – his side being from out Howardstown way and the other from over towards Joyce's country, towards Tankardstown. This stone 'croosting' (as it was called from the Irish *crústa* meaning a clod or missile) was often at the pump cross. Eddie was knocked down one day in a battle in the schoolyard and 'a fellow put a broken tip of a shoe through the palm of my hand. I have the mark too today. That was the great charge,' he said in 1966.[101] In his sixteenth-century treatise *De Rebus in Hibernia Gestis*, Richard Stanihurst had observed among Irish foot soldiers a particular skill in throwing stones.

Then there was 'Balling the Cap' which it is hard to see appealing to many young people today, at least as de Valera described it in the 1960s. About half a dozen boys would place their caps upside down in front of a wall and, from ten yards back (about three metres), each tried to pitch the ball into his own cap. The thing to avoid was landing the ball in another boy's cap, because when this happened:

> the boy in whose cap the ball was could stand behind, and all the others had to face the wall, bend themselves horizontally with their fingers touching the wall; and they presented a very fine target for the boy behind. He had a shot at each one in turn … with boys like we were who were used to 'croosting' – throwing stones – he could give you a pretty smart smack [on your backside].[102]

If this seems like a strange 'game' to play, there was in some parts of Ireland an even odder form of 'croosting'. This was at wakes where people gathered around a corpse before it was buried. Ó Súilleabháin writes that 'Even persons who were no longer young took a hand in the "croosting." Besides turf, the shanks of clay pipes were also broken off by those who did not smoke and used as missiles; the targets were usually unpopular individuals or crusty old men, who were easily angered. Whatever was ready to hand would be used: potatoes, water or anything convenient. "We'll have a night of croosting," the young folk would cry with joy, whenever they heard that some old person had died in the parish.'[103] Taken with other 'rough games' mentioned by Ó Súilleabháin, games that could leave one permanently injured, and with the more general practice of dangerous faction fighting that was common at fairs into the mid-nineteenth century, de Valera's references to 'croosting' are a reminder that a labourer's life in rural Ireland was not genteel.

Uncle Pat himself was happy in later life to talk of a distant relation on his mother's side who had been a leading 'faction' fighter. This was Martin Gabha (Irish *gabha* meaning 'smith'). He was a great-granduncle of Eddie and a brother of 'the Dyer'. 'The Dyer' was said to have owned a tannery in Charleville and, as 'he was well-to-do', helped to look after Eddie's grandmother Carroll when her husband died:

> A great, big, brawny blacksmith known as Martin Gabha (Carroll) used to go to the 'Fair of the Well' (Debarah's Well) in the parish of Ballyagran and also to the fair of Dromin … His battle cry was 'Here is Carroll O'Gorman or otherwise Martin Gabha'. He carried two big black-thorn sticks and a frieze coat. When the battle cry was raised he used to pull the coat after him in the puddle ['trailing your coat' was a form of challenge]. Whoever would stand on the tail of the coat would hear from the sticks… and then others would follow their leader and the faction would begin.[104]

Rabid dogs were a great danger when Eddie was a boy. As late as 1898 four people in Ireland died after being bitten. De Valera recalled rabies being 'not uncommon' and that people were sometimes 'terrified' of a rabid dog in the area: 'Those bitten used to go to the Pasteur Institute', which was in Paris and which in 1885 had developed there the only effective vaccine. It attracted patients from as far away as America. The Poor Law Guardians might fund such a trip, as they did in the case of Paddy Cullinane of Co. Waterford.[105]

There were superstitions in the Bruree area, and Eddie was not immune to them. One night he was crossing a stream near where the boreen from Barrens reached the main road. A small bird, hopping from bush to bush, seemed to be following him and 'I was thoroughly frightened by the time I reached the churchyard, which lay on this way. A black dog was supposed to meet travellers at this point, but the dog did not appear, but the bird continued to follow me until I reached the brook beyond Walsh's gate. And so I became a firm believer for a time in the local superstition that spirits do not follow over running water.' He was told that people used to put up ropes in the rafters and pulled them as if milking cows, 'and this was to get the milk from other people's cows'. Houses were lit by candles and paraffin lamps, with candle lanterns hung outdoors. The girls and boys from Mortells' farm often came to his house and told yarns in the flickering light, especially ghost stories: 'I used to be frightened of them.'[106]

His grandmother too scared him rightly one time. On that occasion, as he recalled, 'she came home at Christmas time – home from the village – with an icicle on her face. I was alone and when I saw a mask, which was a horrible one, I got frightened at this strange creature peeping in through the half open door. I got a very great fright indeed. I think she was very sorry.' But Granny Coll could be kind to strangers. It was customary for a number of people to travel around and stay for a period in each parish. Eddie's grandmother allowed one of these, 'Pegín from Kerry', to make down her bed by the fire when she was coming through the Bruree countryside. He could hear Pegín praying at night.[107]

De Valera later said that in his youth 'all but well-to-do farmers came to Mass by horse or donkey with a common car'. The well-to-do had traps (of various kinds) with iron rims on the wheels. He rode with his grandmother and Pat for Mass in the village chapel each Sunday. As well as 'serving Mass' for the priests (assisting them during the service), he often got to ring the church bell to summon Mass-goers. He liked that. He tolled it too for funerals.[108] In 1934, when denying that he was Jewish, he told Dáil Éireann:

> I say that on both sides of me I come from Catholic stock. My father and mother were married in a Catholic Church, on September 19th, 1881 [no record of such marriage has ever been found]. I was born in October 1882. I was baptised in a Catholic Church. I was brought up here in a Catholic home. I have lived amongst the Irish people and loved them and loved every blade of grass that grew in this land. I do not care who says, or who tries to pretend that I am not Irish. I say I have been known to be Irish and that I have given everything in me to the Irish nation.[109]

Besides going into Bruree to serve Mass on Sundays he appears to have spent little time in the village itself ('to me 'twas "the town"') – 'except just passing through' to catch a train: 'It was the place that I went to school.'

This did not stop the station being 'a favourite playground of mine with some of the other boys'. They 'used to be always anxious to get a jaunt' on empty wagons that were let freewheel down the slope to the buffers. Perhaps it was here too they smoked their ratan 'cigarettes' (below). Once on board to Charleville 'I utilized any time I had in the train to make up my home lessons. That was the only time I had for this except at weekends.'[110]

Meanwhile, in the land of his birth, his mother was not writing to him as often as he would have liked. Any letters that she did send in these early years do not appear to survive, but one that he drafted or sent to his Aunt Annie is extant. Dated at his home in Knockmore on 26 December 1889 it shows that he was annoyed at his mother. Perhaps he had expected money or some other Christmas gift that did not come:

> Dear Aunt, I am writing these few lines to you hoping Mamma Katie, Sister [his half-sister Annie, born July 1889], Uncle [Charles] and yourself are well. I am sending these little cards one each to Mamma and Sister and the other to you. Tell Mamma I am angry to her for not writing. Tell her also I will write her a long letter soon. No more at present. Wishing you all a happy New Year. Mamma [presumably this meaning his grandmother, Aunt Annie's 'mamma'] wishes you the same. From your fond nephew, Eddie De Valera.[111]

Aunt Annie came back to visit in 1891, the year that he made his First Communion and Confirmation. She was there again in 1895 when he was thirteen, the year his grandmother died:[112]

> My task on the Saturday as I grew older was to sweep the yard in front of the door. There wouldn't be much more, I am sure, than about twelve or fifteen feet on each side, but it was a task which I disliked intensely. I remember my aunt tried to make it lighter for me by giving me sixpence. I think that must have been when she had returned from America. She came back after an absence of some years and was as kind as she had always been. What wonderful dresses she had, and that great big trunk with a wonderful box of trinkets. She was a gallant picture on Sundays as she went to Mass with her grand American dresses.[113]

But Annie went back to America and Eddie was left alone again with Uncle Pat. He took to smoking, and to more daydreaming. He and other young boys used to smoke ratan: 'There's a certain cane and it's very porous and if you burn it you can suck the smoke through it.' He added 'Turf was very common too. We smoked turf and this chap Mortell – 'twas he introduced me to the "lucky bag", a penny lucky bag, and in this lucky bag one of the things you'd be hoping to get was a miniature pipe, but you'd put turf in it. Although I heard that some people used tea!'[114]

Eddie and Tom Mortell practised hurling on the side of what was called 'Mortell's Hill'. One day when they were hurling 'up on the hill field at Knockmore' they got tired and sat down for 'a fairly long time'. He had been warned not to sit on wet grass, so instead sat on the broad part of his hurley. As he recalled this episode in old age he thought that he had served as an altar boy at a requiem Mass in a woman's house that morning long ago, and now in the afternoon the funeral itself was taking place and they could see it 'passing at a great distance from us, but it could be seen dimly from the hill'. It set him pondering on life and death and 'that set me wondering about the world around me – whether it really existed or whether it was a dream'. To satisfy his curiosity, he said, he pinched the other boy – Tom Mortell – 'to see if we really existed. This was my first philosophical thought.' It was a practical experiment: 'The response I got left me in no doubt as to the actuality of the world outside me.' Mortell punched him.[115]

Much later in life, when he was elected president of Ireland, de Valera sometimes welcomed at his official residence Dr W.H. Heitler and his wife. Heitler was the professor of theoretical physics in the University of Zürich but had worked during the Second World War at the Dublin Institute for Advanced Studies that de Valera created at the time. In 1982 Heitler recalled one such visit:

In his charming manner he told us of his boyhood and how he developed a passion for collecting frogs' eggs, like so many boys. The reason was that he could not have enough of watching the ever-recurring miracle of the birth of a tadpole and then the transformation into a frog. He added that this confirmed for him, more than many a learned proof, that there must have been a creator at work. He was deeply religious, but we also agreed about the difficulty of understanding the world in general, living nature to start with. I suppose that many scientists who still think that their primary task is the understanding of nature will agree with de Valera when in the end he said with a sigh: 'I wish the Lord had made it a bit easier for us'.[116]

As he got older Eddie's grandmother sent him to an itinerant dancing master to get some lessons in dancing. He learnt the side-step, the jig and one or two set dances: 'But I can't say that I learnt very well.' There were some 'local balls', but does his bland remark that he 'went to one at McCarthy's – paid a shilling' indicate that he went to *only* one?[117]

With his mother absent, no known father, and a foreign name, it might be expected that he would have been bullied. The loose stones that filled potholes around Bruree crossroads were telling ammunition. He came home one day with a cut on his forehead. He said there was a fight because he stood up to those calling his uncle 'Dane Coll' – as if Pat was foreign and not Irish. He didn't tell Pat that they called Eddie himself that same name. He learnt later that this could have been just the local way of pronouncing 'dean' and not the word 'Dane', and that they might have been referring not to Vikings but to the fact that Fr Sheehy sometimes asked Pat to lead the congregation when it was time to recite the rosary in Bruree chapel. There may also have been an actual dean in the extended Coll family it seems. But had Eddie a nickname besides the occasional 'Dane'? Indeed he had, and hated it. It was 'Deliver-us'. There was also 'Young Neddy Cull', and it made him furious. The place was full of Colls ('Cull' it was pronounced). To distinguish them, the different families had nicknames. He said that he gave many a black eye over the name-calling.[118]

Less violently, in the evenings, he played games called 'Duck' and 'Peg Top', as well as 'Pitch and Toss' (with buttons instead of coins). His statement that 'When I was growing up I was able to spin a top and play like the farmers' boys in the evenings' reveals indirectly the social division between farmers and labourers.[119]

As he got older he skipped school more. The boys called it 'leaching' as well as 'slinging' then.[120] He'd wander the countryside, eating haws and other berries and digging up pignuts to take the edge off his appetite.

The pignut can be tasty, 'something like celery heart crossed with raw hazelnut or sweet chestnut and sometimes having a spicy aftertaste of the sort you get from radishes or watercress'. The finest sloes in the country were around Clonbrien he thought. There was a hollow near the top of Knockmore Hill, on Lyons' side, where he picked blackberries, cowslips and mushrooms.[121]

Drinking-water around Bruree was usually drawn from wells then, sometimes hauled up from springs with a windlass. Springs might attract snipe, as Kickham observed in *Knocknagow*, and this was a gamebird that could be shot. Eddie searched for fresh springs, digging and watching the water spurt – seeking something hidden underground, ready to erupt – like his own uncertain past: 'It would seem a peculiar method of enjoyment, and indeed an unprofitable one', thought one man.[122]

One day a boy named Martin Callaghan and himself went 'on the sling'. They met two travelling tailors at work. One of the tailors wanted a story but Eddie stayed quiet and Martin said he had none. So a tailor told the story of John Connors of Bruree. Connors too had been asked to tell a story, said the tailor, but he also had none. So Connors was sent for water then and met men carrying a coffin. They asked for help carrying it. Connors wanted to know who was inside. The Devil, they said. They came to a house. Hearing the rosary being said they passed by. At the next house they were welcomed in God's name, so they went on. But then, said the tailor, they came to a house where the husband and wife could be heard fighting. The Devil said that that was the house for him, and the men lowered the coffin onto its doorstep. So Connors beat a hasty retreat. He ran home and recounted what had happened. The people at home told him he could never again say he had no story.[123]

But what was Eddie's story? He knew nothing certain about his father or his father's people; remembered next to nothing of his first years in New York; had no chance to meet his half-sister or half-brother in Rochester. No story. No prospects. And when his Granny Coll died in July 1895 he became partly a housekeeper for his uncle, even cooking the wedding breakfast when Pat married Kate Dillane just eight months later. So now there was a new 'Kate Coll' in the cottage. There'd be new babies too.[124]

During the 1890s a song entitled 'The Man Who Broke the Bank at Monte Carlo' was popular. Michael Bergin – who went by pony and trap selling tea in Bruree for Foxy Pat Coll – used to sing it as he drove along. The boys began to call him Monte Carlo. One day Dick Coll, a son of Foxy Pat, was absent from school and Eddie was sent to get him because an inspector was due: 'Like most kids I was delighted to get away from the books.' Along the way Eddie met Bergin and asked had he seen Dick. Bergin replied that the boy might be in the barn. When Eddie entered it, Bergin locked him in. In later years Bergin boasted that he was de Valera's first jailer.[125]

Even when not locked in a barn by a trickster, Eddie felt confined in Bruree. He was not content and dreamt of getting away.

– 4 –

'I WAS ALONE
A GOOD DEAL'

DREAMING OF ESCAPE

Eddie passed much of his time in Bruree on his own. He often had
to spend all of Saturday out minding cows. As he got older he combined this with reading. Books were an escape, and an encouragement.
Robinson Crusoe, a favourite of his, is the story of a man surviving
alone on a deserted island.[1] For a long time Eddie saw no chance of
getting away from Bruree and getting on. In the 1930s he told Dorothy
Macardle:

> One thing I had when I was a child that I liked playing with alone: I had
> no one to play with. I was alone a good deal. In the river I had a little
> island, and I used to shape it and make plans about it. This was Ireland
> and I was the ruler of it … And yet, though I dreamed a great deal, I had
> no ambitions or expectations. I had nothing but the spade. I remember
> a boy who lived next us; he was older than I, and he was going to be a
> draper's assistant. I thought that was a big world from which I was forever
> shut out. To be a labourer was what was before me.[2]

His friend Frank Gallagher was to remark that 'a surge of envy swept that
young American-Irish heart, clearly felt more than fifty years later', as de
Valera recalled for him the same moment:

He remembers well the day he and another boy were digging potatoes. The other boy who was older (about 16 or so) told him he was going to Limerick to a job. That seemed to D. like going on a great adventure and he said to himself 'and I am to remain digging potatoes all my life?' He was twelve about that time.[3]

'D.' (de Valera) also told Gallagher that he had thought about why people left the land and moved into cities. It was not just the lack of amenities. He believed there was some deeper urge to go away and get into a place busier and more bustling. He may have had a buried memory of Manhattan that excited him. In another rendering of the same story in the 1960s he added that this boy was 'my nearest companion', namely Tom Mortell, and he thought he was going 'to learn the grocery business'.[4]

Eddie's son Terry would one day paint a nostalgic picture of Éamon de Valera as 'he reminisced fondly of his early times with his uncle and other relations in Bruree, Co. Limerick and spoke with affection of the little house which had tender memories for him.'[5] But Eddie was far

De Valera's beloved Aunt Annie (also Hannie) who cared for him when he first came to Bruree, before herself emigrating. On her two return visits, Annie's 'grand American dresses' impressed him. Photograph by Bostwick, 98 Sixth Avenue, New York. Courtesy UCD Archives P150/213.

from satisfied in Bruree. He thought that one option for him was to go to America. This is clear from a letter he wrote to his beloved Aunt Annie, with whom he opened a channel of communication that appears to have bypassed his uncle's supervision. Eddie's grandmother (Annie's mother) had died the previous year and he was now living alone with Uncle Pat.

On 2 March 1896 he explicitly told his Aunt Annie in America that he was not content in Co. Limerick, that he had nobody to be with there and would much rather be in America. He pressed his 'dear aunt' to persuade his mother to send for him:

> I must again ask you to excuse me for not answering your letters. I would have answered your first one but, as you said you were sending me some pocket money, I thought it best to wait, and that perhaps I would get it in a few days, and so I did and received it a week after. Then when I was going to write again one of the cows calved and I had no chance of writing at all as Uncle would not stay out any length of time. It was only today that he is gone to Bruree that I have a chance.
>
> John Sullivan is very much improved since I wrote last [and] he wants me to tell you that Maria didn't write yet and for you to write to her again. Uncle didn't get married yet. But Paddy Donovan your old friend did: did you remember when you put the beans on the fire of a Christmas Eve, for him – to know if he would get married?
>
> I am going to school regularly and Uncle is as kind as ever, still I am not content here. I would by far rather be over, as I have no one to be with, Tom Mortell having gone over to his uncle in Kilmallock. A woman called Ellen Crotty does our washing and ironing. I do not see J---- D---- [*sic*, but overwritten is the name Jack Dwane] as often as formerly. I told him what you said. Father Connolly asks often about you.
>
> It would not be a bad plan if Mamma was writing to Uncle to say to send me over with someone that was going soon, and perhaps he might let me go. I would like very much to be over for Patrick's Day but it is impossible.

I am joined in the Bruree I.F. [Irish Fireside] Club. I am sending you a bunch of shamrocks for Patrick's Day. I hope they will be in time. I am in a great hurry for Uncle might be in any minute.

I remain my dear Aunt your loving nephew Eddie de Valera.

P.S. Address your letters in care of John Dwane, Howardstown, Bruree, Co. Limerick, Ireland.[6]

Sixty-eight years later de Valera dictated to his secretary the following note about the above letter of 1896:

This letter to my aunt was written some seven months after my grand-mother's death when I and my uncle were living alone. I had to do a good deal of the house-keeping and my attendance [at school] that year was rather low (140 days). I had not yet gone to Charleville C[hristian] B[rothers] School. My uncle's idea was that I should become a monitor [teaching assistant] in the local Bruree [National] School. I disliked this very much. My aunt was with us from sometime before my grandmother's death. We were very fond of each other, and she was urging me strongly to come to America, particularly in view of my uncle's likely marriage. She and Jack Dwane were particular friends, hence my suggestion that she write in care of him.[7]

That last explanation may not be the whole story. He evidently felt unable or unwilling to be found writing to his aunt when Uncle Pat was at home. By suggesting that Annie reply to Eddie via Dwane there was no chance his uncle would open the envelope first and read what she said.

There is nothing in this or any other extant letter that supports a statement by Terry de Valera that, when Eddie reached adolescence, Kate 'invited him on no less than two occasions to return to the USA and live in her new home' there. Terry de Valera does not cite a source for this assertion.[8] In the note quoted above that de Valera dictated later regarding his letter to his Aunt Annie written in 1896, in which year he was an adolescent aged thirteen, he claims his aunt had urged him 'strongly' to come to America but gives no indication that his mother ever supported the idea.

Eddie liked to linger on the hill of Knockmore, or the hill of Knockfenora and then by the brook. It cleared his head doing so. There was a very nice hazel tree, where you could get nuts in autumn. It was on the hill of Knockfenora that he slowly read through Abbott's big biography of Napoleon. That was a man who made his own way in the world. Napoleon Bonaparte forged his own destiny. And Eddie intended to forge his. Meanwhile, he amused himself by observing those who passed through Bruree. There were the itinerant 'tinkers' who 'came around to mend vessels of tin; soldering; they put bottoms into cylindrical tin cans. They had a budget in which they carried their tools – it was usually a wooden box in which they had soldering iron, scissors'. There were the two tailors who, besides making clothes in their own houses 'went about the district to farmers' houses, and while in a farmer's house usually made clothes for the family of the house and for surrounding houses'. They sat cross-legged on the kitchen table as they worked. Neighbours dropped in to hear them talk, for the tailors 'were great tellers of folk tales'. On summer evenings one could see tailors, shoemakers and tradesmen walking about after 7 p.m. in their leather aprons – 'they didn't think it worth their while to take them off'.

He later recalled in detail the interior of rural kitchens about Bruree at that time, with their swinging cranes over the open fire for cooking pots, and a wooden settle bed like a rectangular chest that folded down at night on hinges: 'children very often slept in it'. He recalled no cigarettes being smoked: 'People used plug and rat tail tobacco, also snuff.' For alcohol adults had stout and whiskey, with 'five gallons of porter for hay-making the reek and out in the fields'. When farmers around Bruree killed pigs they distributed black puddings and fresh pork steak – *griscín* – to neighbours. The ordinary meat was bacon, for very little 'fresh meat' (beef) was eaten locally. When Uncle Pat bred up young steers he and Eddie brought them to the fair to sell. He later recalled often standing in the fair at Charleville. One very cold morning there he went into a hotel after his uncle to warm up. A woman brought him to a fire and got him some bread and butter and brown stout: 'She put the poker in the fire and got it quite hot and put it in and warmed up the stout. I thought 'twas a wonderful drink!'[9]

In Eddie's youth hay and corn were cut with scythes, occasionally with a hook. He said he saw the introduction of the mowing machine. The Sullivans lived a short distance up the road from him. Eddie used to follow the tumbling rake for them. He said there were no hay barns then, just simple 'reeks' (ricks/stacks, or *síog*).[10]

Later, in Dáil Éireann, he conjured up memories of his days working on the land while at school, using them to identify himself with rural Ireland:

> We [in the Fianna Fáil Party] believe we are just as much interested in the welfare of the workers of the country, as any members of the Labour Party are. Few of us were born with silver spoons in our mouths. Deputies have been speaking as if we knew nothing about agriculture. There is not an operation on the farm, with perhaps one exception, that I as a youngster had not to perform. I lived in a labourer's cottage, but the tenant could be regarded as, in his way, a small farmer. From my earliest days I participated in every operation that takes place on a farm. One thing I did not learn – how to plough. Until I was 16 years of age, there was nothing of any kind on a farm, from the spancelling of and milking of a cow, I had not to deal with. I cleaned out the cow-houses. I followed the tumbler rake. I took my place on the top of the rick. I took my place on the cart and filled the load of hay. Let nobody talk as if we were reared in some exotic atmosphere and knew nothing about the life of our people. We have been intimately associated with the life of our people, and with the ordinary, plain people of the country. I took milk to the creamery. I harnessed the donkey, the jennet and the horse, and I know just as much as any Deputy in this House about these things.
>
> Should farmer-Deputies want to come along and discuss farming matters with me, they will find they are dealing with one who has not got his knowledge from books. We are interested in the working people of the country. We are interested in the small farmers. We are interested in everybody who works whether, as it was put here, with hand or brain.[11]

The statement that he lived in one of the labourers' cottages but that 'the tenant, in his way, could be regarded as a small farmer' obscures the fact that labourers spent much of their time working for others who were better off. His uncle had him labouring for neighbouring farmers

Eddie appears to have shared with Uncle Pat a pleasure in riding a good horse. Pat once told his own daughter Lizzie a striking story that she related to de Valera years later: 'My father [Pat] was ten years when his father died and he always said that day was the greatest day of his life. He was left in charge of a neighbour's saddled horse and kept racing up and down the road on horseback while the owner was at the graveside.'[12] As a way to deflect the trauma of loss this was perhaps as good as any.

Eddie did not ride only the usual farm horses around Bruree. One day he was on his way home from Charleville when he met Willie Daly, a brother of one of his teachers, on a horse named March Boy that had won the Charleville Plate. The man seemed 'very tipsy' and Eddie was fearful that the rider – a member of a famous hunting and racing family – might fall off and be killed. Just then, local landlord John Gubbins came along with his steward, and they got the man off the horse and into their sidecar for his own sake: 'I have a picture of him kicking like a child as he was being lifted,' Eddie recalled. Gubbins asked Eddie to ride the horse instead: 'I had ridden horses for farmers around but I had never been on a racehorse before.' He was 'delighted' as he said, and had a great time cantering back and forth near them. At Gubbins' back gate at Garrouse, 'to my great disappointment, I had to surrender my mount'. Gubbins, the sometimes controversial landlord of Bruree House as seen above, was also a highly successful racehorse owner and breeder who twice won, among other top races, the English Derby – in 1897 with Galteemore, and in 1902 with Ardpatrick. The incident mentioned here gave rise to the story that Eddie rode one of them that day near Bruree, but it was in fact another horse. De Valera long remembered the celebrations in Bruree when Galteemore won, with tar barrels still smouldering as he went to school next morning. On another occasion he was on his way to a funeral with his uncle in Co. Limerick, the two of them in a covered car, when a man named Philip Barren gave Eddie a chance to ride Barren's chestnut mare. Barren was a very heavy man, 'and seeing a youngster in the car he thought it would be better for his horse that I should be on its back' –

De Valera as a boy enjoyed riding horses. Seen here on horseback later in life. Courtesy UCD Archives P150/194 no. 4.

and he instead sitting in the car: 'I of course was delighted with myself. I rode the whole way and back again.' Barren gave him another chance, more thrilling, to ride the same horse – which Barren was then putting in for the Charleville races and for which he had no light rider. Eddie had been sent to Barren's house to return a horse lent to his Uncle Pat to plough the cottage garden. Barren on that day invited Eddie to go down to a long field and mount the racehorse again. She went off like a shot. It was Eddie's first time riding really fast: 'It took my breath away and I held on tight for bare life.' Eddie was heading for a trench and he had never jumped on a horse before. But she went over it like a bird. He was hardly shaken in the saddle, and the same speed on the return: 'To be on the back of a racehorse and to let her go as fast as she could go! She went!'[13]

In 1936 Éamon de Valera was to lose his third son, Brian, in a riding accident in Dublin's Phoenix Park – the place where he himself subsequently lived for fourteen years of his life when elected president of Ireland in 1959.

He may have dreamt of riding a horse out of Bruree and into a different kind of future. But how could he rise above a life of labouring in the fields? The priests said education was a key to getting ahead, and he began to try harder for good marks, even when tired from his other work. Maybe he himself might become a priest: 'My grandmother hoped that she might be able to apprentice me to be a carpenter. I would have liked that alright, but fundamentally I think my desire was to become a priest. I'm not sure that I had any very definite ideas about it however.'[14]

Pat sometimes needled Eddie about his schoolwork. De Valera later recalled a boy in his class called Jack Potter, who used to come to school on a donkey with a beautiful leather saddle. When Eddie rode the Coll's donkey to school, he had only an old sack to sit on, and cord over the back as stirrup. Potter had free time to learn very well, and in second class Pat used to hold him up as a model to Eddie. 'Why don't you be like Jack Potter?' He knew well why. Pat had Eddie otherwise occupied. But Eddie was already watching out for his interests. He liked to recall especially how one time he was kept at home in bed because he had measles. It was the day of an examination by a schools' inspector. Eddie feared that missing the examination might hold him back from advancing at the end of the year. 'I was determined that this would not happen.' He heard Jack Potter coming into the Coll's kitchen – as he sometimes did on his way to school. Eddie's grandmother was still alive then. She told Potter that Eddie would not be going to school that day: '"That's right, Mrs Coll"', says he, "measles are dangerous; it would be bad for him to go out."' Eddie felt rivalry: 'I thought 'twas the ruse of a chap who was very interested in keeping me in bed'. Although he seemed to have a fever, Eddie pulled on his clothes and ran to school and was examined: 'I got a cold however, and had some trouble with my eyes for a time afterwards.' Excepting that incident, he said later, 'I do not remember any very special circumstances connected with my school life.'[15]

Eddie appreciated that Pat had given him a home and, when later working at Carysfort College, he supported his uncle in an application to the Land Commission for an allotment at Athlacca near Bruree. The surviving draft of a letter he prepared when teaching in Dublin has Eddie telling the commissioners 'I am considerably indebted to him for my upbringing. I am anxious to assist him and it struck me that my willingness to do so might have some influence with the commissioners.'[16] Yet De Valera was not to name any of his own children Patrick, which was both his uncle's name and that of Eddie's grandfather Coll. Indeed, he did not name one child after any of his grandparents, or even after his own mother. Only his unknown father was to be so honoured.

If his uncle was a 'severe' man with 'very high standards', as Eddie had said, he was also a labourer who – like Eddie himself – showed an inclination to rise above his station in life. He got one of the first labourers' cottages, engaged in farming activities beyond the half-acre attached to their cottage and took an active and successful interest in local politics. Uncle Pat also won a race of donkeys and cars down a hill after the first session of 'a mission' (preaching and prayer) in Bruree church. On this and the following night both Eddie and his grandmother were seated in the car. On the second night some people, whom de Valera later described merely as 'they', decided Pat should not win again: 'We were half-way between Schoolhouse Cross and Rourke's Cross when out came the wheel of the car. Some prime boy had taken the linchpin. We weren't thrown, curiously enough. There was a jolt, the axle came to the ground against a slope, but none of us fell out.' While de Valera coupled this story with one about a harmless practical joke played on an old lady with a donkey and cart, in his family's case the outcome could quite easily have been serious or even fatal. If this was mere entertainment, it was 'curiously enough' dangerous if not also malicious.[17]

Later, on a public stage, Pat could not resist mocking Eddie's work on the land. This was during a song and dance '*Aeridheacht*' (outdoor entertainment), organised by Fianna Fáil in Co. Limerick. One newspaper recalled it when Patrick Coll died in 1938. Pat was, wrote the reporter:

A man of splendid physique. He was six feet four inches in height and many stories are told of his remarkable strength. Many years ago he was a member of the Kilmallock Rural District Council … He had a sense of humour racy of the soil … On one occasion at least Mr de Valera was made the victim, if the expression may be permitted, of the late Mr Coll's banter. When speaking at an *Aeridheacht* at Loughgur, Mr de Valera made an allusion to his boyhood days in Bruree and mentioned that he used take special pleasure at the hay-saving operations. His uncle, who was on the platform, interjected – 'And a damn bad hand you were at it.' This sally created roars of laughter, in which Mr de Valera joined in heartily.[18]

De Valera could scarcely have done other than 'join in heartily' in the circumstances. Later again, when he was aged eighty-four, he would write of his 'many happy recollections' of his boyhood in Bruree, and of his pleasure in visiting the 'old haunts' there as often as possible.[19] Yet, as a boy, he ached to leave.

WHAT EDDIE READ

There was informal education, pleasure and sheer escapism to be had from reading, with printed books becoming cheaper and therefore more plentiful as the later nineteenth century was marked by technological change: 'When I was minding the cows, of course, that was when I was able to read. I remember reading *Robinson Crusoe* for instance. Then, later, I used to read books on the hill of Knockfenora.' Yet there were still 'very few books' in any house when Eddie was a boy, so far as he remembered. It is possible to piece together from a number of sources a list of titles he later said he had read as a child.[20]

Abbé James MacGeoghegan's *History of Ireland* was a favourite of Uncle Pat. Eddie read it too, as well as Jane Porter's *The Scottish Chiefs* – an early and widely read imaginative account of William Wallace and the battle for Scottish independence that mixes fictional and historical characters. MacGeoghegan (1702–1763), priest and historian, is said to have been the son of a prosperous Irish farmer. He wrote in French his account of Ireland until the 1691 Treaty of Limerick, decrying the Williamite political settlement and the penal laws against Catholics that ensued. Patrick Kelly's English translation of MacGeoghegan's history, published in 1831–32 with a new edition in 1844, is said to have become an Irish nationalist classic during the nineteenth century.[21] For her part, Porter (1776–1850) has been frequently neglected and deemed a minor author, but 'she played a significant role in using the historical novel to promote a heroic Scottish identity'. Bies and other authors have analysed the function of such romances in forming nations' perceptions of the place of virtuous heroes in the fight for independence. De Valera thought he had *The Scottish Chiefs* perhaps through the Uncle Remus Club (below).[22] An indication of the reach of Porter's book is that a character in Kickham's *Knocknagow* is reading it. *Robinson Crusoe* also features in that Irish novel.[23] Remarkably, as noted above, the popular *Knocknagow* is not a book that de Valera included in the list of what he read. Uncle Pat also had *Handy Andy: A Tale of Irish Life* by Samuel Lover, published first in 1880.

As seen earlier, Eddie also read Abbott's *Life of Napoleon*. He read some stories by William Carleton, including humorous ones about a 'gauger' or exciseman. At least one of these – the tale of a clever boy who gets his way by practical tricks – found its way into oral folklore in Irish.[24]

De Valera said that Paddy Joyce, when working at Bruree national school, formed the 'Uncle Remus Club – *Weekly Freeman*' and in that way the boys got to read a variety of books. This was part of an initiative that, in conjunction with the Irish Fireside Club, allowed one to acquire certain titles from the paper at low cost. Eddie is said to have been secretary of the Bruree branch at the age of thirteen. 'In the Uncle Remus Club we got books like *The Bog of Stars*'. Written by Standish O'Grady and published in 1893, *The Bog of Stars* is a collection of sketches of Elizabethan Ireland (1558–1603). O'Grady stated in its preface that his object was 'to bring the modern Irish reader into closer and more sympathetic relation with a most remarkable century of Irish history; a century which, more than any other, seems to have determined the destiny of Ireland.' He added 'The events are in each case related either as they actually occurred or with a very slight dramatization and infusion of local and contemporaneous colour.'[25]

Scott's *Ivanhoe* 'was one of the first long books that I remember reading when I was going to school', said de Valera. Indeed it was 'the first novel I ever read'. The historical romance *Ivanhoe*, one of the Waverley novels by the Scottish poet and novelist Walter Scott (1771–1832), has been described as 'essentially a moral work' that adapts history to its author's purpose. Scott explores the clash between heroic traditions of the past and practical visions of the future. Although set in a distant period *Ivanhoe* is said to have 'a political modernity which makes it one of the most remarkable novels of the nineteenth century'.[26]

De Valera also said that he read *The Wild Rose of Lough Gill: A Tale of the Irish War in the Seventeenth Century* by Patrick G. Smyth. Published in 1883, this was another historical romance; *Twenty Years After* 'by Victor Hugo' (actually by Alexandre Dumas as a sequel to his *Three Musketeers*) and some stories by Captain Frederick Marryat of the Royal Navy, particularly *Mr Midshipman Easy*.

Then there was – 'of course', as he said – *The Story of Ireland* by A.M. Sullivan. It was 'the book that I read from most' and the first history of Ireland he 'really' read. Published in 1867, it was intended for children. Maume has written that its 'emotive, gripping, pictorial and literary narrative', incorporating Young Ireland ballads and uncritically recycling the idealisations of earlier antiquarians, 'was immensely popular; it reflects the Young Ireland project of creating patriotic popular history. The book went through innumerable editions, and has been criticised for popularising a simplistic and teleological nationalist narrative.'[27] Sullivan was a polemical journalist, sometime supporter of the conservative wing of Young Ireland and editor of *The Nation* but unsympathetic to the Fenians. He also produced with his two brothers that same year the very popular nationalist text *Guilty or Not Guilty? Speeches from the Dock*.

The *Freeman* was not the only paper circulating daily or weekly in the neighbourhood. The Mortells next door used to get the *Cork Examiner* and the *Munster News*, with one of the Mortell nephews getting the illustrated *Shamrock* nationalist weekly as well as comic cuts – 'wild westerns' such as *Buffalo Bill*. As regards the *Shamrock*, 'Mick McQuaid, with Terry Geraghty, was the famous character in it,' noted de Valera.[28]

In March 1888, on her visit back to Bruree, Eddie's mother brought with her a copy of Thomas Moore's *Melodies* which Eddie's Aunt Annie used to read: 'I have a great recollection – I can see them all – sitting round the table on Sunday afternoons reading aloud songs from the *Melodies*,' said de Valera later.[29]

Reading aloud was common in families at that time of limited literacy, but it was also a form of entertainment. Charles J. Kickham – author of *Knocknagow* – had heard at home Dickens, Goldsmith, Defoe (*Robinson Crusoe*) and even Shakespeare being shared in this way.[30]

Uncle Pat not only read the *Weekly Freeman* – the weekend edition of the Catholic/nationalist *Freeman's Journal* which was Ireland's leading daily newspaper then – but also took out of it a number of its political and social cartoons that he liked and pinned these to his bedroom wall.[31] The striking coloured lithographs that came with the *Weekly Freeman* as supplemental sheets reflected strong opinions on current political and social issues. They were supportive of Irish parliamentary politicians and, for example, highlighted farm dispossessions. De Valera described one of them on his uncle's wall as showing an Irish soldier in the British Army refusing to take shamrock off his tunic. This was probably the cartoon published on 2 April 1892 entitled 'The

"THE CHOSEN LEAF."

Uncle Pat pinned to the wall cartoons from the *Weekly Freeman* such as this from 2 April 1892. Courtesy King's Inns Library.

Chosen Leaf'. It showed 'Colonel Bull' pointing at a man in uniform while saying 'Look here, you Irish soldier! I hate that beastly weed you are wearing in your cap. Put it away immediately.' But 'Private O'Grady' retorts, 'Never! And I'd like to see the man who would lay a finger on it – and what's more, if that little "beastly weed" was not at Waterloo and Inkerman [in the Crimea] and Delhi, and elsewhere, you would not be as fat today as you are.' Underneath are the words 'Young Irishmen, please NOTE above.' The fact that the Irishman in the cartoons was often named 'Pat' may have added to their attraction for Uncle Pat.[32]

Demond Ryan has written that de Valera's 'home had strong Nationalist traditions'.[33] But Pat's support for Irish parliamentary party candidates and his readership of the mainstream nationalist *Freeman's Journal* suggest that these 'traditions' were not exceptionally radical. If that newspaper and the books that de Valera listed shaped Eddie's mind, it was a conventional media and literary diet for an Irish Catholic of the time. The reading of romances about virtuous heroes fed many youthful imaginations then but did not necessarily inspire revolutionary violence.

An English book that he studied at school particularly impressed him. This was *Our Village*, by Mary Russell Mitford (1787–1855). It was a collection of literary sketches of English rural life in Berkshire, begun as pieces for *The Lady's Magazine* in 1819. Eddie often thought how one could write a similar book about Bruree, but did not feel experienced enough to try to write it himself: 'I wasn't sufficiently intimate with the life of our village to pick out the droll characters.'[34] Was there more of this English idyll than there was of Kickham's *Knocknagow* in the ideal Ireland that Eddie later imagined during his famous radio broadcast of 1943 – 'a land whose countryside would be bright with cosy homesteads, whose fields and villages would be joyous with the sounds of industry, with the romping of sturdy children, the contest of athletic youths and the laughter of happy maidens, whose firesides would be forums for the wisdom of serene old age'? Trumpener explains how books by Mitford and Scott were actually seen at the time as functioning both to attract people overseas to British values or lifestyles and to console subjects of the United Kingdom in Ireland and the colonies.[35]

When it came to more traditional storytelling, Eddie was among children kept in after dark, for he once said, 'I wouldn't be allowed out at night to hear the storytelling, but Tim Hannan used to go out, and at school he'd tell us the stories he had heard the night before from Jim Connolly; and one of these was the story of Séadna, in English.' Written by the Cork priest Peadar Ó Laoghaire, this quasi-Faustian tale of a cobbler first appeared in print as a serial in 1894.[36]

WALKING FROM CHARLEVILLE

On 9 October 1896 Eddie spent his last day at Bruree School (his name was formally removed from the roll on 31 December that year).[37] He had become desperate to advance himself beyond his uncle's ambitions for him. The Christian Brothers school at Charleville, about seven miles (11km) away was an escape route. From there, if he worked hard, he just might get into a college. Attending secondary school, never mind university, was much rarer for children then than it is today. As seen above, Uncle Pat thought that Eddie should just take the post of 'monitor' in Bruree National School, a teaching assistance function that would earn him a little money but leave him free for labouring work too.

Eddie pressed his grandmother and uncle hard to let him attend in Charleville, even though each day's journey there and back might be long and tiresome. He later told his friend Frank Gallagher that, 'had they refused to send him to Charleville, he had decided to go back to the United States and had secretly written to his mother telling her so'.[38]

His determination was remarkable, given the usual expectations and resources of a member of his social class when it came to advancement then. Few could hope to pursue formal education beyond national school. However, the Intermediate Education Act passed in 1878 was a reform measure that made money available to schools of any denomination. It created three levels of intermediate examination at secondary school level, providing schools with a direct grant for each student successful in one of the examinations – and in the case of the best students providing a further financial award known as an 'exhibition'.[39] The intermediate system was an incentive to young men such as de Valera.

The establishment of the Royal University of Ireland in 1879 opened up further opportunities. Catholics of all classes had been disadvantaged by such educational opportunities as were provided by the government in London, and were suspicious of what purported to be non-denominational institutions such as the Queen's Colleges and Trinity College Dublin. The Catholic University of Ireland had been established privately in Dublin in 1854, with John Henry Newman as its rector, but it received no royal charter and was itself therefore unable to confer degrees that would be generally recognised. It did not prosper. The new Royal University of Ireland was now empowered to grant degrees to students of the Catholic University. Reformed in 1882, the Catholic University came under the direction of the Jesuits who thereafter prepared students (including James Joyce) for the examinations of the Royal University. It evolved into the present University College Dublin, a constituent college of the National University of Ireland.[40]

Anyone was free to attempt the annual degree exams of the Royal University of Ireland. If they did not attend preparatory courses at the Queen's Colleges or at Trinity College Dublin, they could undertake preparation elsewhere, not only at the Catholic University college in Dublin but also at other 'colleges' including those of St Patrick's seminary in Maynooth and certain Catholic secondary schools. These institutions still had no power to award fully recognised degrees separate from the Royal University. Because the markers of examinations of the Royal University included academics who also lectured in the Queen's Colleges or at Trinity, there was a lingering suspicion among Catholics that such academics were biased in favour of Protestant students.

Writing in 1882, the year that de Valera was born, Arnold Graves – who was to become known as the 'father of Irish technical education' – described 'a great gulf fixed' between the end of one's education in a free 'national school' and admission to a university. He acknowledged that the Intermediate System had been started recently for the purpose of promoting secondary education in Ireland – 'of bridging over this gulf between primary and university education'. However, in 1882 Graves still thought 'The cleverest of the National School boys may as well cry for the moon as strive to gain Intermediate Exhibitions.'[41] Yet De Valera was inspired to strive, for he knew of one boy who had gone to the Christian Brothers school in Charleville, winning at it an exhibition in the first level of the Intermediate examinations. If de Valera managed to do the same then he might aspire to even further advancement. The discouragement that a person of de Valera's social background faced in addition to any denominational or financial obstacles was reflected as late as 1908 when Geoffrey Browne, 3rd Baron Oranmore and a Mayo landowner, told the House of Lords that 'a well-known Irish gentleman, a member of the Roman Catholic Church' had said to him recently 'There is virtually no middle class in Ireland, and we do not want a university for ploughboys.'[42]

In 1985 an historian of Bruree suggested that de Valera was encouraged to pursue his ambitions by his community, his church and his family – in the form of schoolmaster, priest and Uncle Pat:

As de Valera approached the end of his time in Bruree School, John Kelly, the principal of the school, and Fr Liston, the local curate, approached Pat Coll and suggested to him that he should send his nephew to the Christian Brothers' secondary school in Ráthluirc (Charleville), for so brilliant a lad, they said, deserved to be given every opportunity to pursue his studies further. Pat Coll agreed to the suggestion – which called for considerable sacrifice, pecuniary and otherwise on his part – and by so doing helped, in no small way, to shape the future history of Ireland.[43]

This heartwarming version of history is somewhat at variance with earlier accounts by de Valera himself that suggested a lonelier struggle, one that saw him attracted by the possibility of being employed by a bank in America instead of staying in Ireland. In 1955, for example, he said:

My grandmother died on the 31st July 1895. This was a definite milestone in my life. Up to this point my grandmother and my uncle planned my future for me. Henceforth I had to do the planning for myself. I was fully aware of what my grandmother's death meant. She had planned that I should be apprenticed to a trade if I could afford it. She had, of course, at times wished that I could become a priest, but that seemed out of the question. I also doubted if I could be apprenticed to a trade. I then thought that it was right that I should join my mother in America. I communicated with my aunt and arrangements were being made to get me into a bank. My uncle Pat in Ireland wished me to become a monitor in the local school. I had other plans, however. A boy – a young man from my, neighbourhood, Paddy Shea, from the Bridge at Garrouse, whom I had known as a senior boy in the school at Bruree – he was a couple of classes in advance of me – had secured a junior grade exhibition and had gone to St. Munchin's College in Limerick. I thought that what he could do I could do.

In the end Eddie somehow persuaded Uncle Pat to allow him to proceed, and 'in summer or autumn of 1896' his uncle went with him to meet Brother Prendiville, headmaster of the school. Uncle Pat had married recently, another reason for a lad aged fifteen to think of his future if he stayed around Bruree. De Valera said in 1955 that his uncle 'was foolish enough in talking to Brother Prendiville to praise me excessively, telling him that I knew, not merely arithmetic, but that I knew some algebra and geometry. How little that was he was not aware at the time, nor indeed was I fully aware of it myself. As far as algebra was concerned the matter was put to a simple test.'[44] Brother Prendiville had cautioned them, when Uncle Pat mentioned Paddy Shea's name, that Shea was exceptional and that it was not right that others coming like Eddie should hope to do as well. To test Eddie's knowledge of algebra he asked him for the factors of $A^3 + B^3$: 'I gave the first factor A+B all right, but gave the second factor as $A^2 + AB + B^2$ forgetting the minus in the second factor [which he should have given as $A^2 - AB + B^2$], and so my reputation was immediately shattered.' Notwithstanding this, he was accepted into the Christian Brothers' school. Shea was to say that de Valera later told him that had it not been for Shea's example 'I never might have gone there and I'd be still hunting the cows'.[45]

Eddie started school in Charleville on 2 November 1896. The subjects he was told to take were Latin, Greek, French, English and mathematics:

I remember the difficulty I had in learning the Greek alphabet. It was a Sunday and I was given Hime's *Introduction to Greek*.[46] It took me a considerable time – all Sunday devoted to it – before I knew them. My teachers in Charleville besides Brother Prendiville were two laymen. One, Michael Daly whom I had known in Bruree and who was the son of the local R.I.C. sergeant taught me Latin and Greek. O'Riordan, Sonny as he was commonly known in Charleville – from Broad Street – taught me Greek originally and later algebra. Brother Prendiville himself taught me geometry, arithmetic, French and English. I do not know what the scholastic attainments of these two lay teachers were, but they were devoted teachers.

In the exhibition examinations of 1897 he was sent in as a trial but did not achieve the required standard. He was free to try again the following year and was successful, doing well this time. He was thrilled:

When I was informed that I had secured an exhibition I felt that my life's ambition had been realised. I was now, I felt, on the road to success. In those days there was a great deal of competition between the various schools and colleges, and those [boys] who secured exhibitions were fairly certain of being given a place in one of those schools, on the payment to the school of the money received by way of exhibition.[47]

He was understandably proud of his educational achievements. In the 1930s he stressed to Macardle his determination back then:

Charleville was seven miles [11km] away. It was not easy to manage. But I told my Uncle [Pat] I must go. I told him I'd either go to the school or go to America. I was fourteen or fifteen years old [actually still fourteen] … Anyway, I told my uncle that if he would send me to Charleville he would only have to pay the train journey for me one way. I would walk back; so he agreed. It was hard. I used to get up at about half past six and light the fire and make my breakfast, get the train about eight o'clock and then walk a mile to the school. If I missed the train I walked the whole way. I had a penny bun with me for my lunch. It would be half past three or four when I started home and unless somebody driving that way gave me a lift I walked seven miles. I remember the weariness, the terrible weariness! I would lean against a wall for a few minutes and sleep. I remember falling asleep while I was walking.[48]

He said that he had forgotten that Paddy Shea lived much nearer Charleville: 'If I could have got a bicycle it would have meant making things easy, but I could not get a bicycle, and the train service was not by any means satisfactory. The only suitable train in the morning left Bruree station at twenty minutes to eight, and there was no train that was suitable for coming home. The arrangement, however, was made that I should go by the morning train at twenty minutes to eight and come home as best I could, walk, or if I got a lift of any kind to take advantage of it.'[49]

In the 1920s one of a series of diary entries that Frank Gallagher wrote and posted back to his wife in Ireland – during Gallagher's and de Valera's visits to the USA – recorded:

A long chat with D. [de Valera] in which he told of his boyish determination. He had a hard though good uncle. His uncle didn't see the need to send D. to a good school. D. answered he could win an exhibition in the Junior Grade if he would go to Charleville School. Asked to be sent there. Uncle refused. D. prepared his pleas; wrote to his mother in America telling her he either would be sent to Charleville school or else she must send him the passage money to America. Then he went to his uncle and delivered an ultimatum. America or school. Uncle still adamant; preparation for America – school and first victory for E. de V. and he got the exhibition all right and thenceforward earned his way up to Professorship.[50]

Sometimes Eddie got a lift home from school, from the Emmets on one road and the Carrolls on another. In both cases this left a 'substantial' walk of a couple of miles (about 3km). He recalled 'The agony of trying to keep awake. Falling over a fence when walking to wake myself up.'[51] He told Gallagher that 'it would be seven o'clock when I got home and then there was a bucket of water to be brought in and a pail of turnips to chop' for the cows.[52] He used also to cut some hay off the bench and give the cows a *gabhal* (forkful) of it, and looked after them generally.[53] His routine meant that 'I did no studying' on such days.

Many children then used to walk long distances to attend school, albeit not all as long as he did. One evening on his way home, as de Valera later told Fr Farragher, he was so hungry and tired that he actually fell asleep against the ditch at the side of the road and when he woke up he saw his books lying in the gutter. He told Farragher 'Ye don't realise what our generation had to suffer.' This provoked an uncharacteristic response from the priest, who ostensibly had a rapport with de Valera but who also had not been born with a silver spoon in his own mouth. Suddenly – as Farragher later wrote – all the unhappy memories of living on a small farm during the Anglo-Irish 'trade war', after de Valera's Fianna Fáil party came to power in the 1930s, revived like a rush of blood to his head and he burst out 'That is where you are bl… well wrong. You inflicted as bad on us as a family of eleven with your Economic War [1932–38].' De Valera took the comment calmly, this being an indication of his general composure thought Farragher.[54] It was also perhaps a sign of indifference to criticism. In the 1930s Dorothy Macardle was to write down a statement made to her by de Valera that threw light on his single-mindedness: 'I wonder whether the people who get things done are also those who are a little blind to every side of a question but the one side. Some of us are always wasting time and breaking our hearts, wondering whether the other fellow may not be right, going into his point of view, trying to meet him – trying to do the impossible. More work gets done if you could simply dismiss all that. Say – this is what I am going to do and that's all about it.'[55]

The absence of a bicycle may just have been a symptom of poverty, or perhaps a harsh test of Eddie's determination. In 1957 he was to recall being at a race of old penny-farthing bikes. He also said 'I saw the solid tyre in use, and the arrival of the pneumatic tyre.'[56] Was there no affordable way for Uncle Pat to get hold of a bicycle for him? From the late 1880s cycling became popular as the middle and upper classes embraced it enthusiastically – particularly after the introduction of the pneumatic-tyred 'safety-bicycle'. There was 'an amazing total of twenty-five cycle companies launched on the Dublin Stock Exchange in the closing years of the century', no doubt all hoping to be as successful as Dunlop.[57] Founded in 1890, the *Irish Wheelman* was packed weekly with a large number of illustrated advertisements, many for items manufactured in Britain. Yet Pat got no bike then, new or old, for Eddie.

Eddie (back row, 2nd from left) and other 'exhibition' winners at the Christian Brothers school in Charleville, 1898. Brother Prendiville seated centre. Courtesy UCD Archives P150/12.

The national scholarship or 'exhibition' that de Valera won in his second year at Charleville, opened the door to further education. Likewise an exhibition that he won later eased his way onwards to university.[58] In 1935 he told Dorothy Macardle of his sense of achievement when, at Charleville, 'I got an exhibition. It was in '98. I remember being pleased because a photograph was taken of the boys who passed that year and hung on a wall in the school and someone wrote under it "The Men of '98".' The inscription was a humorous reference to the fact that the centenary of the revolt by the Society of United Irishmen in 1798 was being celebrated nationally that year. De Valera added in 1935, with an eye to his reputation perhaps, 'I liked reading about '98 and all those old fights for freedom; but I used to feel sad because I thought nothing of that sort would ever happen in our time.'[59] Among the small group of exhibitioners photographed in 1898 in Charleville were the son of a bank manager, the sons of two RIC sergeants and the son of a candle-maker who was known as 'Danny Dip'. It is said that one of these boys became a bank manager, another a clerk in the Land Commission, another a druggist.[60]

At Charleville he saw no point in some of the English essays they were expected to write. 'They would give us a subject like "Make hay while the sun shines"! We were supposed to enlarge on that. I hated it. It seemed to me that the whole point in writing was to condense. And there it was: done! "Make hay while the sun shines". It was beautiful! It says every thing! Why go and spoil it all! The essays were very goody-goody, I'm sure … I hated the compositions and I was not good at them.'[61]

He had to find time for his homework in the intervals between chores at the cottage and other jobs on the land. Such intervals 'were rare except at the weekends when I had – when going to Charleville – to try to write these abominable compositions: "I make hay whilst the sun shines"; "a stitch in time saves nine", and so on, which could only be written well if one had a lifetime's experience behind to illustrate the points. I had always thought that the writing of "a stitch in time saves nine" was the quintessence of experience. And my mind rather goes from bringing experience down to such a statement than expanding the statement into experience.'[62]

There were a couple of excursions that the Christian Brothers of Charleville organised for groups of boys including himself ('probably those who had succeeded in some examination' he wrote). They picnicked at Kingston Castle in Mitchelstown, and he also remembered being impressed by the 'wonderfully beautiful' Killarney.[63]

While Eddie was attending Charleville, his mother in America lost her only daughter. This was his half-sister Annie E. Wheelwright. The eight-year-old died at Lenox, Massachusetts on 8 July 1897. Her cause of death was recorded as endocarditis – an inflammation of the heart due to infection. Her family appears to have been living at Rochester, almost 300 miles (480km) distant, yet she is also buried at Lenox.[64] In 1956 Éamon de Valera made a passing reference to having at some time received letters from his mother from Lenox, and also from Newport, Rhode Ireland.[65] These letters are not found in the UCD Archives. There is one from him to Kate dated 15 January 1898, in which he tells her he had 'a very pleasant Christmas' but adds 'I suppose yours was not so, since sister Annie had died so recently. Tommie must be a very big boy by this time.' He thanks her and 'especially' her husband for a money order sent to him and Uncle Pat for Christmas. This, as he said perhaps pointedly, 'helped to get me a portion of the books which I required' (just 'a portion'). He enclosed the results of his 'Xmas Examinations which you asked for' and expressed his hope that she will be pleased by them. He reports 'keen competition' between the boys – 'most of them are better circumstanced than I am as they stay in town' – and writes that the school is urging him too to stay in town, or to wait there longer and take the 8.30 p.m. train back to Bruree (whence he is already taking one daily to Charleville about 8.00 a.m.). He tells her that in Bruree they have not had a letter from Uncle Ed 'in a long time', and adds poignantly, 'I suppose Aunt Annie [by then in America] must have forgotten us.'[66]

ROMANCE AND REALITY

One of the first long books that de Valera much later remembered reading when a boy in Bruree was, as noted earlier, Walter Scott's *Ivanhoe*. Eddie's homework for the Christian Brothers at Charleville included writing an appreciation of 'Lockinvar', from Scott's verse romance *Marmion: A Tale of Flodden Field*. Eddie's remark in his homework concerning the poem's hero that 'nothing proves a barrier to his progress' might well have served as his own personal motto at this time. He described 'Lochinvar' as a 'beautiful' poem, and its opening lines were exhilarating for Victorian teenagers:[67]

> O, young Lochinvar is come out of the west,
> Through all the wide Border his steed was the best;
> And save his good broadsword he weapons had none,
> He rode all unarm'd, and he rode all alone.
> So faithful in love, and so dauntless in war,
> There never was knight like the young Lochinvar.

Did its theme of a dashing but vulnerable young hero who crosses water to rescue a woman he loves from her marriage to an Englishman resonate in any way with his own feelings about being left in Ireland when his mother returned to the United States to marry the Englishman Charles Wheelwright? Was he expected, like some émigré Gaelic or Jacobite chieftain crossing the ocean, to fulfil Ireland's destiny – if only he could find a way to do so? He reviewed the lines:

> This beautiful poem by Sir Walter Scott was published in the *Marmion* in 1808. It was founded on some old ballads, especially 'Katherine Jaffarie', which represents a gallant young Scot as carrying off the bride of an Englishman … Nothing proves a barrier to his progress; he goes over mountains and even swims [corrected to 'fords'] large rivers until he arrives at his destination. But he comes too late, for his love has been betrothed to an Englishman; and he enters the hall just as they are preparing for the marriage ceremony.
>
> On being asked by the bride's father what was his mission, he answered that he had long loved his daughter, and that he came before she should be married to the Englishman, to dance one measure with her and drink a cup of wine. He was handed the goblet of wine and when the bride had

raised it to her lips he quaffed it off and then asked her to dance with him. She did so; and when they reached the hall-door, he touched her hand and both darted out. He swung her to the croup [rump or back end of a horse], jumping himself before her on the saddle ...[68]

Many boys may have been inspired romantically by that tale, and perhaps none more so than one who had already enjoyed the chance to ride fast horses.

- 5 -

A HOLY GHOST TRANSITION

ANOTHER MOTHER, 1898–1900

Blackrock College was the making of Eddie de Valera. It opened its doors to him when Limerick colleges kept theirs shut, and he never looked back. 'I remember well how happy I was on that night – my first night in the College. I could not understand why boys coming to such a place should be weeping. I had heard some sobbing: but for me this coming was really the entry into Heaven.'[1]

'Heaven' was to mean friends, intellectual engagement, a chance to advance to university and plenty of sport – most notably rugby but also cricket, boxing and athletics. It was also to mean that he later had a network of influential acquaintances among the rising Catholic middle class, not least within the Catholic Church's hierarchy. On his very first day there he met 'Jack Dalton (as we called him)', a future cardinal and future Catholic primate of all Ireland.[2] Eddie was always to remain literally and intellectually close to Blackrock College, living in the south Dublin suburb for most of his life and cultivating a special relationship with John Charles McQuaid – the college's president from 1931 to 1939 – whose appointment as archbishop of Dublin in 1940 he strongly encouraged.

Blackrock College became de Valera's '*alma mater*', a Latin term frequently used in English speech to refer to a person's former school, college or university, and found in the title of a book about de Valera's time at Blackrock College.[3] But the literal meaning of '*alma mater*' is 'nourishing mother' and this is particularly apt in de Valera's case. The college became a home for him. It provided a kind of alternative parenting for a youth whose birth mother remained in America. Eddie had yearned to get away from Bruree. Blackrock now became his refuge.

His efforts to find a way forward by using the 'exhibition' he won at the Christian Brothers school in Charleville had faltered when – as he later said – he received no reply from two Limerick colleges, Mungret and St Munchin's. Years later Frank Gallagher was to record de Valera telling him that, because he had been 'thinking of being a priest', he had also written to a religious institution at Kimmage or Terenure where he might embark on such a career while being allowed to study for a university degree at the same time – 'but there and elsewhere there were no vacancies'.[4]

Then Eddie got an unexpected break that was to change his life. Fr Liston, the curate in Bruree, was on holiday in Lisdoonvarna, Co. Clare. Returning, Liston rode up to Pat Coll's door one day and called Eddie outside. The curate said that he had met in Lisdoonvarna a certain Fr Larry Healy who was president of Blackrock College. Healy was deeply committed to making education at all levels accessible to Catholics. That same year Healy strongly defended the funding system that had been introduced two decades earlier by the Intermediate Education Act 1878, a system that included grants to schools based on results. He also rejected robust criticism of the Intermediate syllabus voiced by Prof. John Mahaffy of Trinity College Dublin.[5] De Valera later wrote that:

Evidently before Fr Liston went on holidays I had been telling him, because he was aware of the exhibition [that Eddie had won]. Perhaps I discussed with him my failure to get response from either St Munchin's or Mungret in Limerick. This Father Healy whom he had met was a Clareman. He told Fr Liston that if I wrote to him and was willing to come to the College the amount paid in the exhibition would be accepted as my fee. I got in touch with the President – Fr Healy – and was told to come along. I was told what equipment I had to bring. I think there were sheets and night attire as well as a couple of suits of clothes. To get my outfit I went with my uncle to Rathkeale; but it appears that there was no suitable place from his point of view in Rathkeale, and then we went to

Newcastlewest. At Newcastlewest I bought a little tin trunk. I remember my suit of clothes cost sixteen shillings.[6]

His uncle tried to get from Blackrock College a quarter share of Eddie's exhibition award, ostensibly to cover some of the costs associated with kitting Eddie out for Dublin, but Fr Healy ignored the request and held on to all the money. He had already agreed to admit Eddie at a substantially reduced fee. Meanwhile, Eddie was elated. 'From the time I heard that I was to go to Blackrock I was really walking on air. No more long trudges over the interminable distance, as it seemed, from Knockmore to Charleville or from Charleville to Knockmore. No more chopping of turnips for the cows, or the drawing of water, or the attempts to do my lessons in the intervals.'[7] De Valera recalled his departure for Dublin: 'I set out with my uncle and the donkey and cart after the jennet [offspring of a male horse and a female donkey] to Kilmallock Station.'[8]

Sometimes in his later life de Valera told a rambling story about his difficulties in finding his way on first arriving in Dublin. He had to get from the station out to the suburbs, a journey complicated by the fact that he was unaware that the school to which he was going in Blackrock township was known then as 'the French College'.[9]

Although located in the district of Blackrock township the college was as close to the seaside village of Williamstown and to Booterstown as it was to the small town of Blackrock. It had been founded in 1861 by Père Jules Leman CSSp and his two French companions, who came to Ireland to recruit men for missionary services in Africa and elsewhere, and to provide a first-class Catholic education for Irish boys. The *Freeman's Journal* remarked in 1868 that:

> Among the many striking features in the religious progress of Ireland, Dublin more especially, within the last few years, none is more remarkable than the rapid growth and extension of the orders and congregations of religious men and women who are devoted to the education of youth. It is but seven years since a few of the French Fathers of the Congregation of the Holy Ghost [also known as 'Spiritans'] first set foot on Irish soil, yet now we find in Blackrock, apart from a branch house in Rockwell,

Co. Tipperary, extensive and tastefully laid out grounds, several collegiate buildings ... [and] one hundred pay boarders, the essential complement of all which, a suitable collegiate chapel, was yesterday added.

Praising 'this elegant little church, a very gem of Romanesque architecture', the writer reported that some of its decoration was copied from the cathedrals of Notre Dame and Chartres.[10] It was a new era for Irish Catholics.

In 1911, at a lunch to mark Blackrock College's golden jubilee, the bishop of Clonfert, Dr Thomas Gilmartin, was to recall that before Blackrock College opened, all of the endowed schools had been under the control of non-Catholics 'and the few Secondary Schools that private enterprise had called into existence were insufficient to meet the needs of the Catholic population'. De Valera attended this lunch, at which Gilmartin said:

> The aim of the fathers of the Holy Ghost in founding this College on Irish soil was to give such a liberal and practical education to Catholic youth as would give them access to those responsible and lucrative positions in life from which enforced ignorance has debarred them, and would at the same time fix in their minds those principles of faith and conduct that must as long as man is man, form the basis of human character ... I read in its public advertisement 'The moral and religious formation of every student, combined with highest gentlemanly culture, is the foremost aim, and the constant care, of the President and of all the masters.'[11]

Blackrock College quickly developed a middle-class milieu, offering, from 1874, special training for those eager to enter the civil service of the United Kingdom – of which all Ireland was then a part – and for others wishing to get a university degree. De Valera had come a long way from one of the labourers' cottages in Bruree to attend Blackrock College, and he never forgot it. He told Dorothy Macardle in the 1930s that when he woke up in the dormitory on the morning after he first arrived at Blackrock 'I realized I was there on an equality with the others, with the same chance of studying as they. It seemed to me to be Heaven. There were boys who fretted at coming back to school. I couldn't understand that at all. It was Heaven open to me to be there.'[12]

The classes that Eddie took for examination when he went to Blackrock were in arithmetic, algebra and euclid, Greek, Latin, English, French and Religious Instruction. De Valera's education at Blackrock spanned the two final years of secondary school, 'Middle Grade' and 'Senior Grade' 1898–1900, and after that his preparation mainly at Blackrock's 'Castle' building for the BA examinations of the Royal University of Ireland 1900–4. About the time that de Valera was born, Blackrock College had begun to provide facilities for preparing Catholic students for the arts degree of the Royal University.

Eddie first wondered if he should be admitted to Blackrock in its scholasticate, where boys lodged who were destined for the priesthood. But Blackrock's principal Fr Healy thought 'not', and so young Eddie had a place among the lay boarders: 'I had a place, not far from the fire, which was the place that was usually coveted by the new boy,' he later said.[13] It was not all plain sailing for the new boy, however. He later recalled that he had become 'miserable and disappointed', finding it difficult to keep up because he had been taught until now using books that were different from those used by most of the other pupils: 'Had I been punished by the Dean I doubt if I would have remained in the college … But the Dean, however, was understanding …'[14] In later life de Valera was to donate to Blackrock College a few of his schoolbooks, and they reflect the classical syllabus in such Catholic schools then. There were Horace's *Odes*, Virgil's *Georgic IV*, scenes from Euripides' *Alcestis*, Plato's *Crito* and part of Plato's *Phaedo* and some Cicero. He also gave Blackrock two Greek grammars, Goodwin's and Kuhner's. Most of these books were signed by him 'Edward de Valera', but others have 'Éamon de Valéra' (thus) and were presumably signed after he left Blackrock College as there is no indication that he used an Irish form of his name earlier than that.[15]

Like many other Irish Catholic school children then, he became a 'Child of Mary' – in his case on 8 December 1898. As a token of his membership of that Catholic sodality he received a shiny medal, inscribed in French '*Congregation des Enfants de Marie*' – he was after all at 'the

French College' as the 'College of the Immaculate Heart of Mary' in Blackrock was also known. Under these words was inscribed his family name, preceded by the initial letter 'J', from his middle name 'Joseph' adopted at his Confirmation ceremony. There was no 'E' for 'Edward' before the 'J', an oversight. On religious feast days of Mary the boys wore their medals attached by a blue ribbon. Many years later his medal and some prayer books that he had obtained while at school and that he had continued to use in old age were also gifted to Blackrock College. On the obverse of each medal was an image of Mary, mother of Jesus, framed by the Latin words '*monstra te esse matrem*' ('that you may show yourself to be a mother'). He continued to feel keenly his own mother's absence. When he later became a statesman he adorned a number of his annual official Christmas cards with reproductions of portraits of Mary and her infant Jesus. These included in 1972 '*Breith an Linbh Íosa*' ('The Birth of Jesus') by Barocci, in 1970 '*An Óiche Bheannaithe*' ('Holy Night') by Maratta, and in 1966 '*An Mhaighdean agus an Naíonán*' ('Virgin and Child') by Murillo, which were close studies of mother and baby. He also had a copy

Eddie de Valera and Frank Hughes, his friend at Blackrock College and later his 'best man'. Courtesy Blackrock College Archives.

of the Holy Ghost Order's hymnal, from which his secretary read him the *Stabat Mater*. She said it was 'perhaps his most cherished prayer, after the Rosary, in his declining years. Mr de Valera said this prayer daily for many years.'[16] The *Stabat Mater* ('A Mother was Standing') is a very old hymn honouring the emotions of Mary at the cross of her crucified son. It includes these verses as translated in his hymnal:

At the Cross her station keeping,
Stood the mournful Mother weeping,
Close to Jesus to the last:

Oh, how sad and sore distress'd
Was that Mother highly blest
Of the sole-begotten One!

For the sins of His own nation,
Saw Him hang in desolation,
Till His Spirit forth He sent.

De Valera appears to have stayed at Blackrock for Christmas Day 1898. As most of his classmates prepared to depart for their families he asked to be allowed to remain during the Christmas recess with the 'scholastics', those pupils on the path to becoming priests. His unusual request was granted, ultimately strengthening his ties with the institutional Catholic Church. He was also invited to play on the wing for the prefects' team in their annual rugby match with the scholastics. His involvement with and enjoyment of rugby continued for years afterwards. By the time Christmas came again, in 1899 during his second year at Blackrock, he had made at least one close friend there. This was Frank Hughes, who is said to have hospitably invited him to spend part of that Christmas at his home in Kiltimagh, Co. Mayo. A photo of them together shows Eddie resting an arm on Frank's shoulder. Eddie also wrote him a warm keepsake pledging eternal friendship. Each would serve as the other's best man in due course.[17]

In a chatty letter to his half-brother Tom that he wrote on 26 December 1899 (St Stephen's Day), Eddie made no mention of Hughes or of going to Mayo that Christmas. Thomas was then aged just nine:

> My dear Brother, I received your letter and your lovely Xmas card a few days before Christmas. I am very glad you are such a good strong boy and such a good scholar as I saw by your nice letter. My uncle Pat wanted me home for Xmas but as my vacation was so short and the expense so great I thought it would not be worth my while to go home. I like the college and some of my companions are very nice. We have one boy here Cha[rle]s Kane from Pittsburg he is a very pleasant fellow and he tells me a lot of things about America. He has been in New York, Rochester, Washington, the Niagara Falls, at the Chicago Exhibition and at nearly every spot of interest in America.
>
> At the Xmas examinations here I got fourth in my class. The first two were in this class last year but one boy that I beat at the Intermediate Exams got one place before me now, his name is John D'Alton; he is a very holy and intelligent boy and a great friend of mine; he is going on for the priesthood. Dear little brother will you not say a prayer for me every night and morning for you know we have all great need of prayers. Be a good boy and very obedient and loving to [your] papa and mama and you will always be happy and your mama in heaven [Kate or Grandmother Coll?] will love you. I hope you had a very nice Xmas and that you are pleased with the nice presents (I will not say toys for you are I suppose too big for that) that your friends gave you. Have you seen Uncle Ed lately up in Washington [Connecticut]? I am sending you a little New Year's card though I am sorry it will not arrive in time. I am also sending a cutting from the 'Catholic News' of New York with an account of the college.
>
> Again wishing Papa, Mama and yourself a very bright and happy new year. I remain your loving brother Eddie de Valera. Kisses for New Year xxxxxxxx [= kisses]
>
> PS The cutting of the paper I am sending you is not very neat as I got it read from a person who had it in a box for a long time. I hope you will excuse it as I was very anxious to send it to you and I could not get another copy of the paper. EDV.[18]

De Valera later dictated notes of explanation about this letter. In the first note, on 2 March 1957, he stated that 'T.F. O'Rahilly and A. Moran were kept back for two years in the Senior Grade – they got 1st and 2nd place at Christmas Exam above referred to.' In the second, undated but referring back to 'seventy years ago', he stated, 'I had never seen my brother. He was some eight years younger than I was. As I had been brought up alone, having a brother was of particular interest to me. As I regarded myself as grown up and Tom a "baby" I wrote accordingly. Anyway the atmosphere of close on seventy years ago was different from what it is today.' He added, 'To understand the reference to examinations: Tom O'Rahilly and "Gusty" Moran had been in the Senior Grade the previous year, had sat for the examination except for the failing subject, English, so that they could repeat the examination the following year and secure high places. O'Rahilly did secure, I think, first place in Ireland on the second occasion. Moran, also, I think got a high place. In the Middle Grade, I had got first of the Blackrock boys on aggregate marks, and so was ahead of D'Alton. But apparently he beat me at the Christmas examination, as he also beat me at the final examination.'[19]

Eddie's social life at Blackrock included bathing in the sea across the road at Williamstown, and joining friends to admire girls locally.[20] But he had to cope with both normal educational demands and with the fact that he came from a lower social class than many if not all of the other students. He wrote to his mother, ostensibly in late spring 1900, and told her that he was under stress, that he had more work than he could handle and that he had 'scarcely an idea' of what the future held:

> You are I suppose greatly surprised at my not writing to you oftener. I would do so much more frequently but for stress of work this year especially, I have more than I can do. I am sure Brother Tommie received my letter. Uncle [Pat] asked me when writing to you to explain that he would have written but that Aunt [Pat's wife since 1896] has been unwell for some time past. She is nearly well now however. I too felt poorly during winter and spring but as the weather gets finer I get stronger.

Our boys are beginning to play matches for the Leinster [rugby] football cup. We have but just returned from the first match for it – we won easily. I hope we shall win the final also.

Just imagine we have but three months more to prepare for the Summer Examinations – and now our Easter ones which, by the way, are very late this year and are but one month distant. This is my last year for the Intermediate: What I shall do next year I have scarcely an idea, but God I know will make that alright. I suppose this year's results and whatever the president thinks best for me will shape my course next year.

I hope Uncle Charlie, Tommie and yourself are quite well. I would like very much to be able to see you all soon. Tommie, I suppose, is a good scholar now. I am very glad he has got over his illness alright. Aunt Annie wrote to me some time ago. I expect to hear from her soon again. I heard poor Mrs Doyle [who had helped to care for him in New York] has lately died but that the old man is still living. With fond love to all,

Your Son Edward de Valera. Pray for me and excuse writing.[21]

The days were long and demanding at Blackrock College, with a full schedule from dawn to bedtime that involved much study. He liked and was good at mathematics. Although he won no gold medal or single best mark in the 'exhibition' examinations in 1899, he did well enough to secure a grant for his continuing education for each of the next two years. He also got the highest total of marks across subjects among his fellow Blackrock pupils, and the college invited him to become the reader of morning and evening prayers, and to lead the recitation of the rosary at Mass. This was seen as a privilege. He kept a copy of Blackrock College's *Students' Little Manual of Prayers* from then 'to the day of his death, and had the prayers from it read for him in his later years'. He was also asked to read prayers in the refectory during the Retreat: 'I remember one of the readings was from St Alphonsus on death, and I was greatly pleased to speak about the maggots, etc., and the worms which devoured the dead body when the others were at their meals. I felt they would fling a plate at me if they could.' His Religious Instruction grades were high and he took pleasure later in recalling how his marks in this subject were sometimes better than those of John D'Alton, his classmate and a future cardinal.[22]

Being called upon in elocution class to recite a poem of his choice he opted for lines from 'The Downfall of Poland', a patriotic cry for liberty composed by Thomas Campbell that he had learnt from his sixth-class book at the national school in Bruree. De Valera claimed that when he finished reciting, his elocution teacher turned to the class and remarked jokingly, 'I didn't think we had an O'Connell here.' His authorised biographers add to the teacher's comment their observation, that it was 'A truer word than he knew'.[23] The comparison and the observation are strained, for the teacher's remark is scarcely prophetic. O'Connell crucially opted unambiguously for constitutional and peaceful political action. In 1916 and in 1922 de Valera did not.

An undated exercise book shows him at Blackrock writing compositions on topics as varied as Cromwell, the country of China, the challenge to be truthful and 'the advantages England derives from her insular position'. Remarks on this exercise book, seemingly written by a teacher, are quite strict. He is reproached for a form of writing that is stiff, and for an 'abundance of matter, not very skillfully worked up', crowding his writing, scratching out words and flawed punctuation.[24] He was by no means the first nor the last pupil to get such feedback. He later admitted a tendency to be long-winded.[25]

At Christmas 1898 Fr Larry Healy, the Blackrock principal whose kindness had been instrumental in de Valera getting into Blackrock a few months earlier, was in print robustly defending the option of the Irish language as an Intermediate examination subject. He did so against criticism of it in particular by Prof. John Mahaffy, who thought it a 'perfectly useless subject' that was included to pander to 'mischievous sentimentality'. Mahaffy had been tutor to Oscar Wilde at Trinity College Dublin in the early 1870s.[26] Eddie himself did not attempt the Intermediate exam in Irish. In 1901, while he was still at Blackrock College but by then studying for the Royal University exams, the Holy Ghost fathers made a return for the census. This included details of who spoke 'Irish and English' there. The page of the return on which 'Edward de Valera' appeared included twenty-eight students. One in three reportedly spoke 'Irish and English'. Eddie was not among this minority.[27]

The earliest mention of 'Edward de Valera' in a newspaper appears to have been in 1899. On 28 August that year the *Freeman's Journal* published details of the Intermediate examination results, showing that he had been awarded '£30 for two years' for his performance in the Middle Grade exams. The paper reported that the proportion of exhibitions awarded was one to every two students who passed the examination. It noted 'the place of honour has been secured in the present year by Blackrock College, the students of that well-known institution having obtained twenty-five exhibitions', with 'the kindred establishment, Rockwell College, Cashel, carrying off nineteen'. Throughout all Ireland the total number of boys and girls taking any of the four grades of Intermediate examination was fewer than 8,000. It was no mean feat for a labourer's son such as Eddie de Valera to be among them.

De Valera's authorised biographers have written that 'Sport did not figure largely in his life at University College' in Blackrock, but sport was a constant factor in his life then. Even they acknowledged he was an

A schoolboy at Blackrock College in 1899, with a Pioneer pin in his lapel. Courtesy Blackrock College Archives.

athletic youth who ran around the playing fields in the early morning and then drank a glass of milk before getting down to work.[28] His cousin Lizzie remembered him coming from college on holiday to Uncle Pat's: 'He used to go across to the hill of Knockmore dressed in tights and he'd have it arranged with three or four other boys of his age and they had long jumps or high jumps. There was a starter, an old man who worked on the farm – he was their starter.'[29] Farragher believes that 'Dev was genuinely interested in sport of all sorts – in cricket, javelin throwing, boxing, handball, hurling and athletics as well as rugby.' One contemporary was said to remember him as 'a slogging batsman'.[30] The programme for the annual 'Athletic Sports' day in 1899 shows him participating in the pole vault, throwing a cricket ball and competing in the football place kick. He also won a Potato Race. Perhaps his desolate experience of digging spuds in Bruree had given him an edge on some of his competitors when it came to balancing a potato on a spoon.[31] Students were serenaded at Blackrock that day by the Dublin Metropolitan Police Band.[32]

His authorised biographers also wrote, echoing a chivalric tale told more than once by de Valera, that 'he missed his great chance of athletic fame through an excess of humanity, or perhaps just a lack of sporting ambition, although he does not tell the story by any means in his own favour'. The story has it that he had won the mile race and was going well in the half-mile for the President's Cup. The front-runner kept using his elbows to block him passing, so de Valera 'gritted his teeth' and vowed to himself to break the other's heart. At that moment, somehow, the leader crashed to the ground unconscious. De Valera stopped to help him and thus lost the race. However, lest we think de Valera was somehow unmanly, it is added that soon afterwards 'he found himself opposite the same opponent at rugger [rugby]' and again the victim of elbows that were too vigorous: 'This time de Valera reacted remorselessly. "I hopped on him", he used to say, "knees and all".'[33] He had found a distinctive way to 'not tell the story by any means in his own favour'! Another heroic and moral tale that he spun in later years also concerned his athletic exploits. He said that he learnt from this incident on the racetrack a lesson which served him all his life. It was his third race on a particular day – the three miles (5km). Towards the end of it he was so exhausted that he was about to drop out when suddenly the idea came to him that maybe the others in the race were even more weary than he. So he summoned his last ounce of energy to burst forward. His rival was so taken aback that he collapsed and de Valera won.[34]

Photographs of Eddie at Blackrock College between 1898 and 1900 suggest an alert and intelligent boy. Like many Irish schoolboys then and later, young Eddie took the pledge of the Pioneer Total Abstinence Association of the Sacred Heart, founded in Dublin in 1898. A photograph shows him wearing its distinctive pin in his lapel in 1899.

Many Catholic boys have joined the Pioneer Association but then not remained a member. Eddie himself is known to have taken alcohol later – stout, claret and whiskey for example while at Rockwell (Chapter 5 below). He had stout at sports meetings in Kilmallock when back in Bruree for holidays. However, it is said that in 1919 he told his cousin Edward Coll that 'As an example to others and as a further offering of sacrifice to the cause he had stopped smoking and had also given up the use of liquor in any form.' During the following decade he was offered brandy by Frank Gallagher when queasy on board a liner to America, perhaps for medicinal purposes.[35] The US State Department reported years later that the papal nuncio in Ireland believed de Valera at that time 'never smoked, never took a drop of alcoholic drink except in public when as a matter of courtesy he forced himself to gulp down a few swallows of wine …'[36]

KING OF THE CASTLE, 1900–1903

In early 1898 Eddie de Valera was still living in one of the labourers' cottages in rural Limerick. Four years later he was lodged in a 'castle', in one of the comfortable coastal suburbs of south Dublin. The Holy Ghost Order had in 1875 acquired Williamstown Castle, a Georgian structure – fifteen years after founding the adjacent Blackrock College. The priests now used Williamstown Castle as a place in which to prepare young men for entry into the civil service or for passing the annual examinations of the Royal University of Ireland. It was known both as 'the Castle' and more formally as 'University College, Blackrock'. Many of its students later occupied civil service positions in Ireland, Britain, India and other parts of the British Empire. Others got coveted jobs in the Inspectorate of National Schools and elsewhere.

By no means all such students could be accommodated within the Castle itself, however, and De Valera was among those who did not immediately go to live there from his dormitory in Blackrock College, after he finished school in 1900. He first lodged in one of a number of old two-storey houses along Williamstown Avenue, which led from the nearby coastal road up to the Castle. These houses would soon be pulled down. But, in the meantime, students lived in them and gave them nicknames, with some names reflecting Blackrock College's middle-class milieu. There were 'Gray's Inn', 'Lincoln's Inn' and 'Middle Temple', after three of the four inns of court in London. Before 1885 people wishing to practice as barristers in Ireland had been legally obliged to attend one of those four London inns. However, the house in which de Valera first lodged on the avenue had an earthier nickname, 'the Piggeries'. Access was through a yard full of mud and puddles.[37]

Although de Valera earned some money from part-time tutoring and teaching during his period as a matriculation and university student at the Castle, he knew that this income would be insufficient for his needs. Farragher writes that for Eddie, in 1900, 'the priority now was to work hard enough to secure a scholarship in the Royal University examinations each year which could cover his board and tuition over the next four years.' Eddie felt his best chance of a scholarship lay in mathematics, which he liked and where there was less competition than in some other areas. Blackrock was to recruit Michael Smithwick as a part-time teacher specifically to tutor Eddie and just one other young man. Smithwick was a former Castle student who had been born near and educated at Rockwell College. Smithwick captained the Rockwell rugby team on which the Irish internationals Jack and Michael Ryan played, and at Blackrock he became captain of the 'firsts'– the top rugby squad there. He is said to have been a gifted mathematician and an enthusiast for the Irish language, and would later teach at Patrick Pearse's Scoil Éanna.[38]

On 2 March 1901, during his matriculation year, Eddie wrote to his mother. This is his first surviving letter since the previous March. It is short and rather uninformative, apart from his unenthusiastic statement that he might enter the diocesan priesthood that year or the next:

> I hope you are well and that neither Uncle Charlie nor brother Tommie are in ill health. I would like to have a letter from Tommie. I suppose he is a good scholar. There is nothing new about my prospects. I suppose I will go to Clonliffe [Diocesan College], next summer or the next but one, to be a priest in the diocese of Dublin. Do you see any objection to it? I would like to have your opinion. My health is improved – I was rather unwell about Xmas time. I am studying hard and hope to do something this year.
>
> How is Aunt Annie? How many children has she? Is she in Rochester still? I wrote to Uncle Pat for her address. I expect to get it tomorrow, when I shall write to her.

The Castle, Blackrock College, where Eddie lodged in the tower. This drawing is thought to have been made in 1895. Courtesy Blackrock College Archives.

The weather here is very cold. I suppose it is very severe in Rochester so near the lakes.

Hoping there is nothing amiss. I am dear mother Your loving son E. De Valera. Pray for me – write soon.[39]

His hesitancy in going forward to train as a priest may not have been entirely related to wondering if he really had a vocation. Farragher, who met de Valera frequently in later life, writes that Eddie 'could not afford to pay his way at Clonliffe College [a major Dublin seminary], even if accepted'.[40] It is a reminder that the process of becoming a priest was not entirely subsidised by the Catholic Church for those who thought that they had vocations.

Eddie was certainly attracted by religious practice, though. In 1902 the authorities at Blackrock instituted a series of lectures for their students on the rational defence of their faith, a course on apologetics in effect. To encourage interest in this, the examination at the end came with a prize of a Douai Bible for first place. De Valera won this. Much later, on some blank pages inside the book, he set out information about his family and subsequently gifted the Bible back to Blackrock College. Since then it has been lost.[41]

In 1902 Eddie also managed to secure for himself a room in the tower of the Castle at Blackrock, where he might in peace continue his studies for a Bachelor of Arts degree. In 1964 he was to write that 'although, in comparison with present standards the accommodation [at the Castle in 1900–3] may be regarded as primitive, all the essentials were there.' When he moved to the tower he enjoyed a commanding view of his surroundings between the sea and hills, being able to place a deck chair on part of the roof nearby. He gazed at the ships passing out in the evening light to Liverpool and other ports. He could see Lambay Island, which for a long time he mistook for Howth Head.[42]

Eddie was moving up in the world. He certainly did not fully embrace republican sentiments at this time. He was not among pupils who boasted they decided actively *not* to salute Queen Victoria when she passed through Blackrock on her way to Dún Laoghaire (then 'Kingstown') on 4 April 1900.[43] Indeed in 1901–2 he argued in a student debate that 'A Constitutional Monarchy as a form of government is preferable to Republicanism.' The minutes note 'Mr. De Valera maintained that constant elections disturb a nation and are thus not conducive to the prosperity of the people.' He thought 'there is no rule so tyrannical as that of them all'. Even when he later professed republicanism he was to assert famously in 1922 'The people had never a right to do wrong.'[44]

Farragher refers to two Blackrock debates in particular and in the interim between them he perceives a lessening of any romantic tendency in Eddie. In 1901 the question was whether or not 'the old monastic form of charity to the poor was preferable to the modern state social service'. Eddie thought it was, and 'waxed eloquent in defence of the age of chivalry, only to be devastatingly demolished' by an opposing speaker. In 1903 they debated whether or not 'modern progress is productive of human misery'. Eddie opposed that idea and this time, writes Farragher, 'displayed no hankering after the age of chivalry'. The society's minutes record that 'Mr de Valera did not approve of the spirit of romance which prevailed during the Middle Ages; he would not like to be the hero of many of the exploits which were performed in those times. In modern times the poor man had his liberty, serfdom was no more, and the advancement of the individual went hand in hand with human progress.'[45] Eddie appeared to be changing.

One ought not attach too much significance to views expressed in student debates, which can be a form of role-playing. However, raised as he was in the cottage of a labourer, Eddie might well have appreciated the limitations of romantic fiction and the attractions of that bourgeois 'gentlemanly culture' fostered at Blackrock. Nonetheless, his profile later in life was not entirely without a chivalric hue due to his performance as a rebel warrior, symbol of the republic and defender of his faith.

In another student debate he proclaimed that Greece contributed more than Rome to civilisation. In another he praised Napoleon. On one occasion, on the question of free trade versus protectionism he was ambivalent, being 'in favour of a little of both'.[46] There was no sign of his holding political sentiments outside the mainstream. Indeed it may be an indication that he already had his eyes fixed on a respectable career as a university lecturer that in February 1903, during his third year at the

Castle, he composed and delivered at the Blackrock College debating society a closely argued and forceful paper on the future of Irish higher education or, as he styled it 'the Irish University Question'. He favoured a system more amenable to Catholics:[47]

> In opening his address the lecturer set forth Cardinal Newman's conception of a University i.e. a seat of universal learning. Of such a University, and of all the advantages it entailed, were Catholics deprived. The statement, knowledge is power, was never so applicable as at present and in no country was truer than in our own. Catholics could not avail of the existing institutions, the atmosphere of Trinity and of the Queen's Colleges was dangerous to the integrity of their faith; while those institutions more than fully met the requirements of the Protestants and Episcopalians who constituted less than one fourth of the population of the country. The agitation continually kept up disproved Professor Mahaffy's taunt that Catholics were not anxious for a higher education.[48]

As he rose socially, how did Eddie protect himself morally against 'dangerous' ambition, and against imagining himself 'in very glorious positions', temptations of which he warned his half-brother in 1902 (below)? As a boy minding cattle he had read *Robinson Crusoe*, believed to be based partly on the true story of Alexander Selkirk – a Scot marooned on an uninhabited island in the Pacific. When Eddie gazed out from his tower at the Castle, did he recite the well-known lines on solitude that William Cowper based on Selkirk's experience? 'I am the monarch of all I survey, / My right there is none to dispute; / From the centre all round to the sea / I am lord of the fowl and the brute.'

De Valera later remembered being asked by a priest soon after starting at the Castle what he liked most about being there, and replying 'one had some liberty and did not have to ask permission to go from this place to that'.[49] He was a young man, and he pushed himself to do well academically, not least because he wanted the financial support that came with being awarded a scholarship. In 1956 he recorded his routine at the Castle as having been this: 'Arise at 6.30 a.m. – morning prayers; study; Mass; breakfast; class; luncheon; recreation; class until two o'clock, and then final class from 2.30 to half past three; dinner and recreation until five; study five until seven; tea and recreation until eight; study until half past nine (or ten?); library until half past ten.' He still found time to participate in the first Blackrock College branch (or 'conference') of the charitable Society of St Vincent de Paul, becoming its inaugural secretary and subsequently its president. Members of such branches usually distribute charitable donations to poor individuals in their areas, and one wonders what de Valera thought of the circumstances of those to whom the society brought assistance in south Co. Dublin when compared to the conditions of people living in rural poverty in Co. Limerick. He was also secretary of the Castle's Library Society. In this capacity he had access to daily newspapers and to the *Spectator*. He said that some boys used to take papers like the *Spectator* to their rooms: 'The Secretary had permission to go into the rooms and search to see whether these papers were there. I went to some older boys who had been there three or four years before, and took the papers away. There was a penalty.' He added, 'We had supplemental reading of current papers by going to the Carnegie library, Blackrock.' His close policing of the library regulations may not have endeared him to everyone.[50]

Eddie is said to have had a disconcerting experience when he became ill on one occasion. From his room in the Castle he was shocked to find that he was unable to make out the identity of some members of the college staff walking down the avenue nearby.[51] This may indicate that his serious eyesight problems of later years had begun to manifest quite early. Meanwhile, he corresponded with his relatives in America. Not all of the letters that he sent and received survive but a significant one that does so was addressed to his half-brother Tom on 6 October 1902. For some time Eddie had been mulling over the possibility of becoming a priest. Then, just weeks before his twentieth birthday, he had learnt that Tom who was eight years younger than him had entered an American college providing education to boys who believed they had a vocation to the priesthood. The older half-brother – describing himself as 'successful in almost everything I have undertaken aye brilliantly successful' and one to whom the world had already offered 'its choicest pleasures, honours etc.', and as one who has dared to imagine himself 'in very glorious positions'

– now gives the younger one some sage advice about the dangers of praise and ambition:

My dear Brother [an arrow here inserted pointing to a note above it: 'Don't be frightened at the length of this. You can read it at your leisure'].

I cannot tell you how delighted I was to receive a letter from you and still more difficult would it be for me to attempt to express my joy on finding that you were actually in a Redemptorist College and about to become a member of that most sacred order. Of course you must as you said find it difficult at first, but pray for perseverance and remember that each obstacle you now overcome will make each succeeding one less hard to surmount, and that it is only by cheerfully bearing the cross that any merit can be gained. Moreover, the very hardships you have now to undergo will constitute the greatest sweetness and consolation of your later life.

You ought occasionally meditate on the great dignity of your holy calling. You are called to be a minister of the Most High! How sublime! This will always assist you in guarding your vocation as your very life. You will have moments I suppose, I have had them, when the world will offer you its choicest pleasures, honours, etc. for the purpose of ensnaring you, and well for you if you overcome them. It will not be easy, alone they will defeat you. You can triumph only by aid from above.

Be on guard against dreaming, imagining yourself in very glorious positions. It seems a very innocent pleasure but, in my case, it has been the chief method Satan has employed to disturb my peace of soul and make me waver. Hitherto I have been successful in almost everything I have undertaken aye brilliantly successful, more successful I fear than is good for my salvation. Praise is our most terrible enemy. It excites in us ambition, a thing not sinful in itself but highly dangerous to one that wishes to be a man of God. If therefore you are not successful (through no fault of your own) thank God he has delivered you from such a source of temptation. But if you are successful then beware! If you can be humble in praise, as reason tells us we should be, and can offer that praise to Him to whom only it is due, without feeling any pride in yourself, then God has granted you a special favour.

Having unburdened himself of the confession that he tended to imagine himself in very glorious positions, Eddie then introduces a reference to their comparative experiences of family. He points out that Thomas has been lucky to grow up in the company of a mother. Eddie at this point had not seen their mother in about fifteen years. Study itself, it seems, is his 'best friend':

You who have been always at home must find it very hard to be away. This should be no obstacle to you. You have had a privilege heretofore which numbers have not had. You have been always near a loving mother; others who may have almost as much love as yours have to live separated by the ocean from her they love. You can see mother on your vacations. I must be content with the hope I see her one day. So then try and be happy. Never be idle. At first work will be hard, but it will soon be lovable in itself. I love study so much that if it were withdrawn from me I would feel for the loss of my best friend.

You will perhaps be tired of all this preaching. It may be that as often is the case the preacher does not practise his own doctrine and has more need of advice himself than those to whom he preaches. I have great need to look to myself, but what I have said to you can do no harm and may do good in making you content. I as you intend also to become a priest, and I have only told you of what I found advantageous to myself, and warned you of what I find dangerous.

Now for worldly matters. As regards your studies, if you want to succeed it will only be by strenuous work. I could give you advice how to work to the best advantage in Latin, Mathematics, English etc. but I am sure you have someone more competent than I to do it, and moreover I am not very well acquainted with your systems (I have never studied German up to the present but I hope to do so one day). If however you wish for any information, which you would rather not ask from your professors, remember I am always at your service as far as I am able. It would interest me very much to know what books you are reading in Latin and English. It is a pity you are not studying Greek but your superior knows best. Never be content with second place, always strive to be first, but always under the conviction that it is a matter of duty for you towards

God and never to satisfy your own pride. If you do not care about being first [so] much the better reason why you should work for first, as you will then be doing it entirely for God.

He returns to a consideration of their respective positions in the extended family. Annie, his beloved aunt, is seriously ill. He wishes to ensure that neither he nor Thomas causes their mother pain, not least because of 'how good she has been to us' and the 'sacrifice' she makes by being willing to give up 'the joy of having us by her side – all for the service of God':

I suppose you will see Aunt Annie during your holidays. I hope you won't forget to tell her how fond I am of her. You should pray, I know you will, for her cure. How sad to see a young woman, hitherto strong and healthy,

Eddie (left) competes in a slow bicycle race at Blackrock College, Sports Day 1903. Courtesy Blackrock College Archives.

thus affected. She has her little children to care for. Were God to take her away how would they get along without her?

We must always please mother in every way. Don't forget how good she has been to us and consequently we should always strive to make her proud of us by our good conduct, and not cause her pain by doing what we know she would not wish us to do. Remember the sacrifice she is making for us. Every mother loves her child and we are exceptionally blest with a mother's love; yet she is willing to sacrifice our company, to sacrifice the joy of having us by her side – all for the service of God. What a pity sister [Eddie's half-sister and Tom's sister] Annie died; she should have been a nun! But God has taken her to Himself without trying her with the world's consuming [the word 'purging' crossed through] fire. She is praying for us before the throne of God, for us who have yet to toil for the crown that has I am sure been given to her.

I hope you will write to me often, long letters remember (if you can spare time). We are only two, and we should love each other and communicate often with each other. I am going up on my birthday (Oct 14 – my age will then be twenty) for a Mathematical Scholarship in the Royal University of Ireland. I will probably be engaged in the exam at the moment when you are reading this. So pray for me. If I get it, it will enable me to begin and complete my studies for the priesthood. If I fail to get it I will have to remain here teaching some time longer. You will tell me about your studies and examinations in your next letter, won't you? I will write you the result of my exam, when it becomes known. With best love, Your fond Bro. Eddie.[52]

This is the most substantial letter that survives from the first twenty years of de Valera's life, and it leaves one wondering just how full of heartfelt admiration for his mother he really was. If she was 'giving up' Tom by letting him enter a college for trainee priests at such an early age, she had given up Eddie for different reasons as a child and could scarcely be said accurately to be 'sacrificing' him if he now chose to become a priest at the age of twenty. He and his half-brother were to maintain a cordial relationship until Fr Tom Wheelwright's death in a motor accident in 1946.

Besides playing rugby and some cricket at Blackrock, de Valera liked boxing enough to spend some of his very modest income on equipment. He now invested in a pair of boxing gloves. As a photograph taken on Sports Day 1903 shows, Eddie also took part in at least one bicycle race, this time seemingly one where the winner was the boy who could remain balanced the longest while riding the slowest. He was mounted on a bike that he would surely have liked to own when obliged to walk long distances to attend the Christian Brothers school in Charleville.

The time that Eddie passed with other students while at the Castle yielded a variety of anecdotal stories down the years. These are unexceptional, including for example tales of orchards raided, tricks played on staff and walls climbed to go to Keegan's pub nearby. On one occasion, bottles of claret stolen from the priests' store – by other boys it appears – were hidden under the floorboards in de Valera's room.[53] The young men at the Castle also strolled to Blackrock Park to hear the bands playing there, with Eddie sporting an ebony walking cane that some of those whom he taught part-time had given him. There he and his friends engaged in what they 'later laughingly referred to as "totty twigging"'. Fr Farragher explains this as slang for 'watching all the girls pass by'.[54]

In 1904 Eddie was photographed wearing a cloth cap at Blackrock College, but it seems that by then he had already purchased the bowler hat that features in a 1911 photograph of him at an event in Blackrock College.[55] A cloth cap is the type of headgear also seen in a well-known photo of James Joyce as a young man, albeit later depictions of Leopold Bloom from Joyce's novel *Ulysses* – set in 1904 – often show Bloom in a bowler.

While living at the Castle in Blackrock, and completing his second year of studies for the BA examinations, de Valera wrote confidentially to St Wilfrid's – a Catholic secondary school in Staffordshire, England – to see might he come to an arrangement with it similar to that which he had with the Holy Ghost priests in Blackrock. This would have involved paid work as a part-time teacher as well as accommodation on site where he could pursue his private studies. Thus, on 13 June 1903, he told St Wilfrid's that 'for some time I have been desirous of seeing a little of England and English character'. He set out his academic results since 1898, results that were in the top range nationally at Intermediate and matriculation level and that indicated he might be heading ultimately for an honors arts degree from the Royal University of Ireland, where he was concentrating on the study of mathematics and maths physics. He pointed out that he had also been engaged in some teaching of mathematics, along with classics and English, to schoolboys at Blackrock College and that he had three years' experience teaching there. He stated that along with mathematics (pure) and maths physics at the Royal University of Ireland he was studying Latin, Greek and French but specified that he was best qualified to teach maths. His choice of St Wilfrid's – with which John Henry Newman had had an association after leaving Ireland – appears to have been based on the recommendation of a friend. He had not shared his wish to go to England with authorities at Blackrock, asking St Wilfrid's that as regards any communications seeking a reference for him from Blackrock College 'should you be inclined to consider my offer, from motives of prudence I would wish that you would not write here until after July 1st (say) inasmuch as I have not yet intimated to the authorities here any desire to leave – it would of course be foolish of me to do so until I had made arrangements elsewhere.' He wrote that 'secrecy would be gained' by St Wilfrid's sending him its reply in a plain envelope. He could not afford to burn any bridges in Blackrock given his need to earn an income in order to sustain his ambition to complete his degree.[56]

De Valera appended a notable postscript to his letter to St Wilfrid's: 'Perhaps it would be well to add that my ultimate object is the priesthood.' It is clear that he was then still thinking of becoming a priest.

His decision to seek a position in England may have been at least partly motivated by a proposed renovation of the Castle that was to involve substantial alterations and extension and that necessitated his moving from its tower into less attractive accommodation at Blackrock. He had attained a nice perch in the old building but would now lose it. About this time, the Holy Ghost Order also tore down the old houses on Williamstown Avenue in which students including de Valera had lodged, and erected a new entrance to the college.[57]

In the event, in 1903 de Valera did not go to live in England and teach part-time there but, with the backing of the Dean of the Castle secured a full teaching post in mathematics and physics that became vacant at Rockwell College in Co. Tipperary. Two of his contemporaries had already been employed at a rural secondary school during their final year preparing for undergraduate examinations of the Royal University of Ireland. Rockwell had the added attraction for de Valera of having been founded in the 1860s by the Holy Ghost Order, so that from its connection with Blackrock 'many of the staff were already known to him personally, and he to them'. The Rockwell property had been gifted to the Order by a rich French businessman living in Scotland, whose brother formerly managed it until murdered by a tenant he tried to evict. The French donor wanted the place used for training priests to work in Scotland. For a while it was known as 'the Scotch College'.[58]

The priests of Blackrock might not have encouraged Eddie to enter the priesthood but in 1903 they saw how competently he argued at their Debating Society a Catholic case for the reformation of university educational facilities in Ireland. This was an issue of current controversy then. Senior members of the Holy Ghost Order in Ireland were present when he spoke, and one had even given de Valera some assistance with the paper. Catholics felt that they were still being treated unfairly when it came to their desire to have a Catholic university and de Valera displayed determination and originality in his paper. He was and would remain very much 'one of theirs'.

Edward Prince of Wales, who had briefly visited Cork in the same month in 1885 as Eddie de Valera first set foot in Ireland in that county, had now become king. In 1903 King Edward VII made his first official visit to Dublin as monarch, landing at Kingstown (Dún Laoghaire). Eddie appears to have been absent when Edward then passed through Blackrock.

GUNS AND GIRLS: ROCKWELL 1903–5

From the autumn of 1903 Eddie was living and teaching at Rockwell College in Co. Tipperary, while still reading for a degree from the Royal University of Ireland. He returned to Dublin in the summer of 1904 to sit his final examinations. But he had not prepared well enough and achieved only a pass. This was a major upset for him.

He was conferred with a Bachelor of Arts (BA) in mathematical physics and mathematics, which would later be automatically converted into a Bachelor of Science (BSc) when the National University of Ireland (NUI) succeeded the Royal University. He was very disappointed not to have achieved an honours classification in 1904. As a graduate he now had to earn his living and make plans for the future. His first step was to return to teach at Rockwell. He was employed there in all from September 1903 until June 1905.[59]

It appears that he was not completely well when he first went to Rockwell, although what ailed him is unknown. It may have been stress. On his US visits with de Valera in 1927–28, Frank Gallagher noted his account of one odd incident:[60]

> His first job was at Rockwell. He was in bad health and stipulated for cocoa. But all the other teachers started taking cocoa, and the price was too much for the President of the college. So he cut off all cocoa. D. went to him, demanded fulfilment of his bond. President refused. D. went for his hat and coat. 'I am going to the hotel in Cashel' he said 'I will stay there a week. You'll pay the bill. I won't come back at the end of that week unless our contract is to be carried out.' While he was mounting his bike the President called him back and proposed that D. would have his cocoa but mustn't let any of the other teachers take it. D. refused to be a censor on his fellow teachers' food, and went for his bike again. The President caved in then.[60]

Such a 'demand' for cocoa was unlikely to endear a young teacher to a principal. However, Rockwell was a sister house of Blackrock College – Bishop Thomas Gilmartin of Clonfert called it an 'offshoot' – and Blackrock had recommended him for employment. Soon de Valera settled down. He lodged at Rockwell itself, one of four laymen on the teaching staff.[61]

A comment he made to Dorothy Macardle in the 1930s indicates he had been feeling poorly for some time even before he got to Rockwell:

'It was in Rockwell that I became healthy and strong. The life there was easy. I used to wake about six and go out for a run, drink a cup of milk and go back to bed until it was time to get up for the first class! They used to laugh at the way I put on weight and say they could see the fat growing on me. I went up from ten and a half to twelve and a half stones in weeks.' He attributed this partly to 'stout, claret, and good Tipperary beef and a good time'.[62] He was hunting and playing sport, and girls were interested in him, or so it seems. The UCD Archives have a colourful note of his recollections of 'incidents in Rockwell' that gives a flavour of his days there, including exploits with his rifle and his friendship with the Ryan brothers – rugby heroes he had seen play in an international at Lansdowne Road in 1899:

My fellow teachers. Laymen: Spud [Jack] Barrett, [Tom] O'Donnell. My prefect pals: Thady O'Connor – Hocks as we used to call him – Cunningham, Dennis O'Connor. Graf and our visitor Ryans. Some shooting incidents. The first time shooting and the rabbit at the foot of the thistle. Luncheon at a house out in the fields. When I fired at the rabbit as the dog came chasing after him. Might have shot the dog. The old [erasure/s?] gun. Dan Lane on the fence. The shooting of the [erasures]. The time of the thrashing. Wolfe Colgan; up at the pond and the wild duck. The shooting at Rice's bog. The shooting on the left of the road coming from Cashel to the College – just at the little bridge. The shooting of the weasel and the duck. The incident [erasure/s] and the hat. The incident in which I came out the window and slid down the rope and burned my hands so badly. My morning routine. Running down the [erasure/s] and a bath and then the sleep. Cocoa and Fr Brennan. Then going in the window for the pineapple chunks. The muffler. The football matches away in Knock and Limerick. The famous Limerick match. Drank some whiskey and bad results. The journey from Rockwell during Retreat to Waterville. The journey from Waterville to Cahirciveen and back. Regatta. The bicycle on my return. The journey on my first bicycle to Clonmel. The coming back. O'Donnell's fall. The journey with O'Donnell and Barrett to Fethard Races and the bringing back of O'Donnell holding on to my coat tails. Came back by New Inn. Brother Prendiville and

De Valera with his rifle, 'Rockwell 1904' on reverse.
Courtesy UCD Archives P150/41.

wishing to lock us out at night. Paddy Davies the Welshman who replaced 'Squad'. The playing of Nap. in my room. The stuffing of my football togs and dressing up, and Fr Michael O'Shea – the fright he got – going to give me conditional absolution. The break down of the bed when Mick threw me on it. Fr Brendan next day and the [blank or erasure's overwritten with the word 'thunder'] the night before. The trick we played on Cremer with regard to Margaret Ryan. The nights up at Mick Ryan – cards and supper. Mick Ryan's marriage. Mick and Jack at the football [erasure/s] in the College. The decanter of sherry and the dozen of stout in front of them. The famous sweepstake in the Grand National and how our side drew.[63]

In 1965 Patrick Ryan, a son of Eddie's acquaintance and rugby hero Jack Ryan, informed de Valera that Jack had often repeated the story of how 'he told you to "aim at the thistle and you'll hit the rabbit"'. De Valera replied: 'Your uncles Pat and Mick with your father [Jack] and one or two of the fathers who were fond of fowling often went for the day's shooting cross country. It was on one of these occasions that the incident your father told you of occurred. I know now, but I did not know then that my eyesight must have been deteriorating. Your father's eyes were keen and he saw a rabbit lying at the foot of a thistle at the far side about sixty yards ahead. He told me so that I might have the prize. I refused to believe it, fearing a practical joke, and I did not want to waste a cartridge. He [Jack] repeated "fire at the foot of the thistle or I will." I unwillingly obeyed and shot the poor rabbit. I am afraid I had not the qualms I would have now.'[64]

The gun licence issued to him while at Rockwell survives. As a child Eddie had made a rifle with a piece of wood, 'and for trigger I had a penny gun tied on to it'. He said that he had fired his first actual shot from a muzzleloader, with powder horn and shot horn and a measure for judging, and ramrods: 'Only special people would have had at the time a breech-loader'. A photograph survives of de Valera standing in the countryside near Rockwell, clutching his rifle.[65]

Dwane writes that when Eddie returned to Bruree during this period he went shooting locally and that 'there was little in the mechanism of a gun that he did not understand'. Dwane thought that de Valera had a different fowling piece each time he returned, the latest usually superior to the previous one. Eddie was said to have been heard to remark 'I am afraid I shall be a soldier, I have such a love for guns.'[66]

He did more than go hunting with the Ryans: 'The privileged ones amongst us used to go occasionally to the Race Course to your Uncle Mick's place [near Cashel] for a game of cards. We usually had supper there before we returned,' he told Jack Ryan's son.[67] Eddie also played rugby on the Rockwell senior team with the Ryans. So close did he and Mick become that the latter, thirteen years older than him, sometimes made his way to Eddie's private room: 'On one occasion a bout of wrestling started and Mike flipped Dev off his feet and crashed him onto his bed. The bed collapsed on to the ground prompting the President, Fr Nicholas Brennan, to ask Dev next morning had he heard any thunder the night before!' Mick Ryan was one of the select few to whom de Valera drafted a note while awaiting possible execution after the 1916 Rising.[68]

Besides playing rugby at Rockwell, de Valera also took part in athletics there. He later said that while teaching at Rockwell he thought of

improving his little Irish too. One of his students who spoke the language came to his room a few times and 'gave me the pronunciation of
words occurring in O'Growney's first book. For some reason or other
that I do not remember, the lessons were discontinued.'[69]

Eddie celebrated his twenty-first birthday in October 1903, and would
not accept being treated as a child as he saw it. Rockwell authorities
objected to him and others returning very late: 'One night when D. [de
Valera] and his pals cycled back from Cashel they found the door bolted
against them. D. climbed in the window and removed the bolt entirely.
"We didn't join the Rockwell staff as monks", he said. Next night they
were late they found the door bolted against them. D. mounted a ladder
and got in through a high window. This time he couldn't open the lock
so he screwed it off altogether and then went to the lake and threw it in.
The door wasn't shut against them any more!'[70]

As he and his friends roamed local towns in search of recreation, they
attracted female attention. One girl in particular, the daughter of the
owner of Stewart's Hotel in Cashel, is said to have set her eye on de
Valera. Mary Stewart's brother Larry regularly gave concerts at Rockwell
and in return made its teachers welcome at the hotel, where Mary and
her sister Cissie entertained them. It is not known if Eddie and Mary had
a romantic or sexual relationship – although he is said to have been seen
frequently cuddling her pet cat![71]

And yet he left Rockwell in 1905. He explained his decision three
decades later to Dorothy Macardle, saying that he quit because he was
becoming so comfortable that his ambition was deadened: 'The life suited
me so well there I had to leave. I realized that. I realized that I could settle
down there and do nothing else for the rest of my days. It was hard to
make up my mind to leave it, but I did.' He had corresponded earlier
with Trinity College Dublin about applying for a sizarship (scholarship),
and about its entrance fees for maths and science courses. He even registered as a student there a few months before he left Rockwell.[72] He later
wrote, 'Made up my mind that if I stayed further in Rockwell I would
vegetate there. Found I could do very little work except for my classes
which were exceptionally good … gave full notice to Rockwell …'[73]

Eddie may have been distracted at Rockwell, or lost confidence, or simply lacked the level of academic support he had had at the Castle in Blackrock. He had no family to fall back on for advice or encouragement when it came to study, just Uncle Pat who had been unenthusiastic about his educational ambitions in the past. In July 1905 the president of Rockwell College gave Eddie a favourable reference, affirming that he 'is now leaving of his own accord in order to improve his condition'. Joining in celebrations for the centenary in Rockwell in the 1960s when he was president of Ireland, de Valera reportedly said that his years at Rockwell had been 'undoubtedly very happy'. But he appears not to have wished to speak on that occasion about any actual episode or incident from those days. He thought it would be 'dangerous' for him and others to start reminiscing lest they be there until after midnight.[74] Or was it lest others had reminiscences that he might not wish to hear aired?

DEV'S DECADE OF RUGGER

De Valera's name occasionally appeared in newspapers before he reached the age of thirty in 1912. It was in lists of students who won 'exhibitions' or scholarships but, more often, in reports of him as a rugby player at Rockwell and Blackrock. And it was not at all in political contexts.

His later friend and close political associate Frank Gallagher once described him as 'a fine rugby wing three-quarters and a great runner'.[75] The sport of rugby does not generally enjoy a prominent position in the profiles of anti-Treaty republicans. And it was long regarded by many members of the Gaelic Athletic Association as a 'foreign game', the playing or even active support of which used to preclude one from participating in the 'national' sports of hurling and Gaelic football. Yet playing rugby was an enjoyable part of Eddie's life for a decade after he left his uncle's cottage in Bruree and went to Dublin. He was not long at Blackrock before he got involved in it. In his first year there he was injured:

As Dev was not very familiar with the game at this stage, Burke told him he would not let the ball out to him if he saw there was any danger of a heavy tackle. But he could not arrange that Dev's opposite number should not get the ball either, so inevitably Dev found himself having to tackle his opponent without any knowledge of that art. He just got down on his knees to stop him with his head between his opponent's legs. As his opponent struggled free, a stud in his boot tore Dev's ear so badly that he had to be rushed to the college physician in Blackrock, Dr Thomas McEvoy, to receive several stitches. The fact that Dev's first rugby match literally left its mark on him may explain why he took a less active part in the game for some time to come. Not that he lost interest in it.[76]

Eddie, as seen earlier, already bore a lasting mark from the rough and tumble of factional clashes at school in Bruree. His stitches at Blackrock did not stop him subsequently becoming more active on the rugby field, and he was still playing for Blackrock teams a decade later.

Soon after his first Christmas at Blackrock College, de Valera went to see his first rugby international. This game between Ireland and England in February 1899 was played nearby at Lansdowne Road. Ireland won 6–0 and went on that year to win, for the second time, the 'Triple Crown', an annual contest between the four 'home' nations of the United Kingdom. It was also the last time that Ireland won the Triple Crown until 1948. On the team were brothers Jack and Mick Ryan, 'the two giants of Rockwell Rugby Club' in the province of Munster whom de Valera would soon know: 'Not in his wildest dreams,' writes Fr Farragher, 'could Dev have imagined then that in a few short years he would be playing in the Munster senior championship matches on the Rockwell team in the company of the Ryan brothers, with whom he was so closely associated while professor at Rockwell.' Also in 1899 Eddie helped to chair home on his shoulders the captain of the 'Past and Present' Blackrock 'Seconds' team that won the Leinster Junior Cup, a feat of strength of which he later boasted.[77]

Eddie's interest in rugby is also evident from a record of sports day at Blackrock in 1901. Here he took part in the first place-kicking competition, although he was not the victor in that event then or in later years, despite what Fr Farragher of Blackrock has described as 'almost an obsession with trying to perfect his technique in that area of the game'.

But his kicking on the field did win his teams some valuable points in matches. Such was his enjoyment of the game that two boys who later wished to thank Eddie for tutoring them for examinations guessed what he would like. They gave him a ticket to the covered stand at Lansdowne Road for the Ireland v. Wales rugby international on 8 March 1902. The fact that Michael Smithwick, de Valera's own tutor at the Castle, was captain of the first team at Blackrock in 1901–2 no doubt helped to stimulate Eddie's interest in the game. In time he became secretary of the Blackrock Rugby Football Club, and also captained the Blackrock 'Second Fifteen' team of past and present pupils after he returned to Dublin from Rockwell in 1905.[78]

Having seen the Ryan brothers, Jack and Mick (sometimes 'Mike'), play rugby for Ireland at Lansdowne Road, Eddie was indeed delighted to find at Rockwell that they were 'constant visitors' when he was employed as a teacher there from 1903 to 1905. In 1965 he told Jack's son, 'They were

Eddie de Valera (on second chair from right) with other members of the Rockwell Senior Rugby team 1904: standing second and fourth from left are Jack and Mick Ryan respectively. From *Rockwell Annual, 1964.* Courtesy Blackrock College Archives.

neighbours of ours at Rockwell and the lay teachers and the prefects were particularly fond of them.' He added, 'Those days in Rockwell were full of happiness for me and not a little of it centred around your father and your Uncle Mike who were our heroes of the football field. I would give a lot to have those days back again.'[79]

When putting together a senior team, schools could draw on past as well as present pupils. Thus, Rockwell's senior club side was composed of lay masters, pupils – including students for the priesthood – and past pupils of various ages. The captain of that side when Eddie was there was James Mellett, a student who later became well known as a Holy Ghost missionary priest in Nigeria. Mellett was to recall the team being doubtful at first that de Valera's 'slight build would stand up to the strenuous type of Munster play'. But Eddie made the grade, as Mellett wrote, 'even to the extent of getting on the Munster trial for the Inter-Pro [interprovincial tournament]'. The missionary added:[80]

> I recall one incident which might well have ended in disaster for Mr de Valera himself. The occurrence was purely accidental. It was a 'soft' day, slippery underfoot, and we were playing a practice match in the Big Field. A high ball was kicked up field and I backed up as fast as I could. Dev stood waiting to field the ball as I bore down intending to tackle him with the ball before he could get in his kick. He had fielded, released the ball and was poised to kick when I made contact with him. I'm afraid I got the man without the ball, and while both teams stood up laughing and Dev picked himself painfully from the ground I slunk into the background, not knowing whether to clap myself on the back or feel ashamed of myself. And of course I could not forget that I would be in Mr de Valera's maths class next day.[81]

As Mellett's book was published in 1963 with an approving *Nihil Obstat* and an *Imprimi Potest* from the archbishop of Dublin and former president of Blackrock College John Charles McQuaid, the rugby anecdotes are no doubt absolutely reliable.

In 1960 de Valera expressed an interest in seeing old newspaper reports of rugby games in which both the Ryan brothers and himself had played on the senior team for Rockwell. Three reports were retrieved for him from the *Nationalist* paper of 1904. The first was of his team's victory over Clonmel in a friendly on 10 March. The report stated that Rockwell had never been defeated on its home ground 'except on one occasion by the representatives of the sister college, Blackrock'. The Ryan brothers and de Valera were also on a Rockwell team that beat Queen's College Cork in a Munster Cup game at Clonmel on 23 March that year. A local paper described this as 'one of the stiffest and best contests in connection with the above competition'. It added, unsurprisingly, that 'the home team had the advantage of the Internationals Mike and Jack Ryan in the forward line'. A photograph of the Rockwell Senior XV of 1904, including de Valera and the visibly older Ryans, appeared in the *Rockwell Annual* of 1964.[82]

In the Munster Cup semi-final on 30 March 1904 de Valera touched down the first of two tries that saw Rockwell beat a scoreless Cork County. As the *Cork Examiner* reported, 'From the line out the ball went back to T. O'Connor, and then to De Valera, who dived under the posts for the first score, the Cork full [*sic.* full-back?] being unable to stop him.' The losing team was very unhappy about the circumstances of this match, which was a replay following a drawn game at Turner's Cross. It had been suggested initially that the replay take place in Tipperary town, 'but Rockwell were unable to secure the field there for the occasion, with the result that Cork County found themselves forced to travel to Clonmel for the second time in the competition. In the ordinary course it is extremely difficult to secure a full or representative Cork team for travelling purposes, but the difficulties were greatly increased in this instance', with the result that there were seven or eight changes to the team that had drawn with Rockwell in the previous match.[83]

A few days later, in April 1904, Eddie played in the Munster Cup final, for Rockwell against Garryowen at the Markets Field in Limerick: 'Such a match as this had in its wake an extraordinary amount of interest on the part of all Munster Rugby footballers, and the fact of it being played on Easter Monday occasioned an interest enhanced to a still greater degree.' It would not be the last occasion on which de Valera was to participate in an event of great interest on an Easter Monday. On this first occasion his efforts included an attempt at a drop goal that – unfortunately for his team – went wide. In the end, just a single unconverted try scored in somewhat controversial circumstances decided the 'excellent' match in favour of Garryowen. Their man Hogan had received a pass on Rockwell's twenty-five-yard line: 'It was stated that on account of the excitement and the immense throng on the line that Rockwellians thought he was in touch, and from the Press table apparently, stood looking at him scoring far out an easy try.'[84]

The following season's Munster Cup competition began well for de Valera. In March 1905 his team found itself once more playing Garryowen, the cup holders. This match too was at Markets Field, and he shared honours for a first touchdown. He had gained ground before passing to his friend Barrett who 'with a strong run got far over far out for a try'. De Valera, however, failed to convert. He and Barrett continued to make 'desperate efforts'. *The Cork Examiner* credited him with falling on the ball for a second touch-down, although another report noted that he again failed to convert. His side won in the end by two tries to nil. Despite heavy showers there was an 'enormous' attendance and years later de Valera told his secretary that his 'most important match' was the defeat of Garryowen. A commentator who attended the match remarked that it was hitherto 'unknown in the history of Garryowen when they were defeated all over the field. They were beaten forward and back.'[85] In 1946 de Valera's friend Frank Gallagher made a note of him recalling this match with Garryowen when his side won and how, having scored during it, he drank too much whiskey celebrating afterwards:

> It was a cold, raw day and when they went back to Cruise's Hotel [in Limerick City], Ryan (they usually took a bottle of stout) saying they should have a small whiskey. He (C. [Chief = De Valera]), discussing the match, drank eight of them. Remembers arguing with his teammates on the railway journey up (imitated thick voice very well) but in the outside [jaunting] car from Goold's Cross got sick ('luckily nothing but the ground got it').[86]

Mellett wrote of one memorable kick by de Valera:

> Garryowen were within ten yards of our line when the ball came to Dev at centre. He threw it rather high in the air, seemed to stumble but just got his boot to it close to the ground. Both teams gasped as the ball soared high and 'found touch' at a distance which might well have been a world's record … Dev confided 'I'm proud of that kick!' Proud of it he might well be, but he could never repeat it … He told me that he had a similar experience in hurling practice.[87]

The 1905 season included an incident that 'to some extent marred the friendliness' of the competition. This was after Rockwell lost the semi-final cup match in Cork to Cork Constitution on 25 March 1905, despite de Valera having stopped 'a grand individual effort by Tom Ahern' of Cork Constitution. Rockwell objected to the legality of 'Cork Con' playing a man who had been reported by a referee to the Cup Committee. The complaint saw the result nullified and it was decided that the teams should replay the match at a neutral venue.[88] The replay took place only after a muddle that saw Rockwell turn up in Cashel on 5 April, where a large attendance was expecting the game to proceed. But Cork Con did not travel on that day: 'At 4.45 p.m. Rockwell lined up, and going through the necessary preliminaries to claim the match, Mike Ryan scored a try, off which De Valera kicked a beautiful goal [conversion].'[89] But this amounted only to a claim, not a result, and did not stand. Instead, rugby officials designated another date for the replay. It took place at Markets Field on 10 April 1905, before 'a huge attendance'. De Valera reportedly played an active part in this replay too, but his passing was criticised. One pundit even accused him of 'selfishness' when he was put in possession and lost Rockwell ground. He also missed a penalty kick. In the end Rockwell had no points and 'Cork Con' had three.[90]

In 1905 Eddie returned to Dublin. The Jesuits employed him teaching at Belvedere College. He represented Belvedere on the Leinster Schools Rugby Committee and Farragher wonders if he had any part in the training of the Belvedere team.[91] But he was soon playing rugby for Blackrock again. The *Freeman's Journal* reported his conversion of the sole and winning try in an 'important fixture' against St Mary's on 11 November 1905. In March 1906 he was part of a victorious 'mudlark' in which Blackrock beat Wanderers, scoring his side's only try on a sodden and slippery pitch. In January 1907 the *Sunday Independent* reported him on the winning side against Lansdowne, although in December that year his side lost to Old Wesley.[92] Eddie played for Blackrock on both the Firsts and Seconds, even becoming captain of the Seconds.

When de Valera was given permission to return to live again on the Blackrock campus in 1907–8 he agreed to act as secretary of the rugby club there. He is said to have led the Seconds into the final of the Leinster Junior League in March 1908 but to have been blamed by some people for their 6–3 defeat by Dublin University, due to a supposed 'fixation' he had about his ability to take penalties and place-kicks. Farragher remarks that 'reports of his going occasionally to the cobbler to have adjustments made to his kicking boot based on mathematical calculations are all probably the result of after-match celebrations!'[93]

In November 1909 Eddie was on a Blackrock side that drew with Clontarf.[94] He subsequently surprised his teammates, as J.P. Brennan later reminded him

We were practising for some football match in Blackrock College grounds. I remember vividly the astonishment which was felt by all present then on the news of your coming or actual betrothal – we did not know which. But, as far as memory will carry me, that occasion was one of your last practices. I still can see John O'Boyle, Joe Kenny, Peter Daly – perhaps there were others – overwhelmed by the good news.

De Valera replied 'I remember well my last football match. It was in the College grounds at Nutley Lane.'[95] Brennan continued:

I often intended – but somehow or other never seemed to get a chance – to speak in retrospect of the pleasure you often gave me when you played centre to me. From no other player, except perhaps Joe Kenny did I get a pass at full speed, enabling me to score. I remember that I used to stand a little further in the rear from you, and when you made an opening you threw the ball to me when I was going 'all-out', and scoring became easy. I am afraid that like all wing three-quarters I did not give you the proper merit which you deserved. I remember that one day at Rockwell, in a practice match in which you participated, I got four thrilling tries. I don't remember if you were playing the day Mick Ryan fell on Jack's knee and dislocated it. Through some 'magical' twist, Fr Pembroke who was on the touchline, did some manipulation and the bones slipped perfectly into their socket. I also have in mind your great ability as a place kicker.[96]

During the 1920s Frank Gallagher made a note of de Valera's claim that Gaelic Football originated in the 1870s at Blackrock College when Michael Cusack, one of the founders of the Gaelic Athletic Association in 1884, was a teacher there. Cusack became a member of Blackrock's 'French College' cricket team as well as an enthusiastic rugby player for years: 'no playground but a paved or graveled one therefore no chance of tackling and also no opportunity between class to put on togs – so game needed which barred tackling and could be played in ordinary clothes: Gaelic football the result. Told of taking shots with the ball at high windows.'[97] Later, wrote Gallagher, his 'Chief' – when commenting in October 1946 on that year's All-Ireland Gaelic football final between Kerry and Roscommon – said it was a 'fine game, clean, keen; enjoyed the right hook Roscommon man gave to Kerryman who had tried to kick him, but the round ball always annoyed me. It should be streamlined like a rugby ball.' De Valera had gone on again to refer to Michael Cusack:

> Says Gaelic really conceived in Blackrock where Cusack had been a pupil [*sic*, error for 'teacher'] there – they played rugby in the field, but in the playground of the College which had a hard earth surface covered with gravel they could not tackle or scrum so they invented a game which Cusack developed into the present Gaelic. Thinks it a great pity that we could not have hurling for a national game and rugby for an international one in which we would sweep the board. But it cannot be now.[98]

The Rockwell branch of the GAA had been affiliated to that association on 20 October 1887. De Valera played some hurling as a boy in Bruree, but if he also played it at Rockwell it did not attract the publicity that his rugby exploits later did.[99] No president of Ireland who later attended international rugby matches in an official capacity ever knew more about the game that de Valera did, and it may have been frustrating for him in that capacity that his eyesight in old age was so poor.

- 6 -

GETTING ON

DIGS, JOBS AND JEWS

De Valera might have stayed at Rockwell, married locally and settled down. Instead, he gave full notice to his employer, quit and returned to Dublin in 1905. He found it difficult to get a job in the city. If he thought that Blackrock College would ever recruit him onto its staff he was to be disappointed. Meanwhile, he still hoped to proceed to a degree in mathematics at Trinity College by winning a scholarship there.

He was coming to terms with the fact that he had only a pass grade in his arts degree from the Royal University. He wished to better himself but was in need of an income. One option was to emigrate. He decided that engineering might be the way forward, and that studying it while teaching in Britain might indeed be the best way to do so. In 1903, as seen above, he had secretly explored the possibility of going to England to teach at St Wilfrid's Catholic school, and while there continuing his private studies for his final BA exams of the Royal University of Ireland. Now he applied for a job elsewhere in England:

> My one trip to Liverpool in reply to a Christian Brothers' advertisement. Meant to teach in the day and go to Liverpool University at night so as to do engineering. Left Dún Laoghaire on Saturday night, travelled to Liverpool, arrived at 4 a.m., walked the streets until the school opened. Had a look at it. Saw the Master. Wouldn't stay for love or money. Stayed out in the Square in Liverpool listening to the band until time for train for returning boat. First experience of what it was like to be really seasick.

When Howth showed up thought it stood still and was never coming nearer.[1]

During the academic year beginning in September 1905 he found work for some months in Belvedere College, the Jesuit school on the north side of Dublin, but he soon moved on again: 'Made up my mind I wouldn't stay there any longer.' He does not explain why. Farragher describes the job at Belvedere as 'a temporary post' but de Valera clearly states that *he* decided to leave it. During his time at Belvedere, in late 1905, he agreed to fill a very small role at the Abbey Theatre for a night or two, in a play written and produced by Abraham McHardy and Mary Flint whom he knew as part-time teachers of elocution and other subjects. This was *A Christmas Hamper*, staged by the couple's new drama company on the nights of 28 and 29 November 1905. When later, as president of Ireland, he laid the foundation stone of the reconstructed Abbey Theatre, de Valera recalled his performance there. He told a reception that he had agreed to step in at the time when one of the actors became ill: 'The part was that of a doctor and he [McHardy] thought I would fit the part. I told him that I had a detestable memory and if there were any lengthy lines to learn I would have to decline to take part.' Fewer than forty people were in the audience in 1905: 'When I asked afterwards if I had pitched my voice properly, I was told: "Oh, my God, they heard you out in the street." So my bedside manners were not of the best.' One theatre critic thought that 'The tall, thin appearance of Mr E. de Valera as he made his entrance as Dr Kelly at the end of Act 2 caused many to laugh, especially as Mrs Flint was overacting very much at the time. He fitted in better during the death-scene.' However, in its review of the production the *Irish Times* was satisfied that 'Mr. E. de Valeria' [sic] and others had 'acted capably'. The *Freeman's Journal* thought his part well sustained but also misspelt his name. Given his personal circumstances, one wonders what de Valera made of the drama. It dealt with a grandparent rearing an infant sent to her by the child's mother who was dying, a mother earlier abandoned by her husband.[2]

In 1905, four days before Christmas, Eddie wrote to his own mother from his digs at 20 Charlemont Place, Dublin. He told her he was trying to get a scholarship at Trinity College Dublin. His pass Bachelor of Arts degree from the Royal University of Ireland was not the best possible recommendation for a job. He felt downhearted that 'advancement without opportunities is nearly impossible' and told her he had 'a hard battle to fight'. By 'opportunities' he may have meant just plain luck, or the kind of 'connections' or networks that a lad from a labourer's cottage was unlikely to have. His mother still hoped that he would become a priest, and he told her now as if by way of apology or defence that if he were successful – whether he meant in getting a scholarship or more generally is unclear – he 'may be able to do good'. He let her know that she was perhaps not entirely without some responsibility for his state, because 'every time I hear others talking of their mothers I feel more or less an orphan'. But he also excused her by blaming 'fate':

> We are both very good correspondents, but I know you find it very difficult to write whilst I should I admit write more frequently. The truth is I am very busy. I have to teach all day and work for myself in the evening. I am trying to get a scholarship in T.C.D. [Trinity College Dublin] but the [an ink blot obscures a word] is very hard and the disadvantages for work and proper instruction are altogether against me. I am at that stage when advancement without opportunities is nearly impossible.
>
> I could never explain my position so I suppose there's very little use trying. I am glad Tommie [his half-brother] is doing well. Tell him he ought to be very happy and to be a better son than I have been.
>
> Mother you will think it strange but every time I hear others talking of their mothers I feel more or less an orphan. Fate has been rather hard on us. I know how much better I would be had I been under your softening influence, and perhaps I too could have made your path less difficult had I been with you.
>
> Tommie must do it all. I have a hard battle to fight just now. If I am successful who knows I may be able to do good.
>
> Poor Uncle [Pat] at home too has a hard struggle. If I could only get a position that would give me a chance to help him. But I am not able hardly to keep myself going at present.

Hoping you will have a very happy Xmas and a very bright New Year. Your loving son Eddie.[3]

He was struggling, 'not able hardly to keep myself going at present' as he told her. He later said that about that time he was also offered a post in Santiago, Chile, as secretary of a mine but would not take it: 'Colleague did. Married the owner of the mine, so I was told. Earthquake in Santiago about this time. Had another offer for some University in Canada. About the same time as the vacancy occurred in Carysfort.'[4]

As things turned out, he was to teach mathematics and mathematical physics (honours level) at various schools before he stopped teaching in 1916, including at the Dominican Convent on Eccles Street, Loreto College on St Stephen's Green, St Mary's Rathmines and Castleknock. He also taught these subjects for a while at Holy Cross College in Clonliffe, Co. Dublin, and gave grinds to various students. He even tutored at UCD, before it became part of the NUI.[5] At one point he applied to the technical school in Bolton Street for a job, and thought that his uncertain ancestry was used against him. He claimed this publicly in the 1930s when denying that he was Jewish: 'The first time that it was suggested that I had any Jewish connections was when I was a candidate for a position as mathematical teacher in the Technical Schools in Bolton Street. Because I was put in the first place by the Selection Committee, this was used in order to prejudice my chances with the voters. It was used again in America for the same purpose.'[6]

If the half-Jewish Leopold Bloom and his wife Molly had been real people living then on Eccles Street, rather than fictions of James Joyce's imagination, their paths would likely have crossed that of Eddie de Valera. The young teacher was wandering Dublin from one rented room to another, and one school to another –including the convent on Eccles Street. 'From the time I left Rockwell and came to Dublin in June 1905 to my marriage on January 8th 1910, I lived in many "digs", with intervals in the College, Blackrock. These intervals were mainly in the summer months,' he later wrote. He was at 74 Heytesbury Street in August 1905; then 9 Upper Gardiner Street for about six weeks when he first got work in Belvedere College during August and September; next at the Thomond

Hotel on Gardiner's Row – 'nearly opposite Barry's Hotel' – in October; then back briefly to Heytesbury Street; 20 Charlemont Place ('facing the canal between Charlemont Bridge and Harcourt Street') from before Christmas 1905 until sometime the following month, January 1906. Then on to 4 Bushfield Terrace, Donnybrook (off Marlborough Road) where he stayed until late in the autumn with his old school-friend Barrett. In each of the years 1906, 1907 and 1908 he went north for a summer course in experimental science (physics and chemistry).[7]

During 1906 a full-time teaching vacancy arose at the teacher training college on Carysfort Avenue in Blackrock. With the support of the Holy Ghost Order at Blackrock College, de Valera secured this position. It carried with it what Seán O'Faoláin termed the 'trifle magniloquent' title 'Professor of Mathematics'.[8] In fairness, the title 'professor' has long been used in some contexts to designate a person who does not necessarily enjoy the status of a university professorship. De Valera learnt of the vacancy at Carysfort from a priest, when he went to Blackrock to watch a cricket match one summer evening in 1906. The priests of Blackrock had helped him to get the position at Rockwell, from which he walked away after two years, and they had now informed him of the job opportunity at Carysfort. The Mother Superior of Carysfort College, Alice Keenan, was a sister of Sir Patrick Joseph Keenan, the first Catholic to hold the position of resident commissioner of Irish national education. Sir Patrick was chief architect of the Intermediate Education Act 1878 that had put in place the payment-by-results scheme that had so benefited de Valera himself. The new job did not take up all of Eddie's time every day, leaving him free to teach part-time outside the college.[9]

In September 1906 Eddie lodged closer to Carysfort College, in a house at 46 Carysfort Avenue that was owned by a married couple named Stanley. During 1907 the Stanleys themselves moved to 2 Anglesea Terrace and de Valera went with them as a lodger for a few months. He was no longer sharing a room: 'Barrett, who had been with me in Bushfield Terrace and in Carysfort Avenue had got the Patent Office examination about this time, and I was alone.'[10] However, Eddie managed to get permission to return to the Blackrock campus to live there as a lodger for the academic year 1907–8. This was an exceptional

De Valera (extreme right) – in his bowler hat – at Blackrock College celebrations in 1911. Courtesy Blackrock College Archives.

arrangement. He was even elected onto the committee of the college's Literary and Debating Society for 1907–8.

In 1907, while he was back as a past pupil living at Blackrock Castle, his mother and her second son visited Ireland. Eddie had written to her from there on 16 June:

> Your letter [not found in the UCD Archives] was a pleasant surprise for me. The only thing I regret is that you are not coming in August rather than July, for I would be quite free in August. However, the main thing is that you are coming. Uncle Pat will I know be delighted beyond measure. I'll try if it is at all feasible to meet you at Qtown [Queenstown, Co. Cork, where liners between America and Britain left off their passengers for Ireland]. Write before you leave. As ever, your fond son Eddie.

Have written to uncle. Get a through ticket to Dublin [underlined thus] for Exhib[ition]. You must come to see it, and see the college [illegible word here].

[Postscript note by him on the top left of page] I am delighted at prospect of seeing Tom and yourself so soon. Till then good-bye.[11]

The pair sailed via England, arriving safely there 'after a very bad journey', as Thomas informed his half-brother in a postcard sent from London en route.[12] It was only their mother's second visit to Ireland since she had left Limerick in the 1870s, her first and only other return having been in 1888. It was also to be her last visit ever. A pub in Williamstown near Blackrock College offered accommodation upstairs, and Eddie's mother possibly stayed there. However, Thomas seems to have lodged with Eddie himself. Eddie later wrote 'This was the first time that I met my brother.' They are said to have attended the Irish International Exhibition that was held that year in Herbert Park, Ballsbridge. Returning late to Blackrock campus they found the gate locked and had to climb over it.[13] Thomas later wrote of recalling 'many a happy moment I spent, roaming around Bruree, Howth, Bray, Dublin, and cloudy misty Lisdoonvarna. At such times I would long to be with you again in Ireland, or to have you with me over here …'[14] Little or nothing is known of what he and his mother and half-brother did or said in 1907 on that rare visit.

Eddie was almost twenty-five years old in the summer of 1907. According to some accounts, Kate suggested to him during her visit then that he return with her to live in America, although to live where exactly and do what is not stated.[15] He had wished in vain when younger to rejoin her in the USA. Even if she really invited him in 1907 – though there seems to be no hard evidence of this – he did not go then.

In 1908 Eddie again left Blackrock College campus. He lived from late October 1908 until May 1909 at 13 Merrion Avenue, between the upper class Ailesbury Road and Nutley Lane – off the main road to Blackrock from Dublin. Charles Russell, a son of the couple who owned 13 Merrion Avenue when de Valera took 'digs' there, later told him that 'My mother was a native Irish speaker from Mayo, and my father became deeply interested in the Irish language.' He thought that de Valera 'became most eager to learn Irish from my parents'. Charles was born while de Valera was still living there and in 1971 he told de Valera that he believed his parents had asked Eddie to stand as godfather to him. He thought that de Valera consented.[16] That autumn of 1908 was also when de Valera made a decision which had great personal consequences. He joined the Gaelic League, and through it met his future wife Sinéad (born Jane Flanagan).

By 13 October 1909 Eddie was living at 7 Vernon Terrace, Booterstown, where he remained for about four months. He and Sinéad were married at St Paul's Church on Dublin's north quays on 10 January 1910, using Irish forms of both surnames – De Bhalaera and ní Fhlannagáin. After a brief honeymoon the couple went to live at 33 Morehampton Terrace (off Morehampton Road). Sinéad wrote that she was 'almost certain' that the last night de Valera spent at that address was on 'Holy Thursday', 21 April 1916, just days before the Easter Rising.[17] In the meantime he continued to pursue his teaching career and to revisit Blackrock College from time to time. A photograph taken at its golden jubilee celebrations in 1911 shows a smiling de Valera – not long married and already a father – sporting his bowler hat and rolled umbrella, wearing a cravat or scarf, while some others present even wore top hats.[18] He was no revolutionary then.

'ANXIOUS' FOR IRISH

The public life of Éamon de Valera, appears to have begun when he was in his early thirties: 'My public life might be regarded [omission here – perhaps 'as starting'?] when I joined the Gaelic League. I had always been anxious to learn the language, but the desire had never led to real action before. My teaching and other work had led me in other directions, and I had absorbed all the time that I had [in being] devoted to study.' He said he joined the Gaelic League in 1908.[19]

His assertion that he had always been 'anxious' to learn Irish seems exaggerated, given what he we know about him. The declining incidence of Irish-speaking around Bruree was considered earlier, as were Eddie's first impressions of the language (Chapter 3 above). It interested him to hear the old people speak it at Bruree, but it was not then taught at most national schools and he only picked up a few words and phrases. Like many other people he responded to a popular series in the newspaper by a priest who won great acclaim for his attempts to encourage people to speak the language:

> When Fr. [Eugene] O'Growney's lessons appeared in the *Weekly Freeman* [*Freeman's Journal*] in 1893 I remember my uncle reading the notice about the proposed lessons and telling me, now that we could learn Irish. When the first lesson [omission – 'appeared'?] he read it to me, but the lessons did not continue … My next attempt to learn Irish was in Rockwell. Fr Johnnie Byrne, as we called him, the Dean of Studies, used to teach the language, and one of my pupils, Dr Gogarty, later Bishop of Kilimanjaro, had been in his class. He came to my room in the College a few times and gave me the pronunciation of words occurring in O'Growney's first book. For some reason or other that I do not now remember, the lessons were discontinued.[20]

When he attended Blackrock College he was not one of those pupils who were active in Gaelic revival activities or in learning Irish. If he had an active interest in the Irish language this was not obvious. The connections between the two colleges of the Holy Ghost order at Blackrock and Rockwell saw Paddy Conroy and other students come from Tipperary to Dublin to complete their studies. Conroy was later better known as Pádraic Ó Conaire, an Irish language writer. Conroy was one of a small group of students who took Irish as a subject at Blackrock then, although he was soon asked to leave Blackrock College for reasons that are unclear. Together with Michael Collins, he was later a member of Company No. 1 of the Irish Volunteers in London. Albert Power's neat statue of a seated Ó Conaire was to become a well-known feature of Eyre Square in Galway – with locals dubbing it 'Sean Phádraic' (Old Patrick).[21] The Blackrock class also included T.F. O'Rahilly, later considered to be 'the foremost scholar of Modern Irish'.[22] In 1956 de Valera wrote that

When I was a student in Blackrock I missed what would have been a wonderful opportunity had I known it. There was in the College an Irish class.
It included the late Tomás Ó Rathile, who became one of the outstanding
Irish scholars of our time; Pádraic Ó Conaire the writer – sean Phádraic;
Fr. O'Mahony. Their teacher was Tadhg Ó Donoghue, or 'Terna'. The first
copy of *An Claidheamh Soluis* that I ever saw was in Tomás Ó Rathile's
hands.[23]

Farragher reports de Valera as saying that 'had he known that there was
such an Irish group in the College then he would have liked to have
joined them' (not that he '*would* have joined them' note).[24] However, in
Bruree he had made no sustained effort to learn Irish and in Dublin the
Irish language was of no direct value to his immediate ambition – which
was to get a college degree. He admitted in 1956 that 'I had all the subjects that were required for honours in the Intermediate and to take up
a new subject would in any case, even had I been aware of the class, have
been a handicap. So it was not until I joined the Gaelic League [in 1908]
that I had an opportunity of learning the language in earnest.'[25] Farragher
points out that even Ó Rathile's younger brother did not study Irish at
Blackrock, being 'directed by his parents to concentrate on that combination of subjects which was best calculated to win him an exhibition in
the public examinations in order to pay for his education. The same kind
of consideration applied to de Valera, only more so.'[26]

It is not known when he learnt the 'Our Father', or Lord's Prayer, in
Irish –possibly at school in Charleville – but his cousin Lizzie, Uncle Pat's
daughter, later spoke of him teaching it to her when he was home on
Christmas holidays. Given that she was not born until 1897, and that she
said he taught her the Latin for serving Mass at the same time, this does
not reveal anything significant about his linguistic skills then.[27]

Eddie's decision to join the Gaelic League in 1908 and to make a special effort to learn Irish may have been a calculated initiative on his part,
one intended to ensure that he would not be left behind when it came
to applications for jobs. It would be a feather in his cap to be equipped
to speak 'the national language', particularly as there were growing
demands to make it a requirement for some purposes. He was by then

an up-and-coming teacher of mathematics and it could do him no harm professionally to be seen to be enthusiastic about Irish culture, especially if applying for a position in the new National University of Ireland or in the public service more generally. Patrick Pearse and other militant members of the Gaelic League were already campaigning to make Irish a compulsory subject in the matriculation for entry to the NUI – and they were to get their way in 1910 when the NUI Senate announced that from 1913 Irish would be obligatory for admission.[28] The militants could not foresee that in the future this requirement would be little more than a simple formality, a matter of lip service.

While pursuing his new interest in the Irish language Eddie met his future wife, who was four years older than him and who was actively engaged in cultural politics. After they married he was to spend some summers teaching Irish in the west of Ireland, whereas previously he had gone north for summer courses in mathematics in Belfast.

When interviewed for a US television network in the 1950s de Valera said 'Neither of my parents nor my uncle with whom I came to stay [in Ireland] when I was two spoke Irish.' Asked directly 'Do you speak Irish?' he answered 'Some, yes.' 'And where did you learn the language, Sir?' 'I learnt it mainly in the Gaelic League. I didn't have it in my childhood. As you know, I was born in the United States, and though I did come to Ireland at the age of two and a half, still I didn't learn the language. It was spoken though by my grandma and people of that generation, but the next generation lost the language in the main.'[29] He later said that his tutor at Blackrock College had urged him to join Pearse's branch of the Gaelic League:

I joined the *Árd Craobh* [head branch] on the suggestion of Michael Smithwick, my fellow student in the castle [Blackrock Castle] who taught me mathematics for the mathematical scholarship. About the same time I joined the Leinster College; and now I meant to apply myself seriously to the learning of the language.[30]

He was beginning to use a Gaelic form of his name, a practice adopted by quite a few of his contemporaries in Ireland. He gradually replaced Edward with Éamon. But he also sometimes spelt his first name with a double letter 'n' at the end, and even attempted an Irish rendition of his Spanish surname – using the letter 'B' (with an overdot/*buailte* or equivalent linked letter 'h') instead of 'V' (a letter not found in the Gaelic alphabet). Thus, the official register of Irish births recorded his signature in January 1911 as 'Éamonn de Bhailéara' in respect to his first son 'Bhibhian' (Vivian on the register, later Vivion in practice). When signing his first name, he sometimes placed the acute or long accent (fada) not above the initial capital letter 'E' but above the letter 'a' immediately following that initial. When signing his family name, he sometimes inserted in 'Valera' an accent on one of the letters 'a' and/ or on the letter 'e'.[31] Given uncertainties about the identities and actual names of his parental ancestors, as well as the early change of his own first name from George to Edward and the fact that he was sometimes known in Bruree as Eddie Coll, the variations are notable. One may speculate as to their psychological significance, if any.

He began to learn new skills when he joined the Gaelic League. For example, he found himself making appeals and speeches in public places and persuading people outside churches to part with money – not yet for explicitly political purposes but for the cultural activities of the league itself. He did not join Sinn Féin before the 1916 Rising, and he subsequently sought to explain his earlier aversion to it in terms that suggest to historians that he confused that party with the IRB: 'Disliked the Sinn Féin methods in the Gaelic League. Swore I would never join Sinn Féin on that account.'[32] It was in fact the IRB, not Sinn Féin, that was then infiltrating various other organisations. Decades later he spoke to his close Fianna Fáil associate Frank Gallagher about what happened, as he explained it:

Talked about the early Sinn Féin: it must have been in 1910. He was made a teller in the election at the Gaelic League Convention of the *Coiste Gnótha* [Executive Committee]. Seán Ó Murthuile was another teller and D[ev]. saw him [tricking?] with votes getting the IRB men in the Coiste. Seán was a delegate from Sinn Féin or at least a prominent member of it. D[ev] came home that day to wherever he and Sinéad were living (mainly in the kitchen he said); he remembered throwing down the *clár* [programme] on the table and saying 'If there is one organisation I will never join it is Sinn Féin.' Then he added to me as an afterthought 'I must have been thinking politically then.'[33]

If he was 'thinking politically', his knowledge of nationalist or republican affairs was clearly not extensive at that point. Was it rather that he was *not* in fact thinking politically but later wanted a reason to explain his lack of involvement in nationalist politics before 1916? De Valera likewise stated in 1956:

About 1910 the I.R.B. or the Sinn Féin element appeared to me to be endeavouring to get control of the *Coiste Gnótha* [council] of the Gaelic League; canvassing and using methods which seemed to me unfair. I remember when I went home to Donnybrook in 1910 throwing the Ard Fheis book on the kitchen table and saying to my wife that I would never have anything to do with Sinn Féin. I kept up my membership of the Gaelic League ever since.[34]

De Valera himself later agreed to become a member of the IRB when it suited his plans before the 1916 Rising. This was despite purporting to disagree with the nature of such secret organisations, settling in his own mind for conscientious qualifications to his membership rather than the kind of outright rejection he had visited on Sinn Féin when he thought that it was to blame for frustrating his ambitions in the Gaelic League.

When Eddie learnt enough Irish to run a summer school in the language, his mother in America appears to have thought that his language skills had received outstanding recognition from the University of Dublin (Trinity College). So it seems from a letter she wrote when her eldest son was jailed in 1916, after the Easter Rising. Kate cooperated with Irish republicans then in lobbying Washington politicians to put pressure on Britain to reduce her son's sentence, providing Sinn Féin's US representatives with 'some old letters of Ed's, also copy of Birth Certificate and all particulars'. Eddie's officially corrected birth return, now showing 'Edward de Valera' in place of 'the original 'George de Valero', was issued in New York in 1916 and constituted evidence of his

US citizenship. Writing to her other son Thomas, she remarked 'I have realized all the facts about Eddie since I saw in the papers about the Sinn Féin uprising. I knew he couldn't escape the authorities over there when he was a Professor of Gaelic in Dublin University. Innocent or guilty they treat every Catholic alike. Perfidious Albion.'[35] There is no evidence that Kate felt strongly about Irish nationalism before 1916, although she may have shared the antagonism to 'perfidious' England common among many of the Irish who blamed it for their ills, including for massive emigration from Ireland.

Éamon de Valera came to master Irish well enough for most purposes. In a number of photographs taken between 1918 and 1921 he is seen wearing pinned in his lapel a '*fáinne*' [Irish: circle]. This was, from February 1916, a symbol of one's willingness to engage in conversation in Irish.[36] An exchange in Dáil Éireann in 1921, during the debate on the proposed Anglo-Irish Treaty, demonstrates his fluency while also indicating the sensitive nature of the language issue. First he said:

> *Níl mo chuid Gaedhilge chó maith agus ba mhaith liom í bheith. Is fearr is féidir liom mo smaointe do nochtadh as Beurla [sic], agus dá bhrí sin is dóich liom gurbh fhearra dhom labhairt as Beurla ar fad.* [Present author's translation: 'My Irish is not as good as I would like it to be. I can explain my thinking better in English, and for that reason I think it is better that I speak entirely in English.'][37]

Then, in the style of a consummate politician such as de Valera was, he proceeded in his next sentence – which was in English – to obscure his own shortcomings and to imply that it was others who had a problem: 'Some of the members do not know Irish, I think, and consequently what I shall say will be in English'!

Throughout his political career de Valera was to lament the decline of the native language and to call on people to learn it, but the educational policies his governments later adopted in support of that objective were generally ineffective if not also pedagogically counter-productive.

'BRIGHT PROSPECTS' AND EINSTEIN

For sixteen years after leaving school – from 1900 until 1916 – De Valera taught and studied mathematics. Then, at Easter 1916, this career suddenly ended. At its outset, while still a university student, he had tutored schoolboys and schoolgirls; he later also tutored university students (including at Trinity College Dublin) and worked on short contracts as a school teacher. He finally got a job teaching mathematics to trainee teachers at Carysfort College, where he was known as 'professor'; even after that he attended further lectures in mathematics at Trinity College Dublin and at the Catholic University college in Dublin.

Eddie wanted so much to be a university professor. Yet his examination results generally in mathematics did not suggest that he was extraordinarily good at the subject. He was undoubtedly a competent tutor and teacher but his performance in examinations was uneven. An observation by his most recent biographer seems reasonable: 'He might have fared better with other subjects, perhaps taking his career in a different direction.'[38] Eddie majored in mathematics but a pass BA degree did not leave him well placed to secure a job as a teacher of the subject, never mind as a university professor. Farragher describes mathematics as Eddie's strong point, but at the same time notes that he secured honours in Latin and Greek and thinks that his choice to major in maths was partly determined by the fact that there would be less competition in that subject area than in the classics.[39]

Throughout his life de Valera persisted in reading mathematics and mathematical physics, and took comfort in considering mathematical matters. Occasionally imprisoned in Britain and in Ireland between 1916 and 1924 he had maths books sent into the jails and corresponded with mathematicians outside.[40] When he was in government, during the 1930s, he told his friend Dorothy Macardle that he would like to take some sort of holiday because he had not had one for years –perhaps to visit the south of France to improve his French. However, he added, 'If I were to take a holiday here my idea would be to do mathematics. I could get lost in them. Do you know, I might even get to the point of neglecting a dispatch!'[41] His surviving personal notebooks in the UCD Archives include mathematical scribbles and his biographer T.P. O'Neill recalled seeing the symbols of mathematics chalked on the piece of linoleum with which de Valera, when president of Ireland, sometimes covered his desk for the purpose of considering mathematical problems.[42]

Disappointed by his pass degree from the Royal University of Ireland, in late 1904 Eddie considered the possibility of undertaking an MA at Queen's College Galway, but his undergraduate degree results did not merit a scholarship there and he ruled out that option. However, on 21 January 1905 he registered as a student of mathematics at Trinity College Dublin – just one of about thirty-four Catholics among that year's intake of 320 students to what was then regarded by nationalists as a very Protestant and pro-British institution. Despite the fact that, to varying degrees, members of the Catholic hierarchy frowned on members of their flock attending Trinity, Eddie had since 1902 considered the possibility of trying for a scholarship there. It was a personally audacious decision by the son of a labourer, for how many people of his class – Protestant or Catholic – then became students of Trinity College? He needed financial support to complete a course and, even as he was leaving Rockwell, he sat the scholarship examination in Trinity College for the first time, on 29 May 1905. David Fitzpatrick points out that 'his Royal University pass degree provided inadequate grounding and he finished last among the thirteen candidates' for a Trinity scholarship. This was clearly a blow. Notwithstanding his disappointment he proceeded that summer to sit the first-year 'Junior Freshmen' tests of the Trinity degree programme for which he had registered, and sailed through in first place. He had not attended the undergraduate course lectures at Trinity, perhaps because he was confident that his prior learning of mathematics was adequate or because the timetable clashed with his teaching commitments. As a Catholic and as a labourer's son he may also have found the ethos of campus life in College Green then somewhat unpalatable. He stated at that time that his 'ultimate object' was to apply eventually for a civil service job as Assistant Examiner of Patents, in the office where his friend Hughes had found work. Then, on 21 May 1906, during his second year registered at Trinity, he again took the scholarship examination. Once more this proved much tougher than the undergraduate examinations for which, as a teacher of mathematics, he was already well equipped. The scholarship examiners were looking for a more complex level of ability, and he fell far short – not quite last this time but ninth out of the ten who tried that exam. This second failure marked the end of Eddie's involvement in the degree course at Trinity, which in a revelatory article in 1983 David Fitzpatrick observed had hitherto gone 'unnoticed by his biographers'. Eddie did also attend public lectures given in Trinity College by Dr Edmund T. Whittaker, who was the Royal Astronomer of Ireland and Andrews' Professor of Astronomy at Trinity College Dublin. Although de Valera as a politician was to be critical of aspects of the college's ethos, he was later to be gratefully remembered there, because it was his government that included Trinity within its scheme of university grants in 1947 and so strengthened the college's financial footing.[43]

While Eddie certainly had abilities as a mathematician, abilities that were about to see him employed as 'professor of mathematics' at a teacher-training college, his two dismal efforts to win a scholarship at Trinity are difficult to reconcile with a popular image of him as a bit of a genius at mathematics.

After his appointment as a 'professor' of mathematics at Carysfort College, Blackrock, in September 1906 Eddie displayed considerable initiative in writing and getting printed for his students a special book-let of forty-four pages entitled *Examples in Arithmetic and Mensuration: Theory-Questions and Notes*.[44] He told Frank Gallagher in 1927 that he had trained nearly a thousand teachers, many of whom became friends: 'They, at least, never believe the propaganda against me. They know it isn't true.'[45] What 'propaganda' he meant is unclear. The following year de Valera elaborated for Gallagher on his time at Carysfort:

At lunch today he talked of his teaching days and how comforting it was to have a class of mature minds to whom he could teach the abstract philosophical side of mathematics and how he had to wear a mask because they were all girl students. 'Used you do well?' I asked. He did. One year his ninety pupils got 90 E – ninety excellents – which was apparently top-notch. They were in a state of continual revolt against being brought outside the course but the results proved the value of it. At one time he used to give a gold watch out of his own pocket to the three best girls in his three classes. He did it for five years until the nuns stopped it, on the grounds that it was unfair to other teachers.[46]

For financial or other reasons he never managed to complete any post-graduate degree in mathematics. In 1908 he decided to apply for a job as schools' inspector with the National Board of Education, where Blackrock men had filled a notable number of positions. He elicited some fine references to bolster his chances of an inspectorate position. For example, H.C. McWeeney, fellow in mathematics at the Royal University, wrote on 26 November 1908:

> Mr E. de Valera, B.A., had a distinguished career in the Royal University, especially in Mathematics, in which subject he got Honours at several Examinations [but not an honours degree]. He also gained a Mathematical scholarship [there]. Apart from his public record, I can testify to his attainments from personal knowledge, as he attended my (M.A.) lectures during several sessions at University College. He was an able student and an energetic worker. He has had considerable experience in teaching both University and Training College students.[47]

That was the year he also joined the Gaelic league, undertaking a beginners' class in Irish at its Leinster College where his future wife taught. It might help to get him a job

If he was unable to afford to register for, or had not enough time free to complete, a further degree programme at Trinity College or elsewhere, he was evidently free to continue attending some university lectures on mathematics. This is clear from another reference provided for him that month, by no less a figure than Dr Edmund T. Whittaker, Royal Astronomer of Ireland and Andrews' Professor of Astronomy at Trinity College Dublin

> Mr Edward de Valera has attended several of my Professorial Courses of Lectures on Spectroscopy, Astro-Physics, and Electro-Optics during the past two years. In the personal intercourse which has thus been brought about, I have been much impressed by the intellectual vigour with

which he has interested himself in the most difficult problems of Natural Philosophy. His knowledge is both broad and deep.

The letter was addressed from Dunsink Observatory in Co. Dublin.[48] During the Second World War, de Valera was to consult Whittaker about plans for a school of theoretical physics in the Dublin Institute for Advanced Studies, and Whittaker became one of its first board members. The institute was an initiative of de Valera in government. In early 1959 he would recall for Whittaker's widow his own memories of her late husband's lectures. She had written from Sussex to thank him for 'a beautiful Christmas card with good wishes' that he sent her and she stated that her husband was 'immensely proud that you were one of his students and followed your wonderful career with the greatest interest, as long as he lived'. De Valera then replied:

I recall the first time I met your husband in the lecture room at Trinity College. I have a mental picture of him as a lithe, slim figure, tense and pale-faced, as if he had been burning too much of the midnight oil. Had he a moustache at this time? I have never seen a photograph of him with one, yet the mental picture I have of him on this first occasion as he came gowned from the door to the blackboard is remarkably vivid. I have always pictured him, when recalling that occasion, with a fair golden coloured moustache. Have I been wrong?

She confirmed that Whittaker had a moustache at that time, adding 'I do not suppose that you can ever have known that his friends in Edinburgh thought he bore a certain resemblance to yourself! This pleased him very much for, as you know, he had a very real admiration and a great regard for you.'[49]

From a third reference that de Valera elicited also in 1908 there appears to have been no intrinsic intellectual impediment to his getting a master's degree. Dr A.W. Conway noted that Eddie had attended Conway's lectures in mathematical physics at University College, Dublin and 'I have no hesitation in saying that in mathematical knowledge he is well up to M.A. standard.' The dean of studies at the college explained that although de Valera had read there for a Masters 'His duties connected with his official position at the training College, Carysfort, finally necessitated the postponement of his M.A. Examination.'[50]

De Valera was not made a schools' inspector in the end, and 'felt outrage' at this because he thought he was better qualified than those who were appointed.[51] So he now looked to enhance his skills in a new way. Where in 1906, 1907 and 1908 he had attended summer courses in Belfast to help him advance in the mathematics profession, in the summer of 1909 – swept off his feet by his future wife at Irish classes – he forsook the north to join her in Tourmakeady. This was an Irish-speaking district of the west of Ireland where he might improve his knowledge of the language. In 1910 he received a chief diploma (with first place in the examination) from the Leinster College of Irish in Dublin, as he strove to become fluent in Irish. In 1911, 1912 and 1913 he got vacation work as director or principal of the annual Tawin Irish Summer School at the Irish-speaking seaside location of Oranmore, Co. Galway. There, each August, teachers and others went for Irish classes in the forenoon and boating, bathing or walking in the afternoon, with '*céilidhte* [Irish dancing] two or three nights in the week'. They were advised to bring '*camáns*' (hurleys) and music. The school did not thrive.[52] On 9 September 1911 Arthur Griffith published in his *Sinn Féin* a letter highly supportive of the Tawin school. It came from L.P. Carolan-McQuaid, a resident of Cambridge, England, who at that time was staying in Co. Galway at Tulira Castle, the home of Edward Martyn, patron of the arts and formerly president of the Sinn Féin movement. The correspondent referred to the principal of the school 'Edward de Valera B.A. (who holds a Diploma from the Leinster College of Irish 1st place, 1910)' and to de Valera's native speaking assistants, and wrote that he had 'derived great advantages in being under their supervision during its present session'. He hoped that pupils would flock to Tawin next year and spelled out its advantages in some detail, writing that 'one can scarcely imagine a more suitable situation for such a school. Yet it does not seem to have attracted that influx of students which its position and management would lead one to expect.' De Valera reported on its problems to its financial backers, among whom was Roger Casement.

Meanwhile, Eddie had also enrolled at UCD for the academic year 1909–10, this time on its new Diploma in Teaching course. He thus became one of the first five candidates ever awarded what later became known as the 'Higher Diploma' or 'H. Dip' – regarded as very desirable for secondary school teachers. UCD was one of the constituent colleges of the new NUI and had just appointed Fr Timothy Corcoran as its Professor of the Theory and Practice of Education. In this way De Valera was now a pupil of 'a great propagandist' for Catholic values in Irish education, one who would soon support his application for a professorship in NUI Galway.[53]

As he continued to teach at Carysfort he sometimes received letters from America. His half-brother Thomas wrote to him just before Christmas 1909, from St Mary's College, North East – a town in Erie County, Pennsylvania, 185 miles (298km) from Rochester where their mother lived. It was a long chatty letter, his first in seven months. Given Eddie's fondness for his Aunt Annie who had followed his mother to America, he may have found Tom's short reference to her frustrating. Thomas was still on the path to becoming a Redemptorist priest and looked forward to graduating from St Mary's (a preparatory high school seminary where young men 'discerned their vocation to the Redemptorists' way of life or to another of life's pathways' instead) and to entering the novitiate. Tom's letter indicates that he had had some kind of unexplained 'break down' and had to be 'very careful' of his health for the coming year – to the extent that at a recent athletics meeting in his college 'the only event I dared to enter was the mile walk – the other events I thought too strenuous'. The fact that there is no explanation of what constituted his 'break down' suggests that such an explanation was contained in an earlier letter from him that is lost, and to which Eddie replied before being kept waiting 'seven long months' for further word. Lost too is Eddie's letter to his mother of late August 1909, which apparently 'overjoyed' her by indicating that he had 'bright prospects' and by his saying he would try and visit them in America in the summer of 1910. In fact he would not go to America until 1919, and that visit was primarily for political purposes. Quite why she was 'silently' looking forward to such a visit is unclear. Did she see herself as an heroic, long-suffering mother whose silence somehow signalled the depths of her hidden pain or sacrifice? Must they dutifully 'try not to disappoint' her expectations lest she be hurt more than she was already hurt by giving up Eddie and by the death of her daughter Annie? Thomas wrote to de Valera:

My Dear Brother,

When you receive this letter I am sure you will say, '*Mirabile dictu*! [Latin: 'wonderful to relate'] Tom has written again.' Yes, after keeping you waiting seven long months for some word from me, I am again about to send you a letter. To explain my delay in writing I must have recourse to the same old excuse – often too busy to write, sometimes (I am ashamed to admit it) too lazy to write, frequently interrupted in the midst of a letter to you. Although this is a very poor excuse still I feel certain that you will pardon my negligence.

Before telling you how I have spent the last half year, I must wish you a Merry Christmas and a Happy New Year. I hope, dear Brother, that your Christmas will be replete with God's blessing, and that good health and success will accompany you throughout the New Year.

I will now say a few words about myself. Soon after I wrote to you last spring, the Annual Examinations came along, bringing with them a great amount of cramming, numerous headaches, and many deep and heavy sighs. But like everything else in this world they too had their end. Although I received no 'excellents' in the examinations, still I think I did fairly well in most of the branches.

The examinations ended amid exclamations of joy, and then the glorious summer holidays unfolded themselves to our eager view. There is no need to tell you the emotions we felt when we began the holidays, for you know better than I do, how a student feels when the prospect of two months' vacation is before him.

Often during the summer months my mind would travel back two years, to the time [in 1907] when we were together and many a happy moment I spent, roaming around Bruree, Howth, Bray, Dublin and cloudy and misty Lisdoonvarna [Co. Clare]. At such times I would long to be with you again in Ireland, or to have you with me over here.

With the exception of a couple of days I remained in Rochester all during vacation. I spent a very quiet but happy summer, because I had to rest up for the coming year. You see I have to [be] very careful of my health now, or else I will break down again.

I read a great deal, slept a great deal and ate three or four hearty meals every day.

Mother was overjoyed when she received your letter near the end of August. Of course she was glad to hear that you had bright prospects but what pleased her most was the paragraph in which you said you would try and pay us a visit next summer. I am sure she is silently but eagerly looking forward to the time when she will see you again. Try not to disappoint her.

Vacation ended before I knew it, and then I returned to St Mary's to begin my last year there. The annual retreat was the first thing of note that took place after our return. It was a very practical retreat and I feel that I did not spend the three days uselessly. Character building was the keynote of the whole retreat.

Class followed on the heels of the retreat. My! It was hard to begin to study again. I could not get my mind down to my books. Gradually, however, I became accustomed to study and after the first month I found it not only an easy but sometimes a very congenial occupation. Of course at times one is rather hard-pressed, and on such occasions one wishes the books to be a thousand miles away.

About the first of Oct. we began a three day *Triduum* [a period of prayer] in honor of St Clement Hofbauer (the newly canonized Saint of the Redemptorist Order). During the celebration some of the students presented the moral [*sic*, for 'morality'?] play 'Everyman'. The rendition was very good.

Summer mellowed into autumn and with the changing and the falling of the leaves came the ripening of the college's vineyards. One sunny morning we received the order to pick the luscious clusters of grapes that dangled on the vines. This is a most pleasing occupation and one that is eagerly looked forward to in college. Autumn passed and now all the vineyards, the campus, the lawns and the surrounding fields and woods are covered with snow. But at St Mary's we enjoy winter nearly as much as we do summer, for there are numerous ponds around here, on which we can skate, and on our own property there is a high hill which affords excellent coasting. On Thanksgiving Day, we had a little athletic meet on the campus. There were no world records broken, but still there was as much interest displayed around St Mary's as there was at the Olympic Games. The only event I dared to enter was the mile walk – the other events I thought too strenuous. I came in first by a slight margin; I suppose it was owing to my long legs.

I had almost forgotten to tell you of my studies. Latin, Rhetoric and Trigonometry are the only new branches I am taking this year. I do not find any of my studies, with the exception of Greek, very difficult. Still I have enough to do, to keep me busy most of the time, for we have two English, two German and one Latin composition to write every month.

Now I think I have told you pretty near all about myself. I frequently hear from home, both Mother and Father are very well. Aunt Annie, I am sorry to tell you is not in good health. I do not exactly know what her illness is.

Don't think, dear 'Ed', that I forgot about your birthday in the middle of October, for I did not. I was so 'pushed' for class-work that I had no chance to write to you. However I prayed for you and I feel certain that you will forgive me for not writing. Every day I say a prayer for you, and I want you to do the same for me. In six months I will enter the Novitiate and I want you to pray that I may persevere.

Please answer my letter as soon as you can, for I am just 'dying' to hear from you. Tell me all about yourself. Remember me to Uncle Pat and his family when you write to them. Wishing you again all the joys and blessings of the Christmas season, I am Your Affectionate brother Tom Wheelwright.

P.S. I hope that your health is good and that you are succeeding well with your classes. T.J.W.[54]

During 1910 and 1911 Eddie attended further mathematics lectures given by Conway and McWeeney.[55] This appears to have been with a view to completing a master's degree eventually, but he never finished one due to the fact that he was –according to Ryan – 'compelled to postpone it by his duties in the Carysfort Training College'.[56] Nevertheless, in April

1912, de Valera decided (even dared) to apply for the professorship or 'chair' of mathematics in University College Galway. He again collected and sent with this application a range of flattering testimonials, including once more from Conway and McWeeney. But Conway, professor of mathematical physics at UCD, did not explicitly repeat his opinion of 1908 that de Valera was 'well up to M.A. standard'. Instead he described him now as having mathematical abilities 'of a high order' and of being 'possessed of great brilliancy and originality'. He added that in the past two years de Valera had 'gone deeply into the subject of quaternions (below), and is at present presenting an important original research in them which promises to be of considerable interest'. Moreover, this time in 1912 Whittaker did not give De Valera a new reference. He told the young man that he had already agreed to provide one for another candidate for the same job. He did add that de Valera was free to reuse the reference that he had written him in 1908. There was also a letter of support from Fr Timothy Corcoran. With his application for the professorship, de Valera sent a cover letter and gave details of the various MA lectures he had attended. Drafts of this letter show how he attempted to turn to his advantage the fact that eight years of attending various postgraduate lectures had not led to his passing any further examinations in mathematics leading to a qualification beyond his original pass degree: 'As my maths studies for these eight years was altogether unhampered by examination requirements they have been wider and far deeper than would have been possible were I compelled as an M.A. candidate to cover in a year or two certain selected portions of the field.'[57]

Eddie was not appointed a professor in Galway. However, in October 1912 Dr Daniel Mannix (1864–1963), president of St Patrick's College, Maynooth, wrote to him to tell him that Henry Kennedy had resigned as the college's lecturer in mathematics and physics. Mannix invited de Valera to send in testimonials if he was interested in the position temporarily, as the bishops looked forward to having a resident professor in the near future. In the event Fr Pádraig de Brún was made professor but, meanwhile, de Valera filled the temporary vacancy. The 'brilliant' De Brún had been tutored at Rockwell and Holy Cross College by de Valera himself and had gone on after university in Ireland to obtain a doctorate from the Sorbonne in Paris on problems in integral equations. He and de Valera remained lifelong friends.[58]

If Galway was not to be his, Cork might. In May to July 1913 de Valera again organised some testimonials, this time in order to apply for the professorship of mathematical physics at University College Cork (UCC).[59] His ardent admirer Dwane writes that de Valera found himself competing with the nominee of the president of UCC, Sir Bertram Windle: 'Each of the Munster County Councils had a representative on the governing body. De Valera put forward excellent credentials, but many of the county council representatives at that time were not disposed to give due weight to credentials – if they gave any at all – hence the result.' Nonetheless, de Valera would still have won (according to Dwane) had not the representative for Co. Limerick missed his train at Kilmallock by one minute and so been absent for the vote.[60] Caught between the UCC president and those backing a candidate who grew up in Limerick, perhaps the county representative was diplomatically late for his train.

One of those whom de Valera approached to support his bid for the professorship was J.J. Horgan. Horgan was a solicitor and a leading member of the Irish Parliamentary Party machine in Cork, who declined an opportunity to run for parliament. He was very active in the Gaelic League. In May 1913 de Valera turned up on his doorstep, as an 'unexpected' visitor. He was following in the footsteps of Patrick Pearse, who just three months earlier had stayed with the Horgans. They planned to send their children to Pearse's school in Dublin. One wonders if Pearse suggested to de Valera that he visit Horgan.[61] McCartney provides considerable background that shows how de Valera canvassed actively for this job in Cork, ostensibly asserting his support for Home Rule in order to marshal the backing of members of the Irish Parliamentary Party for his candidature. His efforts paid off to the extent that the governing body of UCC ultimately gave the same number of votes to their top two choices, E.H. Harper and de Valera. Horgan sent de Valera a telegram to tell him the result.[62] However, the academic council of the university described Harper as 'incomparably the best candidate', and did not even include de Valera in their choice of the top three applicants. McCartney writes of de Valera having got so far that 'It can only be assumed that a very successful canvass had been carried out on his behalf among the public representatives, the clergy and the teaching representatives' on the governing body. In July 1913 the senate of the NUI proceeded to appoint Harper, with de Valera not even being proposed at that level. UCC's eminent president Sir Bertram Windle and those best equipped to make academic judgements do not appear to have rated de Valera as a serious contender. The highly politicised governing body, however, had been prepared to make him professor of mathematics with support from the Catholic Church and the Irish Parliamentary Party, notwithstanding ostensibly better candidates.[63]

Horgan's account of de Valera's approach to him, if accurate, reveals a de Valera whose political life did not begin when he later joined the Volunteers in November 1913 (as de Valera claimed) but earlier. The fact that Horgan was married to the daughter of the president of UCC might have deterred other candidates for a job in that college from appoaching him, fearing that such a visit would be taken as a cheeky or inappropriate canvass. Not de Valera. And he brought with him a detailed letter of introduction from Fr Timothy Corcoran, who had both taught Horgan at Clongowes Wood and taught de Valera on the Diploma in Teaching at UCD. The letter, recalled Horgan, asked for his 'support and influence' on behalf of de Valera:

> My visitor, whose modesty was only equaled by his charm of manner, was equally acceptable on other grounds, for it appeared that he was not only an active member of the Gaelic League but also, like most young Irishmen at that time, a supporter of John Redmond's Home Rule policy. If I had to secure for the candidate the support of our party in Cork, this would naturally be a desirable qualification. I accordingly set to work …

Horgan, who had very much helped John Redmond's political career, noted that his father-in-law as president of UCC had in the end 'quite properly' supported the candidature of Harper and 'used his powerful influence' to secure Harper's election. Academic considerations ultimately trumped party politics.[64] However, there was some good news elsewhere for the defeated candidate. When Pádraig de Brún went to Germany for further mathematical studies before taking up his professorship at St Patrick's College, Maynooth, de Valera was employed to continue teaching there for another year. Ordained during 1913, De Brún served as professor of mathematics and mathematical physics at St Patrick's College from 1914 until 1945.[65]

In 1914 the new NUI awarded de Valera a BSc. This was an NUI statutory award available without examination to graduates of the former Royal University of Ireland who already held a BA degree and could furnish satisfactory evidence of being engaged in mathematical work *for* a postgraduate award. By 1914 De Valera had indeed attended many relevant postgraduate lectures, although he was never actually awarded a postgraduate degree.[66]

It is beyond both the competence of the present writer and the scope of this book to assess or rank de Valera's mathematical abilities. McCartney thought that 'a great deal of folklore' has surrounded the subject, although he acknowledged that Eddie's secondary school and Royal University examination results 'were highly credible' – if 'not always particularly outstanding, especially at the university level'. In his warm testimonial for de Valera in 1912 Dr Arthur Conway, professor of mathematical physics at UCD, acknowledged this fact when he asserted that Eddie was 'adapted to excel in research work rather than to do himself justice in examinations'. However, no matter what Eddie's research into quaternions 'promised' in the opinion of Professor Conway, unexamined 'promise' is a very shaky basis for a decision by any university to appoint a young man to a professorship – even where Eddie also had experience of teaching and tutoring.[67]

De Valera liked to recall how, when leaving Limerick for Blackrock College in 1898, 'on the train, with my little tin trunk, I set out for the metropolis. I do not remember the details of the journey very much, except occasionally trying to estimate the speed at which I was travelling by counting telegraph poles.'[68] This anecdote suggests a particular interest in calculation. As Conway indicated, de Valera evinced a special fascination with the fundamental formula of the Irish mathematician William Rowan Hamilton on quaternions – reportedly even scratching

Hamilton's key equation on his cell wall in 1924 when imprisoned in Kilmainham Jail after the Civil War. He also discussed it in the 1930s with British Secretary of State for Dominion Affairs Malcolm MacDonald during difficult political talks. In 1865 Hamilton wrote that decades earlier he had cut his famous equation $i^2 = j^2 = k^2 = ijk = -1$ into a stone of Broome Bridge on the Royal Canal near Dublin but the inscription had 'long since mouldered away'. In 1958 de Valera unveiled a plaque at Broome Bridge commemorating Hamilton's flash of insight nearby. [69]

In 1965, responding to a request from the *New York Journal* 're President de Valera's mathematical reading and studies', de Valera approved this statement for release:

> The President's great regret is that the time he can devote to maths is necessarily very limited. However, he has read to him from time to time articles on modern physics – atomic particles, quantum dynamics, etc., and books such as those by Professors Synge and Lanczos, Dr McConnell, etc. etc. He works from time to time in analysis – tensor analysis, biquaternions and octonions, Grassman's Algebra of Extension and Boolean and other algebras.
>
> The President uses dark green linoleum (found to be most effective from his eyesight point of view), covering the top of his large desk in his private study here in *Áras an Uachtaráin* [his official residence], as a blackboard on which with chalk he draws geometrical figures and pursues such algebraical expressions as he might find difficult to visualize otherwise.[70]

As earlier noted, de Valera's examination results in mathematics after he left school were far from universally excellent.[71] Whether or not he was quite the mathematical 'genius' that some of his family and followers seem to have thought is debatable:

> My father's time at home was limited and his moments for recreation few. In these precious moments he loved to lose himself in his beloved mathematics, a subject in which he altogether excelled, so much so that Einstein said when speaking about his Theory of Relativity that there were

only nine people in the world who really understood his theory and that de Valera was one of them.[72]

A leading American magazine likewise wrote of Éamon de Valera being credited by 'legend' with being 'one of only thirteen scholars who understood Einstein's theory of relativity'.[73] Some of his detractors suggested mockingly that in fact de Valera and Einstein alone understood it – and that there was even a doubt about the *latter*. But when the wags have had their say the fact remains that de Valera had an abiding and informed interest in mathematics

De Valera's establishment of the Dublin Institute for Advanced Studies (DIAS) in 1940, with its schools of Celtic Studies and of Theoretical Physics (and later of Cosmic Physics too), partly reflected his affection for mathematics and his wish to see it studied at the highest level.[74] His initiative was clearly inspired by the establishment of the Institute for Advanced Study at Princeton, New Jersey, in 1930. One of the Princeton institute's first professors was Albert Einstein. The passage of enabling legislation for the Dublin institute through Dáil Éireann gave a leading opposition politician the chance to make personal remarks about de Valera's status as a mathematician. Fine Gael's James Dillon TD claimed that:

The proposal [to include mathematical physics in the Dublin Institute for Advanced Studies] is incorporated in this Bill for one, and one only, silly, childish purpose, and that is to lend verisimilitude to the myth that the Taoiseach is a great mathematician, which he never was and never will be. He is a man who takes an interest in mathematics, but there are thousands of decent secondary teachers who were his colleagues before he entered politics, and who are as good mathematicians as he is – and there are hundreds of them far better. But the myth has to be created in the world that in Ireland we have a scholar Prime Minister and that, in pursuit of the age-old passion that has inflamed his heart for pure science and truth, he could not resist the chance of conferring the reflected glory of his learning on the rising generation of the Irish people. That is all cod, and we in Ireland know it is cod, but there will be articles published in the Melbourne *Argus*, the *Irish World*, the *San Francisco Leader*, and they may even get into *Life* or *Time* under the heading of 'The Scholar T.D.'

Dillon went on to say that de Valera, 'who is notoriously a person who has all his life taken an amateurish interest in mathematics, was seeking to hold himself out for the kudos which would accrue to him as patron of mathematical learning and as a kind of pedagogue amongst the proletariat.'[75] Tones of begrudgery and political bile were certainly struck in the debate. The same fundamental Fine Gael resentment of their civil war foe was still evident thirty-five years later when, in what purported to be a dispassionate if critical tribute to de Valera by a committed supporter of Fine Gael, Senator Alexis FitzGerald claimed that de Valera 'made no mark as Minister for Education'.[76] Given that de Valera held that political brief for only a few months when he was also taoiseach, the foundation of the DIAS was surely quite a 'mark' compared to the achievements of some other ministers for education.

Abraham Flexer, founding director at the Princeton Institute once said 'I am not unaware of the fact that I have sketched an educational Utopia. I have deliberately hitched the Institute to a star; it would be wrong to begin with any other ambition or aspiration.'[77] There seems no good reason to deny de Valera's *bona fides* in respect to his motivations as both taoiseach (prime minister) and minister for education in 1939–40 when the enabling legislation was passed. De Valera continued to take a great interest in the Dublin Institute, attending lectures there and maintaining contact with some of its personnel. It is said, for example, that he used to telephone Erwin Schrödinger for information on mathematical points when the latter – who had earlier jointly won the 1933 Nobel Prize in Physics – was its director. At a colloquium on the combination or relativity and quantum theory held at the Dublin Institute in 1942, while chatting during a tea-break with one of its senior professors, de Valera 'excused himself for taking time off to attend the colloquium by explaining that he had not had a holiday for some years and that the colloquium was really a relaxation for him'.[78] In a brochure in 1982, the DIAS brought together a number of papers to honour its founder, and this brochure cannot be read without concluding that leading members of it believed he remained active as a mathematician to the end.[79] In a memoir of de Valera for the Royal Society, the distinguished Irish mathematician and physicist John Lighton Synge stated in 1975 that it was wrong to think that de Valera's interest in the mathematical sciences was sentimental or superficial.[80] A lengthy dissertation assessing de Valera's mathematical leanings remains unpublished in the library of UCC.[81]

The last word here is left to de Valera himself, or at least to a note of what he said, according to his close ally and friend Frank Gallagher on Good Friday (11 April) 1941: 'His own position [is] as a continuer or a minder of other people's work. As if he inherited a series of houses and repaired the roofs, walls etc. and mended doors and windows. Same in maths. Did some neat things but not original things. Founded F.F. [Fianna Fáil party] at others' suggestions. Others had more character.'[82] With becoming modesty, de Valera does not appear to have claimed to have been or to have regarded himself as a mathematical genius.

PRIESTLY AMBITION

For more than a decade – from at least 1894 until 1906 – Eddie de Valera thought that he might become a priest. He was firmly encouraged in that regard by his absent mother in New York. The latter appears to have made it very clear to him that this was her wish, even after Thomas, her second son, committed himself to the priesthood in the United States. Eddie's grandmother in Limerick also, 'of course, at times wished that I could become a priest, but that seemed out of the question'.[83] He does not explain why it was 'out of the question'.

It was common then for young Catholics to think that they might have 'a vocation'. For those prepared to tolerate celibacy the priesthood offered quite an attractive way forward. There was prestige attached to the life, as well as opportunities for professional advancement in academia or elsewhere, and certain material comforts. However, a boy could not just decide that he had a religious vocation and enter a seminary. Church authorities had to agree that he was suitable. Moreover, those lacking the means to support their training might never qualify to be ordained. Men of a lower social class or limited education were some-times encouraged to become a 'brother' instead of a priest.

From what we know of Eddie, he seems to have been somewhat discouraged by clerics from thinking that he had a vocation to the priesthood. It is unknown if this was because of his personality or his means or his parents' uncertain marital status or for some other reason. Speculation in that regard is no substitute for evidence. In any event his thoughts about a vocation, as well as his enjoyment of prayer and theological questions, partly shaped his character and gave him always a certain 'priestly' veneer.

He told RTÉ in 1966 that, even before his grandmother died in 1895, he 'fundamentally' desired to be a priest, although 'I'm not sure that I had any very definite ideas about it'. Unfortunately, the interviewer appears not to have explored the matter further.[84]

Frank Gallagher once noted de Valera telling him years later that, as he was 'thinking of being a priest', he decided in 1898 to apply to a preparatory institution at Kimmage or Terenure where he might embark on training while studying at university at the same time, 'but there and elsewhere there were no vacancies'.[85] This was during the period when he was finishing at the Christian Brothers' school in Charleville and also seeking entry to colleges in Limerick based on his success in the exhi-bition examinations. Indeed, it may be recalled that when Eddie was unexpectedly admitted to Blackrock College in Dublin, thanks to the initiative of a priest in Bruree, his first thought was to be admitted to the scholasticate, separate quarters where boys lodged who were destined for the priesthood. But for some unknown reason Blackrock's principal, Fr Healy, thought 'not', and instead assigned young Eddie a place among the lay boarders.[86]

In later life de Valera had many conversations with Fr Seán Farragher, whose book on the former's long association with Blackrock College appeared in 1984. Farragher at one points states, presumably on the basis of his discussions with de Valera in old age, that 'all along he [de Valera] had felt from time to time that he had a calling to the priesthood but not the secular priesthood: he was sure of that, as he felt he needed the sup-port and the safeguards of community life' (i.e. with a religious order).[87]

But in that regard Farragher appears to contradict himself when discussing the first ever ordination of a priest at Blackrock College, that of one Joseph Shanahan on 22 April 1900. Remarking that De Valera told him 'how impressed he was by that ceremony', Farragher continues:

> It may well have served to re-awaken in him the desire to become a priest himself, as soon after he wrote to his brother, and again later to his mother, that he was thinking seriously of going on, this time to Clonliffe, to study for the diocesan priesthood. In this he may have been influenced by the examples of his classmates John D'Alton [later a cardinal] and Michael Toher. He mentioned that his chances of getting into Clonliffe depended on his securing a university scholarship; so hard work would be the name of the game for him.[88]

Farragher writes that de Valera 'could not afford to pay his way at Clonliffe College (a major Dublin seminary), even if accepted'.[89]

But Eddie had made no mention of needing such a scholarship for the priesthood in his letter of 2 March 1901 to his mother (Chapter 5 above), where he simply said 'There is nothing new about my prospects. I suppose I will go to Clonliffe [Diocesan College], next summer or the next but one, to be a priest in the diocese of Dublin. Do you see any objection to it?'[90] Nor was there any such barrier mentioned in his letter of 6 October 1902 in which he told his half-brother Thomas (Chapter 5 above) 'I as you intend also to become a priest'.

What does that sentence 'There is nothing new about my prospects' signify? That he has no better option to pursue? Or that he had been and remained intent on being a priest if he could overcome the obstacles? If Eddie's mother replied to her son's letter of 2 March 1901, and one assumes that she did, that reply and any advice in it seem to have been lost. However, it is clear that the option of his becoming a priest remained very real for him. When he thought of moving to England in 1903 and then wrote seeking work at St Wilfrid's College, he remarked in a notable postscript 'Perhaps it would be well to add that my ultimate object is the priesthood.'[91]

Farragher certainly thought that de Valera continued to see himself as a future priest. In 1904, when Eddie had completed his final BA exami-

De Valera disguised as a priest, undated between 1917 and 1923. Courtesy National Library of Ireland, NPA DEV44.

nations but was 'still blissfully ignorant of the results', he was once more thinking of entering the priesthood – as Farragher wrote:

> When he came to Blackrock first he had expressed serious interest in going on for the priesthood. At various times in the intervening years that suggestion kept cropping up in his mind and even in his letters. At last, whether off his own bat, or on the advice of someone else, he decided to do a weekend retreat with the Jesuits at Rathfarnham Castle and to discuss the matter in depth with his confessor. He revealed the state of his soul to the best of his ability to his '*Anamchara*' [Irish: soul friend]. The priest in question was in a talkative mode at the end of the retreat and spoke about many topics. At last Dev, rather impatiently, asked 'But what about my vocation?' 'Oh! your vocation. You have what is known as an incipient vocation.' Dev laughed and said 'If that is all I have after all those years, it

is time I forgot about it'. He recalled that he whistled merrily all the way as he cycled back to Blackrock![92]

How likely is it that de Valera 'after all those years' would have shaken off so lightly his possible vocation – 'incipient' or otherwise? In fact the term 'incipient vocation' has long been used in the Catholic tradition to indicate someone who might well become a priest but has not yet fully committed himself to that life. The Jesuit to whom he spoke was not necessarily rejecting him, and this assertion that he 'whistled merrily' – as if suddenly freed from a burden or a misconception – seems too neat.

On 1 October 1905 his acquaintance John Keogh still thought that Eddie had it in him to become a priest. Keogh, who had been at school with him in Blackrock, wrote to 'my dear Edward' to say that he himself had entered on a course for the priesthood in Carlow:

> In view of what you said as to finally turning in also I want to put this case before you. You have done a fine course in Maths. Why stay out any longer? Would it not be better for you to come in at once and begin your life work? You have a very high idea of the Priesthood. So much the better – do you think that staying out any longer will enable you to realize your idea better? I am sure it would not. Whilst the flush and glow of power is in you is the time to start and do your best. In addition to your own good, look at the great field for work there is. We are suffering terribly from lack of university training. Now one of the ways of partially supplying that is to train our priests: they are the great levers by which the people are to be raised, and our progress is so slow because through a great part of the country they are so badly trained that they do not fully appreciate the necessity of educating the people before anything really good can be done for them …[93]

Eddie did not then 'come in' but he was still actively considering the matter. On 7 January 1906 he had a meeting with the president of Clonliffe College, where he had been engaged to give some tuition. The president noted in his diary that 'De Valera consults on entering eccl. [ecclesiastical] state.' They met again three days later, and the president once more made a note: 'Advised him not to come in now. To give up

Trinity scholarship, to read for th. [theology] and RNI [religious knowledge instruction] and to read what may be useful to begin th. study next year.'[94] Eddie had told his mother a fortnight earlier that he was trying to get a scholarship at Trinity College but said nothing in that letter about the priesthood. He told her he felt discouraged generally: 'I have a hard battle to fight just now.'[95] But the advice he had received from Clonliffe was realistic rather than discouraging. It closed no doors and challenged him to make up his mind. He did not subsequently adopt the course of action in favour of studying theology, as advised by the reverend president of Clonliffe. In fact, four months later, he sat the scholarship examination at Trinity.

During 1906 Eddie was appointed to teach at Carysfort College and John Keogh wrote to an acquaintance about this development: 'De Valera is lucky at last. I wonder will any of these "fair ladyies" hook him and leave our Holy Mother without him. I am watching him with very curious eyes. I think a humdrum home circle will hardly ever satisfy his eager straining spirit – he might be a St. Paul in his own way if he came in [to the priesthood].'[96] He never did 'come in', although he was to don the garb of a priest as a disguise at least once when avoiding capture by his enemies in the troubled years between 1917 and 1923.

Eddie feared that he had disappointed his mother by not being ordained, as a note that he wrote to her from Dartmoor Prison in England in July 1916 indicates. He seems to have hoped that his own sacrifice in joining the rebellion in 1916 might have redeemed him somewhat in her eyes. Referring to the fact that his half-brother Thomas had just been ordained in the United States, he wrote:

My dear <u>mother</u>. A word to ask you not to worry about me. I hope that Tom's ordination day was one of unclouded happiness for you, his father and himself. One son at least gone the path you would desire but as an Irishwoman do not be ashamed that the rake is here [in a British jail].[97]

Again in 1924, this time from an Irish jail where he was interned by the government of the Irish Free State for a total of eleven months for his part in the civil war, Eddie wrote to his mother somewhat apologetically: 'I sometimes smile as I think how nearly your wishes as regards my vocation have been met. I have spent a fair number of years now in a very 'enclosed order'—where the world's distractions cannot reach me!'[98]

By marrying in 1910, Eddie closed off the possibility of becoming a priest. His decision to do so, as will be seen shortly, came as a surprise to his mother and the news of his marriage did not seem to outweigh her evident disappointment.

During the Civil War, when he realised that he had backed the losing side and appeared to regret becoming the political leader of the anti-Treatyite forces, he told the hard-line Mary MacSwiney that reason rather than faith was his master: 'I must be the heir to generations of conservatism. Every instinct of mine would indicate that I was meant to be a dyed-in-the-wool Tory or even a Bishop, rather than the leader of a Revolution.' She responded 'Please don't be so hard on yourself as to think you were meant to be a <u>Bishop</u>. A dyed-in-the-wool Tory is a much more respectable thing!!!'[99]

Although he did not become a priest, de Valera remained close to his Church. Even when disagreeing with Irish ecclesiastical authorities during the fruitless Civil War, blaming 'the bishops who more than the military forces of our opponents have brought our cause to this pass', he insisted on trying to justify himself in terms of Catholic teaching. And when he died more than half a century later, he was laid out in a habit of the Carmelite Order of which he was made an honorary member in 1958. His connection with the Carmelites was long but not entirely spiritual. The order in 1919–20 actively assisted the Irish freedom movement in New York, and in 1965 one of its members helped de Valera himself to ensure widespread distribution of the American edition of Dorothy Macardle's *Irish Republic*, published that year.[100]

Any analysis of de Valera's complex relationship with the Irish hierarchy, through his support for the violent anti-Treaty minority in the Civil War, his drafting of the Irish Constitution of 1937 and his dealings with the powerful Catholic archbishop of Dublin John Charles McQuaid lies beyond the range of this book. However, that relationship cannot be fully appreciated without reference to his earlier 'incipient vocation'.

MARRIAGE AND MOTHER

Eddie had asked his mother if she saw any objection to his possibly entering Clonliffe College to study for the priesthood, but he did not ask her opinion on his forthcoming marriage. It came as a 'great surprise' to her in New York: 'I have not much to say,' she wrote to him frankly when he informed her by letter in late 1909 that he was about to get married to Sinéad Flanagan. He does not appear to have invited her to his wedding, even at short notice.

Kate sent a blessing but no hearty congratulations. Her letter was not a warm one. She hoped that 'the girl is a Catholic'. Given that Kate herself was married to an English Protestant, father of her second and third children, this was somewhat rich. 'I always hoped to see you here unmarried,' she added from New York.

It is not known if Eddie had been with a woman before he married Sinéad. Any sexual experiences he had had by then are not recorded. We know that he went 'totty-twigging' in Blackrock with his school friends, and that there was some kind of involvement with a girl in Tipperary who liked him, but we do not know what exactly this involved. Even a high-spirited Catholic boy at that time was restrained (in a way that can be difficult for many young Irish people today to imagine) by a concept of mortal sin and by the related requirement to confess sins to a priest – often a priest one knew. Contraception was also limited. A pregnancy outside marriage had serious and often very unpleasant social consequences. Many youths had not 'gone the whole way' by the time they married.

The term 'totty-twigging' that de Valera used was laughed off by the late Fr Farragher, biographer of Eddie's days at Blackrock, as 'Tipperary grass-roots slang' for 'watching all the girls pass by'.[101] In fact 'totty' was a term found more widely at the time. The *Oxford English Dictionary* gives it as 'British slang. As a mass noun: people, especially women, collectively regarded as objects of sexual attraction or desire. Frequently in "a bit of totty".' The *OED* defines the verb 'twig' as meaning to 'pull, pluck twitch'. The term 'pulling' a woman today means something more than just 'watching'. Of course schoolboys like to talk big, and in the case of Eddie and his Blackrock friends it may be that any pulling was confined to themselves, much in the way that James Joyce's fictional Leopold Bloom enjoyed the sight of Gertie McDowell on Sandymount Strand during the same period. However, Dev's encounters with a particular girl when he was a teacher at Rockwell College in Co. Tipperary may have been more intense. They occurred at a time when he enjoyed the glory of local rugby triumphs and was known to be consuming beer and whiskey in celebration.

'We hardly knew each other until we were engaged,' Sinéad was to say of their relationship. They met in late 1908 at the Gaelic League and attended some *céilís* (dances) together. Eddie was smitten by her and they became engaged in June 1909, within just eight months of first meeting. They were married seven months later, in January 1910. She once wrote that he was given to weighing up decisions about small matters cautiously but tended to 'go boldly forward' when a big matter was at stake. There is nothing to suggest that she was pregnant when they married.[102]

She had been born in Balbriggan, Co. Dublin, in the summer of 1878 and was thus a little more than four years older than Eddie.[103] Christened Jane, she was known within the family as 'Jennie', being one of eleven children of Laurence Flanagan, a carpenter from Co. Kildare, and his wife Margaret, who appear to have once emigrated for a while. Census returns show that the couple's second child Mary was born in New York about 1871. However, they were back in Ireland two years later when another child was born. Jane's brother Laurence became a tailor while she herself and her younger sister Brigid were both teachers. Jane's other younger sister, Katherine, was married in Balbriggan. Three of their other siblings were triplets who 'barely survived birth', while three more died in infancy. By 1911 her parents lived in Dublin with Mary, Laurence and Brigid at 34 Munster Street, between Phibsboro and the Royal Canal. Jane wrote later 'I had auburn hair when I was young and was always very small for my age.'[104]

From the turn of the century Jane was active in *Inghinidhe na h–Éireann* and the Gaelic League. *Inghinidhe na h–Éireann* was established in 1900 by advanced nationalist women – 'all of whom adopt Gaelic names' it proudly proclaimed. Jane was beginning to call herself Sinéad Ní Fhlannagáin. The association, under its president Maud Gonne, aimed to encourage the study of Gaelic culture and 'to support and popularize Irish manufacturers'. Arthur Griffith helped and promoted it through his weekly political papers and otherwise. Its first public action was to present him with a blackthorn stick for having literally whipped the editor of the Irish *Figaro* who insulted his friend Maud Gonne. Griffth had been sent to jail for two weeks. *Inghinidhe na h–Éireann* held monthly 'ceilidhthe' (dances) at which papers were read by members of the society. Maud Gonne read the first one in October 1900, with Máire ní Chillin, the fiancé of Griffith's close friend William Rooney, speaking next. In April 1901 de Valera's future wife Sinéad ní Flannagáin spoke about '*An inghean dubh*' ('The Black Girl', Fiona MacDonnell, lady of Tyrconnell). Eddie himself was still then an undergraduate.[105] By 1901 Sinéad was also providing Irish classes to children who availed of a support scheme that saw it taught in some schools as an extra subject.[106]

Sinéad was the only woman among five 'professors' in charge of classes at the Gaelic League's *Coláiste Laighean* (Leinster College) when Eddie first signed up for classes there. The Gaelic League had opened the college in Dublin in October 1906, largely to teach the Irish language to professional teachers who could then teach it to children. Sinéad herself had sat and passed the college's advanced class examination in June 1907 before beginning to teach courses there that same year. Eddie later said that his first class in Irish was taught by Sinéad in October 1908.[107] He wrote 'Met my wife at the *Ard Craobh* [head branch, Gaelic League]. Went [summer 1909] to Tourmakeady [a '*Gaeltacht*' or Irish-speaking part of Co. Mayo] because she was there. Engaged 6 June 1909.'[108]

In 1917 Michael O'Toole, a member of the IRB and an Irish-speaker who was then a recruiting sergeant for Roger Casement's Irish Brigade in Germany, wrote of Sinéad:

Before her marriage she had already a distinguished place in Sinn Féin and Gaelic League circles particularly in the line of the beautiful little Gaelic Dramas which have been 'bringing new soul into Erin'. She always played the Fairy in Douglas Hyde's 'Tinker and Fairy'. In that piece she was it. In

Sinéad and Éamon/Ed on their wedding day in 1910.
Courtesy UCD Archives P150/142

the Colmcille [a slip for Celtic?] Literary Society (affiliated to Sinn Féin) she and I conducted the History Lectures. She looked after the children's section through which many 'grown ups' also learned to know and love their country's history. She had a unique method of making history most attractive to the learner. She would tell the story in simple language in coherent style and the children themselves would help by singing solo past songs illustrative of the events. She thus managed to give Dublin youngsters not only a fair idea of Ireland's story but at the same time gave them a fuller knowledge of Irish and Anglo-Irish music and song.[109]

It is not known when exactly Eddie wrote to inform his mother of his imminent marriage – for that letter too is lost – but she replied from 22 South Goodman Street in Rochester on 20 December 1909:

My dear son,
Your letter was a great surprise to me as I always hoped to see you here unmarried. But God's ways are not our ways. So Blessed be His Holy Will. Now I have not much to say but there are a few things I would like you to do. First I hope the girl is a Catholic, then I hope you will be married at

a Nuptial Mass [i.e. not just a plain religious or civil marriage ceremony] and then, unless you intend to come to America next June or July, go housekeeping immediately or else you will be worse off than you have been. I hope the girl – as I don't know what to say otherwise – will be able to cook and if she doesn't let her go to some place where she can learn. I think cooking and sewing are really the most essential things together with economy and of course patience. Those are qualities which if she has them you'll have found a jewel.

If you give all the handling of your money to her keep a little for your expenses as you being used to handle your own money so long it will be very humiliating to have to ask money for every little thing. I hope she is of a lively disposition as if she is not I fear you will be sad. Don't waste your time or money in too much company, only just what is necessary for recreation, and above all don't have any intoxicating liquors in the house.

Was Kate's fear of hard liquor in the house based on any personal experience? She concluded on a somewhat more positive note, revealing in the process that she was unaware of Sinéad's name and background:

Now I give you my blessing. That is all I can do. If you will answer this quickly I want to send you a little box [gift], but I can't do it at present as you may have changed your address and there are so many parcels going through mails on account of the holidays.

If I knew the day you were going to be married I would have a Mass said for you both. Tell me her name and where her home is. There are three jewels in married life and also three demons so I hope you will possess the jewels. They are fidelity, to be ready to share each other's joy and sorrow, and fear of the Lord. The demons are jealousy, covetousness and pleasure seeking. I know Uncle Wheelwright is in the receipt of the money order.

Kate writes to Eddie that somebody 'will be awful sorry to lose you, tell me what he'll say [sic]', but the identity of that person is missing – perhaps she meant Uncle Pat. She urges her son 'Be sure and answer Charlie's letter as soon as you receive it. He is very anxious to have you come over if it [is] only for a holiday.' Kate bids her son 'Tell me all the news about home' and adds 'Tom is well. He is at North East College. I am anxious to have this go tonight so will come to a close. Wishing a Merry Xmas but it will be over when you get this and I hope you will have a bright and prosperous New Year. Your loving mother. God bless you.'[110]

Eddie had presented his mother with an almost accomplished fact, and she could hardly do otherwise than give him her blessing. He was to be married within three weeks of her writing her letter. But there were no warm congratulations or best wishes, and she did not even know the name of the woman he was to marry. Although Kate sent him to Ireland when he was aged two, returning to see him just twice in twenty-seven years, she does not appear to have hesitated to advise him on his possible 'vocation' and personal relationship. He had checked with her about his inclinations to become a priest but, perhaps fearing that she would oppose him, decided not to ask for her approval to marry or to share details of Sinéad with him.

The couple married on 8 January 1910 at St Paul's Church on Arran Quay in Dublin, in a simple Catholic ceremony in Irish. The official marriage register shows he used one of the forms of his name that he sometimes adopted to try and give his surname a Gaelic appearance, in this case 'de bhalaera' (and he spelt his first name here with two letters 'n' at the end as he sometimes did). He was now coming to use the name 'Éamon' in preference to Edward, although family members continued to call him 'Ed' or 'Eddie' also.[111]

The newly-weds honeymooned at Woodenbridge, Co. Wicklow: 'Back within a week to teach at Carysfort. Got an ovation of course [presumably from his students],' he wrote.[112]

Kate need not have worried about Sinéad being a 'jewel'. The newly wed woman gave up her job as a teacher after they married and was to support de Valera in many practical ways. He left their children to her to mind when he went to join the Easter Rising. She was popular and respected in later years, avoiding political controversy and raising a large family for a husband who was often absent or working very long hours. In due course she became known as an author of stories and plays for children, her gentle features a contrast to her husband's often gaunt appearance. She sometimes amused him, as Frank Gallagher noted: 'Soon after they were married Mrs. [de Valera] was called upon by a man named (I think) Byrne who collected rent of the house they were occupying at Ballsbridge. As she was paying it he told her that his wife had died and she immediately poured out her sympathy on this lonely old man. "Yes, maam", he said, "and I raised a monument to her memory" – at which Mrs. poured out sympathy anew – "by marrying again". Mrs [de Valera] thought her sympathy the most wasted thing in life. Delighting himself telling story.'[113]

De Valera would later amuse himself by writing doggerel into one of his notebooks. It referenced the editor of a famous Victorian cookbook, while complimenting his wife:

> Mrs Beeton wrote a book
> Teaching housewives how to cook.
> Judging by the things I've eaten
> My wife's cooking can't be beaten.[114]

Sinéad was strong enough to tell him 'not to try to come home or bother about us' when the cause required otherwise, but she sometimes felt 'lonely and depressed'. She was encouraged to join him briefly when he was in America for eighteen months in 1919–20 but the visit proved unsatisfactory. Afterwards she wrote to his personal secretary Kathleen O'Connell – about whose close relationship to Sinéad's husband unsubstantiated rumours and malicious gossip circulated. She wondered if O'Connell thought her 'a real idiot that day I left Washington. I suppose I was a bit tired and therefore extra emotional.' Back in Greystones, she confessed to O'Connell 'I can feel nothing much else but regret that I went to America. It was a big mistake to go for such a long journey for such a short stay. Since I came home I find it hard to be content or to get along in the old groove.'[115] However, she settled back down.

At the time of the planned auction of certain personal letters from de Valera to his wife in 2000 (below), the historian Tom Garvin told a newspaper reporter that it had always been his strong impression that Éamon and Sinéad were 'enormously in love'. He thought 'Dev was in many ways a normal Victorian gentleman of the period. He had a dour public image, but he had an emotional life. He was not buttoned up. In private, people found him genial and charming.' Another historian, Dermot Keogh, told the same reporter that people took de Valera out of context and dehumanised him: 'He has been judged rather than studied historically'.[116]

MAKING BABIES

In December 1910 their first baby was born. They named him 'Vivian'. The census of 2 April 1911 shows them living at 33 Morehampton Terrace, Donnybrook with an illiterate domestic servant named Mary Coffey who was a Dubliner.[117] At Easter 1911 Éamon received a postcard from the Redemptorist novitiate at Ilchester, Maryland, wishing 'My Dear Bro.' and 'your wife and the Little Chap' well. Thomas wrote that he was happy in the novitiate and that his health was 'O.K.' He was to be 'professed' within his religious order on 2 August that year and to continue to prepare for later ordination, which was to occur in 1916.[118]

It was also in 1911 that Éamon was appointed director of the small and ultimately unsuccessful annual Irish-language summer course at Tawin, Co. Galway, supported financially by Roger Casement. Their first child was just a few months old and Sinéad did not accompany him there. He missed Sinéad, writing at one point:

> I need a kiss, urgently ... I want to press my wife to my heart, but we are 150 miles (240km) apart. Darling, do you think of me at all? Can you sleep without those long limbs wrapped around you? Those same limbs are longing to be wrapped around you again – two weeks, fourteen days – how can I endure it? You do not know how sorrowful I am ...[119]

He was back in Tawin the following summer too, addressing Sinéad as his 'dear little Mummie' in a letter of August 1912. It was four months since the birth of their second child, Máirín. A copy of this letter was seen by Tim Pat Coogan and quoted at length in his biography of de Valera, but its current whereabouts is unknown. In the letter as published de Valera tells Sinéad among other things that 'I am very lonely

without my own sweetheart and her babies. I'll never be a cross husband again … I am always thinking of you darling'. She was at home
in Donnybrook. He poured out his feelings: 'There is a big vacancy in
my heart. I feel empty, joyless without you. I do not let myself think on
for I know in a short time I'll have my own darling in my arms … Ah,
love like our's is grand.' He told her that when he read of the *spéirbhean*
in books he found words inadequate: 'I say my Mummie is a great deal
nicer than all that.' He quoted at length from a poem in Irish to describe
how he felt for his 'darling wife' and promised 'Ah yes, sweetheart I will
be a good boy to you when I go home.' He was remembering her in his
prayers. He said that the Irish words '*beal beosac*' had come into a poem
a few days earlier: 'We translated it as 'nectar lipped', but I understand
what the poet meant. Those wild kisses.' There is eroticism in the tone,
offset by that maternal form of address 'mummie'. He signed off 'Kiss *our*
babies' (his emphasis).[120]

His actual mother kept in touch with the family. At Christmas
1912 a letter that Kate sent him addressed to 'my dear children' from 18
Brighton Street in Rochester, New York shows that she was experiencing
difficulties. While this letter is extant, her reference in it to 'all the letters
that Sinead and yourself wrote' her at that time is a reminder of much
that may not survive, for the UCD Archives contain no such trove of
correspondence for that period. In her letter, she wrote that

> No doubt you will be surprised to get a line from your very negligent
> mother. Please don't be too hard on me for I have been having a very hard
> time of it for two years, on account of the illness of Uncle Charlie. After
> Tom went to Ilchester [the novitiate in Maryland for those training to
> become Redemptorist priests] his father got very severe headaches. The
> doctors said it was from very high blood pressure, and that he was in
> danger of apoplexy. The situation [job] he was in he had to give up, and
> we are at present in our own house [instead of a dwelling provided by an
> employer]. I had to raise a mortgage on the house, so of course I don't
> really consider it our own on that account. I was to see Tom on Aug 2nd
> – he was well and happy. I was glad I went for I couldn't have gone if I put
> it off until later, for Charlie was very sick since.

I promised to send a little box some time ago, but never got around to do so until yesterday. The things in it are for all of you to divide as you please. The Rosary, pin, chain and cross are for Sinead[121] and the scarf pins are for you. The catseye is a lady's pin so if Sinead would like it give it to her – it is set in oxidized silver. By the way I think this is Vivian's birthday [his name spelt thus by her].[122] I expected to be able to send him a little money present for shoes or coats and am only sorry I could not do so. I hope himself and Mary [the couple's first two children] are well.[123] Also hope Sinead and yourself are enjoying good health. I was very pleased to hear of your appointment [that as a temporary lecturer or professor in St Patrick's College, Maynooth in 1912, presumably]. Pat told me about it. I hope you don't have to work too hard and above all try and go to bed early. Those who study very hard must rest their brain or else they will not have as good a memory when they grow a little older, nine hours sleep at least is needed. I got all the letters that Sinead and yourself wrote. I also got Vivian's picture. So I think he looks something like you did as a baby.

Kate wanted to shelter her Thomas from bad news. While her first son had forsaken a vocation, as she saw it, her second son was now well on the road to becoming a priest:

I haven't told Tom about his father, nor have I told him that we left 22 S[outh] Goodman [St.]. I don't intend to tell him because it would worry him too much and he might leave and come home and as he has taken his vows his whole life would be blighted. I have told no one yet but Aunt Annie, and unless someone goes to see him from Rochester he will not hear it. These Crosses come from the hand of Almighty God and we must bear them patiently.

Aunt Annie is fairly well and so are all the children.

I haven't written to Uncle Ed [Kate's brother in America] since last Christmas so you see I don't do much writing. I had a letter from one of his daughters about a month ago. The whole family were well then. Now when you write tell me all the news. Also tell Sinead to write me although she hasn't much time now with the two babies. I will send some photos later. I

have no time just now. When you answer this, seal a letter to me and send it to a friend of mine enclosed in another envelope. Address Miss Hartness, 53 South Goodman St., Rochester, New York, USA. Excuse this. Now my dear children, I hope you will have a very Merry Christmas and a Bright and prosperous New Year replete with God's Grace and blessings. It's the sincere wish of your loving Mother. God bless you all. Pray for me.
[P.S.] Dear Sinead, the Rosary is blessed and indulgenced with all the Church can give at present. Also the little crucifixes have the indulgences for a happy death and the Stations of the Cross attached to them. Write me if you have time. Mother. Excuse this. Once more a Merry Xmas.[124]

The level of religiosity in this letter may seem exceptional by today's standards but was not particularly unusual for an older Irish Catholic woman of the early to mid-twentieth century. What is striking is that Kate does not wish him to reply directly to her, as if her husband Charles might be upset to see such communication between her and her first son.

By the end of 1913 Sinéad de Valera had given birth to a third child, 'Eamonn de Bhailéara' (as registered). About this time she wrote to Kate in America. The first four pages of this letter appear to be missing from the UCD Archives. What survives underlines the distance between Kate and her first son, whose own children have never met this grandmother in America and who cannot conceive of Kate as their father's mother. Reading Sinéad's expression of sympathy in the first paragraph of the letter below as it survives, one wonders if she may be thinking 'and sorry too Eddie lost you' when she refers to Kate losing her daughter Annie Wheelwright. For she exclaims 'I often think of you as the first woman who loved him'. Is there tension or even a criticism implicit here, and might this be why she avers, 'What I should like is that you and I should be very good friends for Ed's sake'? She wrote thus:

Viv and Maureen have brown eyes and are more like your side of the house. Little Ed is a Flanagan. He has fair hair and blue eyes. My father and mother are very fond of all three but I think Maureen is their darling. I always feel so sorry you lost your little girl. It must have been a hard trial for you and her father but the thought of her happiness must bring much consolation. Maureen finds it hard to know who Daddy's mother is. She speaks of you as 'Daddy's Granny' as my 'Granny' is here. She wanted to know would 'Daddy's Granny' like her and would Tom like her. I wish you could see them all.

Is Saturday a fateful day with you? Ed tells me he was born on Saturday – so was I. And we were married on Saturday and Maureen and little Ed were born on Saturday.

Next time I write I shall send you another photo of the children. Ed had a letter from his cousin Mary. If you write to her will you please ask her to continue her prayers for us? Later on I shall write to her myself. It was very kind of her to remember us. I must write to Tom soon. How faithful he is! And we treat him so badly. But really I have very little spare time. The children take up all my time during the day and when they are gone to bed there are hundreds of little things to be done which are so important that they can't wait. Ed never makes any complaints about my housekeeping and he is ever so good at coming punctually to his meals and giving me as little trouble as possible. I only hope the children will be as good as he.

Lizzie [Uncle Pat's daughter] is at home on holiday at present. I shall give her your messages when she returns. I had a letter from her before Easter. All were well then except Uncle Pat had a cold.

I hope Uncle Charlie is quite well and that next time we hear from you you will have good news all round. I shall try and write more regularly in future. Now, please don't think of sending us any gifts. It strikes me you are always thinking of others and not of yourself. What I should like is that you and I should be very good friends for Ed's sake, for I often think of you as the first woman who loved him. Best love from each one and kindest regards to your husband. From Sinead [she places no accent here on her own name].[125]

By the time of the Easter Rising in April 1916 Éamon and Sinéad had four children, aged between nine months and five and a half years. There was also another baby on the way, one who would be born in November 1916 after the children's father had been arrested and imprisoned for his participation in the rebellion. In all they were to have seven children by

1922. As may be seen below, de Valera was conscious of his responsibil-ities as a father when deciding that he should risk his life, liberty and livelihood by participating in the uprising. It is not clear what weight (if any) he attached to Sinéad's opinion on the matter. His actions in 1916 meant, in effect, giving up his paid job of training teachers in Carysfort. This is turn meant his family had to leave their rented home at Morehampton Terrace in Donnybrook. In May 1916 they went to live with her parents at 34 Munster Street in Phibsborough on the north side of Dublin and a year later she was still there when she told Frank Hughes 'You have no idea of what my life is like'. It was during these months that she sold de Valera's boxing gloves, to help 'fight off starvation' according to Farragher.[126]

The career of de Valera as a mathematician was over. His work as a political leader was about to begin. His daughter Máirín de Valera – born in April 1912 – later spoke of how in 1916–17 her mother 'had no income':

> she had to leave our home [with the children] and return to live with her parents, brother and sisters … my [Flanagan] grandparents were very old and both were semi-invalids. My eldest aunt was living with them and was suffering from a very painful form of cancer … my mother had to undertake all the work of nursing her, as well as the housework, cooking and care of the babies … my elder aunt died in August 1916, my brother Ruairi was born in November that year and my grandmother [Flanagan] died in January 1917.[127]

Some sixteen months after moving in with her parents in Phibsboro – her mother now dead – Sinéad and her children moved again, but this time to superior accommodation. They went to '*Craig Leath*', a fine house on Kinlen Road in the exclusive and very Protestant and unionist Burnaby district of Greystones, Co. Wicklow, where they were to remain until late 1922. They employed there a new maid, Hollie Brien.[128] It is not clear how they afforded such a house, but in July 1917 Sinéad told their friend Frank Hughes not to bother about her as 'I am very well off for the present.' She later wrote 'there were generous donations sent from America and Australia' after de Valera was jailed in 1916. Before accepting the presidency of Sinn Féin in 1917 de Valera also negotiated for himself a presidential salary of £500 per annum – an income such as the movement's founder Arthur Griffith had never enjoyed or sought – and this left him free to devote all his energies to the struggle for independence.[129]

CROSSING THE RUBICON

Four months after UCC rejected his application to become a professor of mathematics, Éamon joined the Irish Volunteers. He had been encouraged politically to think that he stood a real chance of getting the Cork professorship, only to have his hopes dashed.

The Irish Volunteers organisation was founded in 1913 in reaction to the activities of the unionist Ulster Volunteer Force (UVF), which had recently declared that it intended to oppose – by violence if necessary – Home Rule for Ireland. The UVF had been armed with the support and connivance of senior members of the British political and military establishment. About 180,000 men were to join the nationalist Irish Volunteers by the time that the organisation split in 1914. De Valera's future son-in-law Brian Ó Cuív, one of the foremost Irish-language scholars of his generation, would later write that members of the Gaelic League were to the fore in answering Eoin MacNeill's call to join the Volunteers.[130] De Valera was one such member.

When the split in the Irish Volunteers came in 1914, at the outbreak of the First World War, it revolved around a decision by the Irish parliamentary party leader John Redmond to suspend demands for immediate Home Rule pending the outcome of that war. Redmond actively encouraged Irishmen to serve in the British Army – 'thereby establishing a claim on the gratitude of Great Britain' he hoped.[131] As a protest against this policy, 11,000 members seceded from the main body of Irish Volunteers and formed a separate force, with Eoin MacNeill as their chief of staff. Among them were public figures such as Arthur Griffith and Patrick Pearse, and others such as De Valera. This relatively small minority (little more than one in eighteen Volunteers) retained the name 'Irish Volunteers', while the larger body became known as the 'National Volunteers'.

De Valera later described his joining the Irish Volunteers in 1913 in ways that are worth considering because they provide different retrospective narratives. The first version given here was recorded in New York by his close associate and friend Frank Gallagher, when he accompanied de Valera to the United States in the late 1920s. It is notable not least because 'the Chief' (de Valera) reportedly told Gallagher in New York that he had been *against* the Rising in 1916 just a few days before he took part in it:

> Chief as we walked told me (in between the roar of elevated trains which pass along here and make conversation impossible every few minutes) of the time he joined the Volunteers. He had a long tussle with himself. He was married and had children. His duties towards these seemed to conflict 'because' he said 'when I signed that attestation I signed knowing that [Edward] Carson's action had put an end to political progress and that sooner or later there would be war. However others regarded the attestation, I knew it must lead to a rising and it was that rising I had to consider in relation to Sinéad and the children.' In this and a score of other things he shows that his actions are almost always deeply and wisely founded, seeing years ahead. Earlier he had told me of his attitude towards the Rising. He was against it until headquarters had taken the decision on Good Friday. Then he could see no grounds for a call-off, and when the call-off came he was so borne down with it and the lack of considered judgement and sincerity that it implied that he thought nothing would ever be done by the Irish in his generation and he even thought of emigrating. Some time before the Rising Pearse said to him one night 'It is a wonderful thing to have taken a decision', from which he understood Pearse to also have had a mighty struggle with himself before deciding on the plunge.[132]

In 'tussling' with himself in 1913 or 1916, did de Valera ask the mother of his little children what she thought he should do? If he did so, there is no indication of it. How much he discussed with Patrick Pearse, and was guided by him, is an open question upon which the de Valera papers in the UCD Archives throw little or no light. They are largely silent on Pearse, one of a number of lacunae in the surviving papers that raise questions about the extent to which they are representative of de Valera's life's work and experience. It has been seen above that both Pearse and de Valera resorted to visiting J.J. Horgan at home in Cork in early 1913 to lobby for their particular professional interests. It was also in 1913 that Pearse delivered a signal address on 'The Coming Revolution', arguing that the Gaelic League as such was 'a spent force' and that the 'vital work' now to be done in the new Ireland would be done in other ways by men and movements who have 'sprung from the Gaelic League or have received from the Gaelic League a new baptism and a new life of grace'. J.J. Horgan wrote later of a 'strange development' in Pearse's thinking about that time. He noted Pearse's declaring in May 1913 in his school publication *An Macaomh* that 'Ireland will not be happy again until she recollects that old proud gesture of hers, and that laughing gesture of a young man that is going into battle or climbing to a gibbet'; Pearse said of the rebel Robert Emmet (1778–1803) more than once – in language that Horgan thought was 'bordering on the blasphemous' – that he had been 'faithful even unto the ignominy of the gallows, dying that his people might live, even as Christ died'; Pearse told the boys in his school that 'as it took the blood of the Son of God to redeem the world, so it would take the blood of Irishmen to redeem Ireland'. Did de Valera himself imbibe directly from Pearse in the Gaelic League such 'strange and terrible principles' (as Horgan described them)?[133] In 1915, in his play *The Singer*, Pearse had his character Macdara declare 'One man can free a people as one Man redeemed the world. I will take no pike [symbol of the 1798 rebellion], I will go into the battle with bare hands. I will stand up before the *Gall* [foreigner] as Christ hung naked before men on the tree!' One critic has expressed relief that he personally was 'not required, in the context, to examine the theological implications of these strange lines'.[134] In 1915 Pearse may have foreseen such a sacrifice as possibly being unarmed. In 1916 he certainly made a different choice.

In deciding to join Pearse and the other rebels in battle, de Valera appeared to be indifferent to public sentiment. During 1915 he gave his close friend Frank Hughes some advice:

> You seem to be too sensitive about the opinion of the world. I am far too much that way myself but I am not I <u>think</u> quite as bad as you are. Sensitiveness of this sort is a great misfortune. It spoils one's peace of mind more than anything else I know. Get shut of it if you can. We two are too fond of trying to look at things as we expect other people will look at them and generally go wrong in our estimate. Let what the world and your neighbour think go be damned. Did you ever see the man who tried his best to be popular ever succeed except in a paltry measure – 'The Old Man and his Ass' just occurs to me – Aesop knew what I mean.[135]

One of de Valera's later notebooks includes a transcription of verses from Horace's Ode 3.3 ('iustum et tenacem…') that express similar sentiments. But where de Valera's advice to Hughes appears to be amoral, indifferent on the face of it to the righteousness of a cause, Horace explicitly references the justness of one's actions.[136]

In 1962, giving another account of his association with the Irish Volunteers, de Valera wrote that his 'active political life may be said to have begun when I joined the Volunteers. I did this on the day on which they were formed at a meeting at the Rotunda on November 25th 1913. This was the casting of the die.'[137] But what 'die' was cast that day in 1913? Joining the Volunteers was not a sundering of one's relationship with society then, by no means a certain prelude to rebellion. The Volunteers were a reaction to unbridled threats by the Ulster Volunteer Force. Joining the Irish Volunteers was a declaration of one's willingness to resist the bullying of a unionist minority when it came to Home Rule and was not a proclamation of independence, let alone of a republic. While an element of risk was certainly involved for anyone joining the organisation, membership in itself was not a declaration of revolution or of war. Irish nationalists hoped that the British would see sense and delay Home Rule no longer. Indeed the eventual passage of Home Rule legislation in 1914 – the third such effort in nearly thirty years – indicated that this strategy might have succeeded. However, it was derailed when the British government postponed its implementation of the Act once the First World War began later that same year.

   As observed above, by describing his membership of the Volunteers as the beginning of his 'active political life' de Valera overlooked his earlier active canvassing of the Irish Parliamentary Party for the professorship at UCC. During the 1950s, in contrast, he described joining the Volunteers simply as 'the next step of my public career'. The first step (according to him) was his joining the Gaelic League:

> Next step of my public career was the foundation of the volunteers on the 25th of November 1913. I had read of the intended meeting in *Claidheamh Soluis* [newspaper of the Gaelic League] to be held at the Rotunda ... When I entered the hall and took my seat and looked around me, to my surprise and amazement, immediately in front of me in the next seat was my old Parish Priest, Fr. Sheehy, and with him, one who had been a very fine athlete and the star in the Bruree Hurling Club – Larry Roche. Later he went to France and became Major Roche. I did not like to intrude upon them and make myself known ... When the application for membership form was distributed I hesitated to put down my name. I was married with a wife and children, and I was alive to my obligations to them. I finally decided to sign, however, on the consideration that all the able-bodied men of Ireland would be necessary to make any struggle successful. The unmarried men alone, I thought, would not be sufficient.[138]

This is a measured statement, aligning his personal development with nationalist sentiment and recognising that there was an element of risk in membership should actual hostilities follow. Yet in another account (partly quoted next below) he claimed he had 'no doubt' in 1913 that there would be an armed insurrection and that battle was 'inevitably in the offing', a battle with 'its likely consequences'. It requires explanation as to how de Valera ostensibly foresaw the sort of 'battle' that was to erupt three years later. Many people who in 1913 were more politically attuned than de Valera was did not foresee this. He even uses the idiom 'crossing the Rubicon' – based on Julius Caesar's fateful crossing of that river in 49BC – to suggest that he made in 1913 the kind of irrevocable revolutionary decision that only came three years later when he committed himself to participation in the 1916 Rising:

I read the article in the C.S. [*Claidheamh Soluis*] and went to the meeting [in 1913]. Enrolment forms were handed out and after the speeches I considered whether I should join. I was married and my wife and [BLANK] children were dependent on me. I had no doubt that the foundation of the Volunteers meant that there would be an armed insurrection. The question was – was I justified in entering into an engagement to take part in an insurrection with its likely consequences. I decided that our man-power was such that if the Movement was confined to unmarried men it would not be numerous enough to succeed. So I crossed the Rubicon and joined. From the moment I signed my name I regarded myself as a soldier with battle inevitably in the offing.[139]

He and his wife already had three children. His third child and namesake had been born just six and a half weeks earlier, on 11 October 1913. Sinéad conceived two more children before Easter 1916. Brian would be born on 25 July 1915 and Ruairi on 3 November 1916 (six and a half months after the Easter Rising). For someone whose own father had walked away from his family, whether in ill health or not, Éamon's decision to leave a wife and three children in order to 'cross the Rubicon' and join a battle he thought would have 'likely consequences' was striking, especially as he had not earlier displayed a great interest in national politics. However, such a decision should be seen in the context of other Irishmen voluntarily leaving their families between 1914 and 1918 to risk their lives in the British Army as agents of John Redmond's strategy intended to persuade the British finally to grant Home Rule in practice.

Frank Gallagher later turned his friend's decision to join the Irish Volunteers into an heroic episode. He quoted Osborn Bergin's '*Amhrain Dochais*' ('Songs of Hope') – which he said de Valera himself translated – before explaining how de Valera thought he would die a rebel:

Farewell forever to grief and woe,
Farewell forthwith to our doleful lamenting!
Let us sing songs of hope
In the sweet tongue of Fódla [an ancient poetic name for Ireland],
And stand with spirit
Before the world.

That spirit possessed those among whom he now spent his time and when the Volunteers were founded in November 1913 he joined them but not in any rush of sentimentality or carried away by emotion. The night he took the decision he stood over the cots of his young family and meditated. Had he the regret to risk their future, to widow his young wife, to orphan these little ones. And thinking it all out he decided that Ireland would be kind to them if he were to die for her. For that is what he saw in the Volunteers: not marchings or demonstrations … but death.[140]

He was issued a membership card, his name entered on it as 'Emin Dilvara'. Denis Gwynn, who graduated from UCD in 1911, described de Valera's appearance about this time as 'extremely remarkable'. He thought that before 1916 he was still unknown outside a small circle in Dublin: 'He was exceptionally tall, considerably over six feet in height, a very serious-looking man in his early thirties, with a long nose and spectacles, and a strangely foreign expression. His clothes of rough home-spun also made him conspicuous; and he wore a most unusual cap, with a prominent peak and flaps across the top, rather like an airman's helmet.'[141]

There was soon an election for officers in the Volunteer company to which de Valera was initially assigned. Maurice Kettle, brother of Tom Kettle, was elected captain. De Valera was elected second lieutenant: 'I was disappointed at this because I thought that I had been more efficient than he [the man elected first lieutenant] but voting pointed otherwise.'[142] It is quite common for those who are disappointed in competition to believe that the best person did not win. For his part de Valera had expressed this view in relation to a number of disappointments in his life before 1916, including his failure to get a job as inspector of schools or an appointment as professor of mathematics in a university.

De Valera was a competent member of the Irish Volunteers, participating in exercises and joining Arthur Griffith and many other members on 26 July 1914 at Howth, Co. Dublin, to collect the guns that were brought in on board a yacht that day. He does not seem ever to have had much if any interest in Sinn Féin, founded in 1905 by Griffith, or in any of the advanced nationalist papers that Griffith produced from 1899. It appears from his evidence in the Sinn Féin funds case in 1948 that he may never have been a member of Sinn Féin before being elected an MP for the party in 1917.[143] Griffith came to be seen by Irish republicans of various hues as 'father of us all' – a description from which de Valera may have recoiled given his keenly felt loss of his own father. Griffith was to be highly supportive of de Valera between 1917 and late 1921, but de Valera himself seldom referred to Griffith then in a flattering manner. As in the case of Pearse, the de Valera papers in UCD throw little light on Griffith or on de Valera's relationship with him.

De Valera did join the IRB, to facilitate his promotion in the Irish Volunteers shortly before the Rising. He had earlier declined to do so:

> On my journeys to drill in Sandymount I had one compatriot from Donnybrook, Batt O'Connor. We returned regularly from our drill together, a couple of times a week. On one occasion he asked me if I would join the physical force boys. I declined because I felt that in the volunteers we had an open governed [*sic*] body which was subject to elections at the Convention, and I hated to bind myself to obey orders given by people whom I did not know.[144]

His decision to join the IRB was paradoxical, given that he had earlier blamed Sinn Féin for his failure in a Gaelic League election when his defeat was actually the work of the IRB. The IRB had wanted its own members elected and he was not yet one of them. In a temper he told his wife then that he would never join Sinn Féin because of what had happened. Yet here he was now in 1916 joining the more secretive body. P.S. O'Hegarty, a member of the Supreme Council of the IRB when de

Valera joined the Volunteers, thought that de Valera was among members who were long unsuspecting of the extent of the IRB's influence in the Irish Volunteers, but de Valera learnt to accommodate it and joined the brotherhood before the rebellion in 1916.[145]

When the Irish Volunteers split in 1914, the smaller but more militant members managed to retain the name 'Irish Volunteers'. However, the latter themselves split in 1916 when their chief of staff Eoin MacNeill called off the planned rebellion at a late stage. Some volunteers proceeded anyway. De Valera reportedly told Frank Gallagher that the decision to 'come out' in a rising had first been conveyed to him in March 1915, at a meeting chaired by Patrick Pearse. He said he was under the impression that the rising was then intended to be in September 1915: 'Dev expressed his belief that he would not come through it alive but they pooh-poohed him as a pessimist. He was the only one of the group to survive', when it did take place in 1916.[146]

Was de Valera's decision in 1916 selfless, suicidal or simply egotistical – or driven by a complex of motivations? Was he influenced by the fact that his half-brother in America was about to be ordained a priest and to celebrate his first 'holy sacrifice of the Mass' the following month? This was a destiny his mother had long desired for Eddie. The choice of the annual celebration of Christ's rising from the dead as the occasion for a violent political insurgency in Ireland does not appear to have struck the devout if professionally disappointed young man as blasphemous or inappropriate in any way.

What was required of de Valera in 1916, an ostensibly devout Catholic who had been rewarded for his religious interest as a pupil at Blackrock College, who had seriously considered becoming a priest, whose own half-brother was about to be ordained within weeks, and who himself was married with children? Whatever de Valera's theological or moral reservations in 1916 about his 'sacrifice' of himself and his family –as he himself then described it – he struggled with his Catholic conscience and won, as he would do again six years later when civil war erupted. The extent to which Pearse was influenced by a kind of secular theology of national messianism in other parts of Europe has been considered elsewhere.[147] The extent to which de Valera was driven by a personal messianic instinct throughout his political life is moot.

Gallagher, as seen above, wrote that de Valera later told him that he had been against the Rising until Good Friday 1916. In his biography of de Valera, Ryan likewise wrote in 1936 that 'Although he felt bound in honour to obey the call to arms, de Valera never concealed his doubts as to its wisdom on the eve of that enterprise … he candidly said he was glad he had only to carry out his orders and not vote for or against.'[148] If so, it was only on the very 'eve' of the event itself that de Valera truly 'crossed the Rubicon'. On Good Friday, 21 April 1916, according to Sinéad, she and her husband knelt down in their little kitchen at three o'clock 'and prayed we would all be left together'. Later that day he departed from home and did not return that night.[149]

'When the Rising did come,' wrote de Valera's later friend Frank Gallagher, 'de Valera was Brigade Adjutant but owing to the shortage of leaders he became commandant of the Third Battalion.'[150] From his command post in the Boland's Bakery area he discharged his duties, with a claim that he had some kind of breakdown there being unsubstantiated and contested.[151] He was not present for the most renowned engagement in his district, that which took place between volunteers and the British Army at Northumberland Road and Mount Street Bridge. He was late to surrender because he requested from his superiors formal confirmation of the order to give up.

- 7 -

'DESTINY'

SACRIFICING HIS FAMILY

During the 1916 Rising de Valera wrote to his wife from his command post: 'If I die pray for me. Kiss our children for me. Tell them their father died doing his duty. Had MacNeill let things go [as planned] the day before Sunday we'd hold this position for months. My force here would have been exactly five times its present strength …We showed that there were Irish men who, in face of great odds would dare what they said.'[1]

Where did his duty lie? He later told Frank Gallagher that when it came to his leaving Sinéad and their children this was the question he asked himself, and Gallagher made a note of how de Valera answered his own question: 'After deep inner conflict he decided that if he did his duty by Ireland, God would protect his wife and their little ones'.[2] Not for him or his, ostensibly, the trauma that some others who 'did their duty by Ireland' suffered.[3] Tim Pat Coogan, whose biography of de Valera is generally regarded as critical of the man, generously describes de Valera's decision to take part in the Rising as his 'most selfless moment'.[4]

Many men have gone to war out of a sense of duty, leaving families behind because they felt that it was necessary to fight to protect their homeland. De Valera, with the zeal of a convert, convinced himself that it was necessary to risk his life in the 1916 Rising. Reprieved from possible execution soon after the event, however, he acknowledged on 11 May 1916 that he had caused Sinéad great pain: 'My darling wife: I know the

231

agonies you must have endured during the past few weeks … I needn't tell you I am counting the minutes till I see you. As all letters are read by the prison authorities I cannot write you, love, the kind of letter I would like, or tell you how, through it all, you were ever-present to my thoughts. You and the children were my (only) source of anxiety … Be of good courage.'[5]

The impact on his family was immediate. Sinéad had stopped working as a teacher after they married. Now there was no income provided by her husband. She had to give up their own home in Donnybrook. Their maid, Mary Coffey, lost her job in the process. As already seen, Sinéad moved back in with her own father, mother and sister – the last two being extremely ill at the time. Her three eldest children were sent to live with an aunt, Kate Byrne, in Balbriggan, and – it is said – they promptly forgot whatever they knew of the Irish language: 'Sinéad had a terrible year from 1916 to 1917. She nursed her sister Mary who died of cancer in August, her fifth child Ruadhrí was born in November, her mother then aged about 78 died in January.'[6]

Nine months after the Easter Rising, in January, 1917, Sinéad wrote to their friend Frank Hughes in Co. Mayo. In May 1916 he and his wife had offered to give her a temporary home or to take some of her children 'off her hands' for a while – an offer she declined while admitting 'my mind is in a whirl'. She now told him, 'I never have a minute'. That same month de Valera wrote to her from Lewes Jail to admit how difficult it must be for her to manage and said 'I hope, am certain indeed, that I will not in the future be guilty of so many acts of unconscious selfishness as I was in the past'.[7] Yet a few months later, on Easter Saturday 1917 (the eve of the anniversary of the Rising), he revealed a need on his part for Sinéad to reassure him he had been *not* selfish but selfless: 'Sweetheart I know you will believe me – I know you will not think it was selfishness or callous indifference or senseless optimism that made me so calm when I was about to offer up you and the children as a sacrifice.'[8] In May she found time to send another note to Hughes, apologising for her handwriting because baby 'Ruary' was in her arms and made her hand shake.[9]

From another letter that de Valera wrote to his wife just over a year after the Easter Rising, it seems that he had acted with chilling self-confidence and a certainty that he was about to die, fully conscious of the impact on her and their small children. Given how much he had suffered from having no living father to support himself and his mother, this letter is particularly striking. In it he tells Sinéad that he had actually *foreseen* 'the agonies' before her, and that when he called to see her on the day before the first shot was fired he found that already 'the strain had been too much for you', as indeed he said he had anticipated. He tells her that giving her a parting kiss before the Rising 'as lightly as if we were to meet again in the morning it was simply to save you, to give you some sixteen hours of respite; for in my heart I believed it was the last kiss I would give you on earth'. In 1916 he had some sort of life insurance policy of which Sinéad was then unaware but in any event it might not have been paid out in the circumstances of his dying in a revolution.[10]

In November 1917, released from prison but occupied on political business, de Valera wrote to her that he was sorry to be so often away and wondered why 'when I cannot talk to you, I have so much to say to you, but when we are together I am dumb. Can you understand?'[11] It was a good question. Perhaps he found it preferable to debate matters with himself than to have to face her possible questions.

So what was it that decided him in the first place – as he put it – to 'offer up' his wife and children (in language redolent of the Mass)? Like the biblical Abraham willing to slaughter his son Isaac to prove his faith, de Valera appears to have chosen to place his wife and children on the altar of his ideals. There were peaceful alternatives to a rebellion, and most Irish people supported these. Home Rule was again being promised. Soon a much wider UK franchise would strengthen democratic options. Had the British not so promptly executed its principal leaders, the insurgency might in hindsight have seemed more rash than heroic to later generations.

De Valera was one of the few commandants to survive the Rising and escape execution.[12] Whether this was due mainly to his having only recently become a revolutionary and thus being relatively unimportant, or to the fact that his arrest and sentencing came later than those of many other rebels, or to his American citizenship (as Sinéad certainly thought but he later denied) is a matter long debated. She wrote at the time, 'He would have shared the death sentence with the others only I got the

American Consuls [plural] to interfere on his behalf. I had his baptism certificate showing he had been born in America and then he had never taken out naturalisation papers here. So he was an American citizen.'[13] In any event he survived, and was destined after 1916 to transform himself into the chosen symbol of an ideal Irish republic.

Having avoided execution in Dublin, he was sent to jail in England. A decade later he told his friend Frank Gallagher that 'the time he felt most like weeping was when he was being taken to Dartmoor on his life sentence for the Rising. He was convinced that he would have to serve at least fifteen years – 'it was terrible thinking of leaving everybody for that time'.[14]

It was terrible for his wife too, separated from her small children and losing their home, and living back with her parents who had significant problems of their own. She first faced the prospect that her husband could be killed in action or later executed, then that he might languish in jail for many years. She kept her mother-in-law informed of developments, writing to her in America on 24 July 1916 that 'Ed was sent to Dartmoor prison in England on the 18th May. He was allowed to write to me the following day ...' In the same letter she told Kate 'Viv [aged five], Mairin [aged four] and I saw him for a short time in the prison here before he went away but there was a warder present all the time.' Sinéad believed that 'of course it was the American influence here that got Ed's sentence commuted' (from death to penal servitude). She explained to Kate that she was told that Ed would be allowed to write to her once in May and that it would be September 1916 before he could write again, so she had been surprised to get a letter from him 'this morning' (24 July).[15]

Archived with this letter are four small rectangular notes that de Valera wanted his mother Kate to have. They appear to have been written at different times between July and December 1916 and were possibly smuggled out of jail. What is evidently the first of these notes relates to efforts being made in America, with the support of Kate and her son Tom, to put pressure on the US government to lean on the British to reduce his sentence. De Valera thought that the chances of this happening were low, but also recognised the importance of establishing that he had US citizenship. For his own personal reasons he had long wanted more information about his father and grandfather, and his current dilemma was both another reason to seek it and an instrument for getting it:

> My dear <u>mother</u>. A word to ask you not to worry about me. I hope that Tom's ordination day [7 June 1916] was one of unclouded happiness for you, his father and himself. One son at least gone the path you would desire but as an Irishwoman do not be ashamed that the rake is here. The question of my nationality is at present of some importance. In International Law am I a Spaniard or an American? Was father born in USA or did he get naturalised? Grandfather was living in New York until recently wasn't he? My uncle told me a number of things about the family but I could never be sure of his accuracy – send [whatever] you know about my father and grandfather.

If de Valera made a note of what his Uncle Pat told him about his family it does not appear to be in the UCD Archives.

In another of the four notes he told his mother 'I would like to know more about grandfather's family and business,' and he thanked her for certain information that he stated she had already sent him. It is not clear when she had done so, but there is information in a letter in the UCD Archives from her that may be that to which he was referring. It is missing four pages, including its date. In it his mother refers to having moved house from Goodman Street in Rochester, which she had done in about 1912, and to a 'Souvenir' that appears to have been of her son Tom's ordination in June 1916. Among the de Valera papers in UCD is a pamphlet of four pages, headed 'Souvenir', containing some details of his ordination and first Mass.[16] The part of this letter from Kate that survives begins with what appears to be a reference to her journey to Tom's ordination, before moving on to de Valera's father. She says that letters from his father had somehow 'got mislaid' and is sensitive to the possibility that she might have given him different or contradictory accounts of his parentage:

> [Pages 1–4 missing, starts numbered page 5] ... baggage at the Depot. The carriage goes to meet all trains that are supposed to stop there from the College. Uncle came on the next train. You can imagine their surprise

when they saw me there ahead of them. I was expecting a letter from Tom today; it hasn't got here yet perhaps tomorrow. I promised you to send a copy of the Souvenir, or at least the verse for the rest I could not copy, but will do so later.

Now my dear boy I want to tell you a little more about your father; he used to write some poetry and charades and was a great mimic, his favorite pastime was drawing and writing and at both of these I considered him an expert, I must say that I never saw any person that could write as perfect as he did and his capital letters were a wonder. I have been looking through all my treasures to see if I could find any of his letters but somehow I can't find them. I had them when I was leaving 22 S[outh] Goodman St but where I put them I can't remember. I was very ill for sometime and having strangers around they got mislaid. Your grandfather as a young man was a decorator but later he had a share in some business in Cuba and I think during the wars in that country he lost everything. I think your father told me, if I am not mistaken, it was tobacco and sugar but I am not really certain about it. I must tell about your father's appearance if I haven't done so before: 5 ft 8 in height, weight over 160 lbs [i.e. eleven and a half stone], medium dark complexion, dark brown eyes, and dark brown curly hair, small hands and feet, always ready to play a trick or joke; he had only a few of all his acquaintances that he cared for as a friend, and really I am the same but those who were our friends we always were true to them and they to us. Of all the music he liked the mandolin best.

My memory since I was sick isn't so clear, so please excuse me if I should write the same thing over again in your letters, or if I contradict anything I had told you it is because I forgot or was not really sure of it. I will tell you more next time, or may tell you some of my traits, as I know them myself.

I hope to be able to tell all in person soon perhaps with God's help.

Write as soon as you possibly can. I hope your previous notes will arrive safely, for they are treasures to me.

Joined by Aunt Annie and Uncle Charlie [Wheelwright] in kind love to you, as ever your loving Mother.

N.B. I send you a leaflet. Goodbye and God bless you.[17]

In the same note in which de Valera asked his mother for more information about his grandfather, he referred again to the campaign to put American pressure on the British regarding his sentence of penal servitude. It was a campaign in which she played an active part:

> I cannot see on what ground America can interfere unless the position has been distinctly laid down in International Law or others had been a precedent in my favour. It is fortunate for the lawyers that nationality questions are not as simple as your formula would make them mother. I am in good health and as you see not in bad spirits. Nature has been good to me (I mean *God has* for the Irish idiom is preferable here as it generally is to the English one) in that way. So do not be uneasy. Despair not for my wife and children. Tom's cloister would not be so very different to mine – except the surroundings and the free will. Ask Tom to pray for the souls of my dead comrades rather than for me … Love to you all.

The third note continued his quest for reliable information about his father. He thought that the surname was a well-known Spanish one, and he referred to Cipriano de Valera, a controversial monk. He also observed that 'The foremost Spanish novelist today is Juan Valera (not *de*); he was ambassador at Washington in '82 and is son of ex admiral Valera.' In fact Juan Valera was in Washington as Spain's minister from the end of 1883 until 1886, and had died before 1916. De Valera now asked anxiously 'What was father's occupation? How old was he when he died? My children will be asking these questions of me shortly I expect.' He switched suddenly to mention *Colleen Bawn*, a popular novel published in the mid-nineteenth century under the title *The Collegians: A Tale of Garryown*. Written by Limerickman Gerald Griffin, it was adapted for the stage by Dion Boucicault.[18] He uses it to make a point about how seldom she has come to Ireland. He writes that 'the last time I read it was when I bade you good bye on your return to America – nine years ago is it not? I hope you are well. Best love to Tom, Uncle Charlie and yourself. x your fond son, Ed. Q.95 H.M. Prison, Dartmoor England.'

The fourth and final such archived note on this file was sent in December 1916, by which time de Valera had been moved to another English jail:

> My dear mother. I am sorry this cannot reach you for Xmas. I write it on Dec. 22nd from Lewes Prison. Our position has now been considerably improved. I can write oftener and I hope to be allowed writing materials for leisure hours. I will write a letter to Tom in a short time. I am in good health and spirits. You are both very good to write so often to Sinéad. Tom will be out on the mission very soon [last two words unclear] I expect. I do not despair of yet serving his Mass some time. Love to you all Charlie, Aunt Annie, Uncle Ed [Coll]. Is his son in Europe yet? Best wishes for Xmas, Ed.

This son of that uncle who had brought Eddie de Valera to Ireland in 1885 served with the US Army in Europe during the First World War.

Nearly half a century later and eleven years after his mother died, Kate's son Eddie (by then widely known as Éamon de Valera) will still be hoping to learn from Kate –even indirectly – something more substantial about the mystery of his origins. Thus in 1963 he wrote to Fr Thomas F. Connors, the founder and pastor of her local church in Rochester, to ask if Kate had ever said anything to Connors about the man she purportedly first married. The priest, who was in his nineties and had long known Kate, answered 'As far as I can recall, I have never heard your mother speak to me about your father.' It was quite a blunt reply. De Valera wrote back to say that he was always glad to get the priest's recollections of Kate, for 'being so far from her from my childhood I knew her but little'.[19]

A MONUMENT TO THE MARTYRS

De Valera feared that he would remain in jail for years after the 1916 Rising. US authorities made it clear to campaigners, including his family, that there was no basis in law on which they could make representations to the United Kingdom to reduce his sentence. However, along with many other prisoners he was released during 1917 and returned to Ireland a hero.

Éamon earlier had little active personal interest in politics and was reluctant to support a policy of running republican candidates in elections even while imprisoned in 1916–17 after the Rising. However, in an inspired moment in jail he called on his militant colleagues to salute the leader of the Volunteers, Eoin MacNeill, who had been arrested and jailed with them despite MacNeill having tried at a late stage to postpone the rebellion. Arthur Griffith had originally founded Sinn Féin explicitly as a movement that would bring together different strands of advanced nationalism and de Valera now seemed to be making this his ostensible ambition too. He stepped forward as a strong personality and a leader, while not being quite as boldly triumphant in jail as some accounts have it.[20] His political capital as a surviving commandant and a potential unifier was greatly appreciated by the most militant republicans and they engineered first his election as a member of parliament in 1917 and then his leadership of Sinn Féin from 1918. When Arthur Griffith bowed to the inevitable and graciously yielded to de Valera the presidency of the party that Griffith had founded, de Valera declared to prolonged applause, 'I regard my unanimous election as a monument to the brave dead, and this is the *post factum* proof that they were right.' While the precise extent of his interaction with Pearse before the Rising is uncertain, he willingly became a carrier of Pearse's legacy and the designated chief surviving rebel. When John Lavery painted a series of portraits of Irish and British politicians during talks on Irish independence in 1921, de Valera was uniquely seated in profile (see the present volume's front cover). His pose is redolent of the iconic representation of Patrick Pearse in profile.

De Valera benefited personally from the execution of the signatories of the 1916 proclamation of an Irish republic, being the senior surviving commandant who would henceforth wear their mantle. Ironically he also benefited from the death of John Redmond's brother Willie at the front in Belgium, after the latter had enlisted in the British Army in line with a Home Rule strategy from which the 1916 rebels dissented. Willie's death created a vacancy in parliament for Co. Clare, one that de Valera now filled. Such is destiny.[21]

Having been elected as the member of parliament for East Clare, significantly with the support of many priests there, and being chosen to be president of Sinn Féin, he told a convention of that party in Dublin's Mansion House that the rebels who died in the Easter Rising had – as he claimed Cardinal Mercier once remarked of Belgians killed in the First World War – 'almost got the religious martyr's crown'. By analogy that would make de Valera himself – who had escaped execution – almost an almost martyr. Mercier in a pastoral letter of New Year 1915 had angered the German occupiers of Belgium. While not quite using the phrase that de Valera attributed to him and while distinguishing between martyr-dom 'in the rigorous theological meaning of the word' and the death of 'a soldier falling in a righteous cause', the cardinal still thought that God would welcome the latter 'plain soldier' with love and he spoke of specific Belgian 'martyrs' in the continuing European war. Having referenced

An unsmiling Éamon de Valera with his mother in America.
Courtesy UCD Archives P150/191–2.

240

Mercier's pastoral, earlier brought to the attention of the Irish public by a number of bishops and newspapers in Ireland, De Valera continued:

> They tell us of rebellion, and the theologians of the *Irish Times* and *Freeman's Journal* (laughter) will tell us that rebellion is not justifiable. I have never yet – and I am a Catholic – found the Catholic religion to be contrary to anything I hold in my conscience or anything that common sense dictated (applause) ... I certainly have yet to find that the Catholic Church or any Christian religion is going to allow itself to be made a tool in the hands of the oppressor (hear, hear). I speak of this matter because we are a religious people, a moral people, and we will do nothing that is morally wrong (applause). We want to be instructed properly ... I am not a theologian but as I said now I find the moral instincts which everyone of us have and commonsense never act contrary to the teaching of the Catholic Church as I have ever known it (applause).[22]

'De Valera became, as if by magic, the accepted leader of the Irish nation,' wrote one admirer.[23] But he was politically inexperienced and no electoral wonder-worker. Sinn Féin lost the three by-elections that followed his own election in Co. Clare – the latter being in any case one of the most favourable constituencies in which he could have stood as a Sinn Féin candidate.[24] The party's success in the general election of 1918 owed at least as much to his campaign against the possible conscription of Irishmen into the British Army[25] and to a moderate demand for Irish nationalist representation at the international peace conference expected to follow the First World War as it owed to republican militancy.

Together with Arthur Griffith and many other leading Sinn Féin members de Valera was again arrested and interned in late 1918. During this period of imprisonment his wife wrote to his mother from Greystones, Co. Wicklow, where she was now living with their children. 'My dear Mother', she began:

> I asked Lizzie to write to you since Ed went away so I expect you will have received her letter long before this reaches you. I hope you got my letter that I wrote some months ago.

Writing at present is rather unsatisfactory on account of the censorship. I hope you are keeping well and that you are not worried about us here. Ed writes regularly from Lincoln [Prison]. He says his health is quite good. God will take care of him. I am leaving all in His hands. All the children are very well. Viv serves Mass now and looks like a little priest, Mairin [*sic*, no accent] is a great blessing and comfort to me. The other three are fine, lively, healthy fellows.

This [Greystones] is a beautiful place and so healthy for the children How I wish you could see them. They would love to know Daddy's Mother. I hope Auntie Annie is stronger now. Tell her not to be uneasy about Ed. God can settle all in His own good time.

Of course it is lonely without him but I am hoping that when God gives him back to me our happy life will make up for all. It is a great thing that the children are so young. They do not worry or fret and I want them to get all possible happiness out of life. Please remember me to Uncle Ed and all his family and ask dear Sister Bartholomew to pray.

[Added sideways on page 1] Uncle Charlie, Will you please send the enclosed note to Tom? Please dear Mother send a line soon to say how all are. With best love from Sinéad.[26]

'Ed', as he was clearly still known to his mother, rather than as Éamon, himself sent her a letter from Lincoln Prison on 28 November 1917. He referred to the fact that the world war had ended just that month, to the future intentions of the United States and to the power of the press. But he also spoke of personal matters:

I know you will be glad that I have served all our Masses here. I feel like a little boy again and I pray that my childish faith may ever remain with me. I tell you this because I know it will give you more pleasure than anything else I could write. I hope you will see Tom soon. You must feel lonely without him though I am certain you do not regret you reared him for such a calling. This life is so very short in comparison with the future it counts for little what sorrows and inconveniences it brings. Were it not so short who would be ready to die? With love to yourself and Uncle Charlie. I am dearest mother Eddie.[27]

De Valera was a monument to the martyrs and a symbol of their republican ideal. His standing grew in that role, not least when he escaped from Lincoln Prison in February 1919 in what one admirer has described as 'a story of tension and drama not so often equalled in fiction' and what even a recent level-headed writer described as a 'daring escape'.[28] In fact he merely used or abused his trusted position as a Mass server to make an imprint in wax of one of the chaplain's keys that unlocked a side door in what was then quite evidently not a high-security jail. The imprint had been smuggled out and Michael Collins with Harry Boland arranged a simple plan for him to walk through the door and be spirited away. His escape created a sensation.

He returned to Ireland, becoming president of the new Dáil Éireann set up by Sinn Féin in early 1919. On 10 April that year he and its other members were photographed as a group at Dublin's Mansion House. But he soon removed himself from the dangers of the War of Independence and in June left for America where this 'monument to the martyrs' was feted by Irish-America. The Dáil approved Arthur Griffith to act in his place, which Griffith then did for eighteen months in 1919 and 1920. Indeed, even before de Valera later resigned as president of Dáil Éireann in January 1922 and was formally superseded by Griffith following the Dáil's approval of the proposed Anglo-Irish Treaty, Griffith had acted in the president's role (as substitute) for longer in total than de Valera himself ever acted as president of the Dáil in practice.[29]

The sharp contrast between de Valera's invisibility in much of what was written about the 1916 Rising before he went to America in 1919 and glowing US media coverage of him after he actually arrived there has been graphically demonstrated by Carroll.[30] On a personal level de Valera's visit of 1919–20 marked his first return to the land of his birth and infancy. His mother embraced him as a nationalist hero. She had already campaigned in 1916 to have his prison sentence reduced, and now helped to mislead the media about his whereabouts when he arrived in America. She also posed for a propaganda postcard promoting a US radio broadcast by him. However, a photograph of them standing side by side in America shows space between them and no physical contact. She is smiling in it. He, on

Éamon de Valera and his half-brother Fr Thomas Wheelwright, Boston 1919–20.
Courtesy UCD Archives P150/206, no. 6.

De Valera and Frank Gallagher, sailing to America in 1927–28 to raise money to launch the *Irish Press*. De Valera shared with Gallagher tales of his youth. Photo: US Shipping Board, Advertising Dept., New York. Courtesy National Library of Ireland, Dev49.

Postcard view of orphan asylum from Cobb's Hill, Rochester, New York. In 1927 Frank Gallagher sent one of these postcards home to his wife in Ireland. Author's copy.

the other hand, does not look happy. She had never returned to Ireland after her second visit back, which had been in 1907.

On this trip to America De Valera also met his cousin Edward Coll, a son of that uncle who had brought little Eddie to Ireland in 1885. This cousin had recently returned from his US military service in Europe. When they met at New Rochelle in New York, his cousin described to de Valera 'all the power of British armaments such as I had just left behind me in the First World War – the great tanks, powerful cannon, machine-guns, aeroplanes, poison gas, the great divisions of highly trained and well-disciplined soldiers. I asked him how he ever expected to free Ireland in the face of such opposition. He turned towards me calmly and serenely and uttered these words – "We are reaching for the stars in the hope of obtaining the mountain tops."' This answer indicates that de Valera accepted then that compromises would have to be made on the road to statehood.[31] He also met his half-brother Thomas on the trip, when in Boston.[32]

Ranging out across the United States from his base at the Waldorf Hotel in Manhattan, de Valera was met, during 1919 and 1920, by large numbers of enthusiastic Irish-Americans and hailed not simply as the president of a new Irish parliament but as 'President of Ireland' – an office that did not exist at the time. In 1933 Seán Ó Faoláin – author and admirer of de Valera – wrote of that American reception:

> wildly cheering crowds of rarely less than a hundred thousand people, poor and rich, lettered and unlettered, Irish of the first to the tenth gener-ation – a crowd mad with a frenzy of enthusiasm, yelling, weeping in their emotion, crying out his name and the name of Ireland ... so that it often happened that he would have to stand for a full fifteen or twenty minutes looking down over an excited sea of faces, listening to the thunder of their cries ... he was their Tone, their Emmet, their O'Connell, their Parnell – their ideal leader of a mighty if banished race.[33]

De Valera's detractors were to say that America spoiled him. His recep-tion certainly enhanced his political profile. Some native Americans were even persuaded to bestow on him a status that he later said he had desired ever since he was a boy, namely that of 'Chief'. A 'persistent' and 'scurrilous rumour' had begun to circulate that he was having an affair with his personal secretary.[34]

He would meet his mother again in later years, in the United States because she never again came back to Ireland after her trip with her son Tom in 1907. Thus he visited her in the late 1920s, when he was in the USA to raise money for the launch of a newspaper in Ireland, the *Irish Press*. His friend and political associate Frank Gallagher was with him and, as noted in the second chapter above, tried but failed then to get Kate to talk about de Valera's father. On 1 April 1927 de Valera went from his birth mother's house in Rochester to visit his Aunt Annie who lived nearby, and who had looked after him so warmly in Ireland before she herself left the Coll family home. In a single and singular sentence Gallagher wrote 'In the afternoon D. went off to see the Aunt who was his mother.'[35] While in Rochester, Gallagher picked up a postcard for his wife at home, penning it on the train to Chicago. There are surely few similar postcards showing a view of a local orphanage, and one wonders if Gallagher chose it precisely because of the history of the relationship between Kate and her first-born son Eddie.[36]

Kate died in Rochester in 1932. It was said that she had hoped to come for the Eucharistic Congress in Dublin that year, and the Rochester delegation that arrived at the event was reported to be bearing a message from her to de Valera.[37] Her son Thomas Wheelwright, de Valera's half-brother, died in a car crash in 1945.[38]

CHIEF AT LAST: NAY NAY ONG ABE

As a boy, Eddie had read Porter's influential *Scottish Chiefs*. He had also longed to become an American Indian, or so he said. That ambition was now fulfilled. On 18 October 1919 de Valera was made a chieftain of the Ojibwe (also known as 'Chippewa') nation in the United States – an *actual* chieftain not an honorary one he insisted. It was thought to be only the second time that such an honour was conferred on a white man.[39] Here now was a living Irish 'chief', one who took up the baton

Éamon de Valera, 'an actual chieftain' of the Ojibwe, Wisconsin. Courtesy UCD Archives P150/871, no. 2.

of the heroes of 1916 and even of 'our dead Chief', as Charles Stewart Parnell was dubbed following his downfall in the late nineteenth century. Long before that the clan leaders or kings of Gaelic Ireland had also become known as chieftains.

Already, in the days just before the Ojibwe ceremony took place, one of its Irish-American organisers was referring to de Valera as 'the Chief'. In a briefing note for Harry Boland, who was travelling with de Valera, he wrote that 'I have every proof that the Indians venerate the Chief as a person holding the same idea as regarding Ireland as they hold regarding their own rights.'[40] Another of de Valera's associates, C.S. Andrews, later wrote that in the context of the Sinn Féin movement when de Valera led it, 'Irrespective of the positions of responsibility they held, men were addressed by their Christian [first] names. There was one exception. Nobody called Eamonn [*sic*] de Valera anything but "Mister, De Valera", "Sir" or, if one was reasonably close to him, "Chief".' Exceptionally, it seems, Harry Boland, his companion on his American trips, called him 'Ned'. His personal friend Dorothy Macardle, for example, addressed him as 'Dear Chief' when writing to him from London in 1936 before the publication of her *Irish Republic*, for which he had provided her with a preface and some advice.[41]

The *Irish World* in America reported details of the colourful Ojibwe ceremony, and some Irish papers carried its report in whole or in part.[42] The tribe conferred on de Valera the name 'Nay Nay Ong Abe'– said to mean 'Dressing Feather'. A famous chieftain of the tribe who had secured for it rights under a treaty of 1854 formerly held this title, and because of that fact the chief's grand-daughter and great-grand-daughter were present.[43] Having travelled by train from Milwaukee to Spooner in Wisconsin for the event, de Valera and his party were met by a dozen automobiles, 'which carried them over forty miles (64km) of wild country to the Ojibwe reservation on the edge of Lake Court Oreilles.' There, reported the *Irish World*, 'Chief Billy Boy and Joe Kingfisher welcomed De Valera to the nation. Kingfisher gave him a beaded tobacco pouch and moccasins, and declared "I wish I were able to give you the prettiest blossom of the fairest flower on earth, for you come to us as a representative of one oppressed nation to another".'

The ceremony was preceded in a church on the reservation by a memorial Roman Catholic Mass 'for the Indians who died in France' serving in the US Army during the First World War. An activist priest Philip Gordon, one of just a very small number of ordained Native Americans, celebrated this Mass.[44] He was described to Boland as a 'full-blooded Indian' and 'a most enthusiastic Sinn Féiner!' and he appears to have agreed that Fr Patrick O'Mahoney of Spooner would deliver the sermon. It is evident that de Valera's contact with the Ojibwe was partly mediated by the Roman Catholic Church, with Fr O'Mahony as well as the Ojibwe being among those who met his expenses.[45]

As regards the initiation ceremony itself, Boland was told 'All the Indians, Catholic and Pagan, will be present, as well as chiefs of the Sioux and Cree Nations who will come in from Minnesota.' The event took place on an open field on the reservation, in the presence of more than 3,000 'Indians and white people', and was 'interpolated by a weird series of Indian dances and speech-making' – as the *Irish World* reported. The recipient of the honours sat in the centre of a semi-circle of clergymen and chieftains. In front five men beat continuously on a tom-tom drum, and 'at intervals a score of tribesmen dressed in the full regalia of paint and feathers of a great occasion danced around the guests.' De Valera arose and walked to the centre of the ring. He accepted the headdress of a chieftain with gravity as the tom-toms sounded louder and louder.

De Valera first addressed the Ojibwe and their guests in Irish, but soon reverted to English: 'I speak to you in Gaelic because I want to show you that, though I am white, I am not of the English race. We, like you, are a people who have suffered, and I feel for you with a sympathy that comes only from one who can understand as we Irishmen can. You say you are not free. Neither are we free, and I sympathise with you because we are making a similar fight.' He then announced remarkably that 'As a boy I read and understood of your slavery and longed to become one of you.' He added, 'I call on you, the truest of all Americans, to help us win our struggle for freedom.'

The Ojibwe reportedly listened to his impassioned address 'with owl-like gravity'. When his speech was translated they 'cheered him wildly'. The Irish delegates had their own way of celebrating it, as de Valera told

Dorothy Macardle during the 1930s: 'Harry Boland and Liam Mellows were on that tour with me. When I was in bed that night they came in with red paint on them and towels around their waists and did a war dance and demanded to be made braves.'[46]

According to Terry de Valera his father later told the family, 'As part of the initiation ritual, the chief of the tribe and the chief-elect had to draw a little blood, then to mix the blood to signify their brotherhood', but de Valera himself 'somehow managed to avoid this part of the ceremony without causing offence'. Notwithstanding de Valera's great regard for his status as chief, his children were allowed to play with the headdress he brought home until it became tattered and torn and finally disintegrated. A native bow too was broken and eventually lost.[47]

A somewhat similar honour was to be bestowed on Dublin's Lord Mayor Robert Briscoe in 1962. Briscoe was a Jewish member of Dáil Éireann for de Valera's Fianna Fáil party. De Valera is said to have been close to him, although he never appointed him to the cabinet. In 1962 the Southern Cheyenne Sioux presented Briscoe with a head-dress. People could not resist quipping that he was 'the world's first Irish Jew Sioux'. Owen Dudley Edwards writes that when Briscoe was dying he lay in a coma without moving. Eventually, old and blind, de Valera was led to Briscoe's bedside and spoke to the man 'whom all could see to be wholly beyond reach: '"Bob?" The blind man's hand took the hand of the patient. "Do you know me, Bob?" And from the figure pronounced unconscious for all of the previous week came, desperately weak but wholly audible: "The Chief!" Briscoe died the next day or so.'[48]

Éamon de Valera subsequently made a gift of rifles to those who had honoured him. Fr Gordon, who was also chairman of the tribe's business committee, wrote that 'The De Valera rifles arrived in first-class shape. At the distribution yesterday of these guns, the Indians were immensely pleased and pronounced the guns O.K. in every particular. The name plates were without an error which is very remarkable since Indian names are so unusual and unspellable as a rule.' The entire proceedings had been 'a big success' he thought.[49] De Valera remembered the Ojibwe when he visited Wisconsin again in 1955, describing them to an interviewer as a 'fine section of the human family' and hoping that the administration in

Washington would not forget them.[50] In this respect he seemed indifferent to alienating a segment of the American public that was ill disposed to Native Americans.

BLOOD-RED

'In 1916, before the Rising, Mars was blood-red. I remember it, so remarkable in the Heavens. And I called someone to look at it,' de Valera told Dorothy Macardle in 1936. He added:

> I remember too, in 1922, when I was going down to the south by train I saw the hedges of blackthorn whiter than I had ever seen them in my life. I never saw the trees and hedges so white with blossom before or since; and the people were saying 'there will be bloodshed in the country'. They have always thought that – that it meant bloodshed if the thorns were so white.[51]

Were these in his opinion bloody portents of an unchangeable fate? Some of his later notebooks and diaries are full of scribbles, including political quotations, mathematical problems and notes for speeches. In one he outlined the 'savagery' of England's presence in Ireland during successive periods. In the same notebook is found a typed insert of these few words as spoken by Shakespeare's murderous Macbeth:

> I am in blood
> Stepped in so far that, should I wade no more,
> Returning were as tedious as go o'er:[52]

De Valera's detractors certainly believed that he was not only 'stepped in' but steeped in blood, and that he could have done more to help Ireland avoid civil war. His critics have maintained that his own choices, particularly in 1921–22, made peaceful outcomes less likely but still he persisted even when he knew that compromise must eventually prevail. If he did not cross a Rubicon when he became a member of the Irish

Volunteers or when he marched out to fight in 1916, de Valera certainly entered history in his own right when he quit the Sinn Féin government in 1922 and threw his lot in with those violently opposed to the decision of Dáil Éireann to approve a proposed treaty with Britain for the foundation of the Irish Free State. Indeed, realising the full import of his actions, he told the anti-Treaty Mary MacSwiney at the end of October 1922, 'It is the unlikelihood and not the likelihood of negotiations we have to fear. I see no basis whatever for negotiation. You have crossed the Rubicon now, and prepare yourself for a long war with utter defeat or victory as the result.' He himself did not believe that victory was achievable then.[53]

When Kevin O'Higgins was later murdered by anti-Treaty republicans in 1927 de Valera reportedly told his friend Frank Gallagher that he had seen civil war coming as early as 1919–20. Gallagher noted that they were then talking of the 'execution' of O'Higgins and remarked 'blood calls for blood'. De Valera told him, 'It is an extraordinary thing but I remember – when we were in America and we got word of the shooting of policemen – I turned to Harry [Boland] and said "Look here, Harry, we'll be shooting one another yet".'[54]

On returning to Ireland from America and resuming the presidency of Dáil Éireann in January 1921 de Valera's sensibility to his ostensible symbolic value was reflected in the rationale that he advanced for refusing to go to London later that year to lead the Irish team in negotiating a treaty with UK Prime Minister Lloyd George. The official record notes him telling the Dáil: 'He really believed it was vital at this stage that the symbol of the Republic should be kept untouched and that it should not be compromised in any sense by any arrangements which it might be necessary for our plenipotentiaries to make.'[55] The monument to the martyrs must not be stained by compromise. His was a somewhat monarchical self-image. King Louis XIV of France, for example, is said to have declared 'the state is me'.

De Valera arranged instead for Arthur Griffith to lead a delegation of five negotiators, including Michael Collins. On 6 December 1921 these negotiators unanimously agreed, in fraught circumstances, a provisional treaty subject to approval by the cabinet and Dáil in Dublin. It was so approved, but not by de Valera.

The particular wording of the oath to be taken by members of the parliament or 'Dáil' of the Irish Free State under the proposed Anglo-Irish Treaty greatly agitated de Valera, who resented its symbolic significance. The oath required members of Dáil Éireann to pledge faithfulness to the British king. Lately children in Dublin had been singing a street ballad that envisaged de Valera made 'King of Ireland'. At the age of twenty Eddie had confessed to his half-brother that he had been imagining himself 'in very glorious positions' and he thought this was 'the chief method Satan has employed to disturb my peace of soul'.[56] Earlier, Daniel O'Connell and Parnell had each in turn been dubbed the 'uncrowned king of Ireland'. Earlier still the Aisling poets and others had yearned for the restoration from abroad of the Irish chiefs or a Stuart lord to rule Ireland – a motif of return over the sea from France or Spain deeply embedded in Gaelic culture in the eighteenth century. One sympathetic biography of de Valera published in the 1940s started with the author quoting from a well-known poem addressed to a female personification of Ireland, 'And Spanish ale shall give you hope, My dark Rosaleen'.[57] It was a potent association, with the partly 'Spanish' de Valera being represented as coming from abroad to answer a national yearning.

After most members of both the Irish cabinet and Dáil Éireann voted to accept the proposed Anglo-Irish Treaty, de Valera stepped down as president of the Dáil in January 1922 and was replaced by Arthur Griffith. On 3 February Sinéad de Valera returned £50 paid into her bank account by Michael Collins. She said 'we should not get any money now, since Éamon is no longer President since last month'. But she also recalled how Collins supported her and paid visits to her and her family at their home in Greystones during de Valera's long absence in America in 1919 and 1920: 'I am very grateful to you, and I shall never forget all you always did for me. With every blessing and kind regard, I remain your friend always.'[58] This was a sentiment that de Valera, uncomfortable with Collins even before the Treaty split, was unlikely to utter.

*

Early in 1922 it seemed clear to many observers that de Valera was issuing bloody threats, although he dismissed this as a misunderstanding. On 17 March that year the *Irish Times* quoted him as saying, 'If you don't fight to-day you will have to fight to-morrow, and I say, when you are in a good fighting position, then fight on.' On the following morning the *Cork Examiner* reported that he had just given a speech to about 2,000 people in Carrick-on-Suir, Co. Tipperary. Accompanied by armed IRA members; he said, 'If Ireland accepts the Treaty then full freedom can be got only by civil war in Ireland.' He added, as the *Cork Examiner* reported,

> If the Treaty is accepted the fight for freedom will still go on, and the Irish people, instead of fighting foreign soldiers, will have to fight the Irish soldiers of an Irish Government, set up by Irishmen. If the Treaty is not rejected perhaps it is over the bodies of the boys and young men he [de Valera] saw around him that day the fight for Irish freedom may be fought.

On 18 March too, the *Irish Independent* noted that de Valera had proceeded to nearby Dungarvan, Co. Waterford, where he proclaimed, 'It was only by civil war after this they could get their independence,' and to Thurles the following day where he said that if the Treaty was accepted then the Volunteers of the future would 'have to wade through Irish blood, through the blood of soldiers of the Irish Government, and through, perhaps, the blood of some of the members of the Government in order to get Irish freedom'.

He had struck a significantly different note the previous year when, as president of the Dáil, he was trying to set up treaty talks with the British. In the Dáil on 23 August 1921, just weeks after a truce in the War of Independence was declared, he forecast disagreements but had a policy to deal with them:

> It is obvious that whenever there are negotiations, unless you are able to dictate terms you will have differences. Therefore it is obvious you will

have sharp differences. The policy of the Ministry [his Cabinet] will be that which they consider would be best for the country. The Ministry itself may not be able to agree and in such a case the majority would rule.

He added a line that indicated that he did not contemplate himself being in a minority: 'Those who would disagree with me would resign.' He further said that if plenipotentiaries were to go to London for Dáil Éireann and negotiate a treaty or a peace, as in fact they subsequently did, then

> seeing that we are not in the position that we can dictate the terms, we will, therefore, have proposals brought back which cannot satisfy everybody, and will not; and my position is that when such a time comes I will be in a position, having discussed the matter with the Cabinet, to come forward with such proposals as we think wise and right. It will be then for you either to accept the recommendations of the Ministry or reject them. If you reject them you then elect a new Ministry. You would then be creating a definite active opposition.

After it transpired in late 1921 that he himself was in the minority as regards the treaty, his 'definite active opposition' turned out not to be entirely parliamentary.

From further newspaper reports, it appears that on 19 March 1922, in Killarney, de Valera warned, 'Those who wanted to get on and travel on the road to achieve freedom, such as those men present with their rifles, would have in the future not merely the foreign soldiers to meet, but they would have to meet the forces of their own brothers, their fellow-countrymen, who would be supporting the government.' He reportedly made reference again there to shedding the blood of Irish soldiers and of members of the Irish government.[59] According to the *Cork Examiner* of 20 March, at Killarney that weekend he also said infamously, 'The people had never a right to do wrong. He was certain that the same pluck which had carried them so far would enable them to finish (cheers).'

On 21 March 1922, the political correspondent of the *Irish Times* wrote that 'Mr. de Valera's wild speeches, with their threats of civil war, have been read everywhere with amazement, in view of his earlier declarations

– especially that in Paris during the Race Congress, in which he declared that there would be no internal dissensions, and that the will of the people must prevail.' De Valera later tried to distinguish between warnings and threats when it came to understanding what he had said and, in Dáil Éireann on 19 May 1922, appeared to deny outright certain newspaper reports from Killarney and Thurles as 'misrepresentation' and as 'misquotations'. That day in the Dáil Kevin O'Higgins reproached him:

> Looking back over the controversy we have had in Ireland since December last, it seems to me that the wisest words that were spoken in the course of that controversy were spoken by the Deputy for East Clare: 'There is a constitutional way of settling those differences of ours; in God's name let us not depart from it' [see de Valera's statement of 8 December 1921]. Those were the wisest words that were spoken in this six months' controversy. Would that the speaker had adhered to them. Would that he had not gone later to Killarney and Thurles and told excitable young men there that if they continued to go forward to their objective, as he hoped they would, it would be necessary for them to wade through Irish blood, including that of some members of the Government.

De Valera interrupted O'Higgins to dismiss as 'an absolute misrepresentation' this version of what he had said to the 'excitable young men'. He told him, 'I denied in the *Irish Independent* that I made this statement, and the thousands of people who listened to me know it is a lie.' Séamus Robinson, an anti-Treaty deputy and IRA commander in Tipperary, told the Dáil that he had been present when de Valera spoke and he backed de Valera's version.

However, his 'denial' made by way of a letter to the editor of the *Irish Independent* that both that paper and the *Freeman's Journal* had published on 23 March 1922 was ambiguous. He did not deny uttering the words reported from Thurles about wading through the blood of Irish soldiers and government ministers, but instead contested their interpretation by obliquely indicating that the words should be regarded as sketching a hypothetical scenario rather than constituting a direct threat: 'This a child might understand, but you [editor] depart from its plain meaning in order to give the infamous lead in misrepresentation.' His letter seems more confusing than convincing, and it was not only at Thurles that he had uttered such words in a highly charged context. His letter appeared in print under the headlines 'Mr de Valera makes Charge of Criminal Malice' and 'Mr. de Valera's Speeches: A Reply to Editorial Comments'. It is worth reproducing in full:

A Chara – Your editorials of the 18th and 20th have been brought to my notice. These editorials, in which you picture me as 'encouraging' and 'preaching civil war' and indulging in 'violent threats' and 'in the language of incitement', I can only characterize as villainous. Nothing, it seems to me, but deliberate and, in these circumstances of the moment, criminal malice could so distort the plain argument of my speeches, perfectly clear to all who listened to me, and no less clear to all who read even the summarized reports in your own columns with the desire to know exactly what I said instead of the desire to distort it. You cannot be unaware that your misrepresenting me as inciting to civil war has on your readers precisely the same effect as if the inciting words were really mine.

My argument was an answer to those who said that the London Agreement gave us 'freedom to achieve freedom'. I showed that instead of opening the way it erected in the nation's path two almost impassable barriers:

(1) The Nation's own pledged word, and

(2) A native Government bound to act in accordance with, and to secure, even by force, respect for that pledged word.

The constitutional way was barred, and the way of force barred – the latter by the barrier of civil war. The Irish Volunteers of the future, if they persevered in the cause of independence, would have to fight, not an alien English Government merely, but a native Irish Government; not English troops, but Irish troops – the forces of their own Government – their own fellow countrymen.

This was the barrier of Irish flesh and blood which those who advocated the acceptance of the so-called Treaty would erect, even whilst they shouted that they were securing 'freedom to achieve freedom'.

In your issue of the 18th, the part of my speech at Thurles dealing with this question you report as follows:–

'Up to the present, when Irishmen and women tried to secure independence the people they had to fight were foreigners; the Government they had to fight was a foreign Government, and if they had to shed blood it was the blood of alien soldiers. If they accepted the treaty, and if the Volunteers of the future tried to complete the work the Volunteers of the last four years had been attempting, they would have to complete it, not over the bodies of foreign soldiers, but over the dead bodies of their own countrymen. They would have to wade through Irish blood, through the blood of the soldiers of the Irish Government, and through, perhaps, the blood of some of the members of the Government, in order to get Irish freedom.'

This a child might understand, but you depart from its plain meaning in order to give the infamous lead in misrepresentation which to-day enables you as a further step to feature such libels as that of Padraig O'Maille, T.D., at Tuam, where he said:– 'Mr de Valera's proposal in Waterford and Tipperary was that Irishmen shoot one another down,' – unless I am to take it that you are misrepresenting him, and those whose statements you have featured with his, as you have misrepresented me.

Pádraig Ó Máille's contribution to a report in the *Irish Independent* on 22 March had consisted of just three sentences, the second and third of which de Valera did not quote in his letter. The sentences that he omitted were, 'My God, how any Irishman should say such a thing! Some time ago Mr. de Valera said he would not coerce Craig or his friends; now he wanted to coerce fellow-Irishmen.' Later in 1922 anti-Treaty gunmen shot Ó Máille on his way to the Dáil. In publishing de Valera's criticism as set out here the editor of the *Irish Independent* also stated beneath it:

We think we made no attempt whatever to distort the plain meaning of Mr. de Valera's speeches, and, taken with certain concurrent circumstances, we believe it is the construction which would be placed on them

259

by thousands of others. We dealt with his language as reported in at least three speeches, and we maintain that, taking the particular passages either separately or in conjunction with the entire speeches and the surrounding circumstances, they justified our criticism. Notwithstanding the 'criminal malice' of our 'villainous' editorials, we hope that we do not now misrepresent Mr. de Valera in assuming that his commentary means disapproval of 'preaching civil war' and indulging in 'violent threats'. We hope that in view of the above letter Mr. de Valera will use his best efforts to discountenance any attempt at civil war in the future.

Various historians have commented on de Valera's proclivity to give incompatible explanations of his actions at different times, with John Bowman in one essay observing that de Valera 'never lost his genius for the bespoke formula' and Ronan Fanning referencing the 'fudge characteristic of other pedantic compromises that studded his political career'.[60] De Valera sought, for example, to explain his refusal to go to London for the Treaty negotiations in various ways. His efforts to explain away what he said in early 1922 leave one wondering if he himself really believed that he had not issued threats. He made no distinction between the Volunteers of the recent past who were fighting for independence with the support of the revolutionary Dáil Éireann and those who might now fight on despite a majority of the cabinet and of a democratically elected Dáil accepting the proposed treaty.

In April 1922, *Poblacht na h-Éireann – Republic of Ireland* (a paper founded to support de Valera) published a crude satire of the Treaty negotiations that included its narrator proclaiming, 'We'll not have this treaty executed. Let us rather execute the man who signed it for us.' In Dáil Éireann, on 27 April 1922, Arthur Griffith described this article as 'a deliberate incitement to the assassination of the plenipotentiaries' who had negotiated and each signed in London not a binding document but a proposed agreement for a treaty subject to parliamentary approval in Dublin and London. Less than four months after *Poblacht na h-Éireann* published that piece Griffith collapsed and died. Appalled by the damage done to nationalism by the Parnell split, he had wished and tried for years to ensure that the Sinn Féin he founded would be a movement uniting republican perspectives. He was heart-broken by the Civil War. Michael Collins was killed in an ambush soon after Griffith's death. De Valera survived. The oath that appeared to be an insurmountable obstacle to his entering Dáil Éireann in 1922 turned out to be not such an obstacle when he founded his Fianna Fáil party in 1926 and later formed a government.

*

During the 1930s when Dorothy Macardle was writing her book on Irish republicanism, de Valera told her:

> It is an extraordinary thing that all my life everything that I really wanted came to me. Small things I mean of course; personal things. I could write a very curious sort of book about that. It is frightening, because if you think that the balance has to be adjusted I am going to have a terrible time!
>
> For instance, when I was a child I had a great desire for a gold watch. I suppose I saw one with the priest. I dreamed one night that I had one in my hand and I woke up with my hand curled round it and to find it empty was a grief. Afterwards, in America, when I was given a gold watch inscribed to me as President of the Republic, it seemed just like the watch in my dream, and it gave me as much pleasure as it would have given to the child.
>
> And of course I wanted, even more, to be a Red Indian Chief. But I thought that could never come true. Even if I got a gold watch some day I would never get that wish. Well, when the Chippewa Indians [Ojibwe nation] made me a Chief of their tribe, it meant more to me than all the freedoms of all the cities I was ever given.
>
> No, indeed! It is not an 'honorary Chieftain' they made me! I am a real Chief. It will be handed down in the tradition of their tribe. They gave me a belt and moccasins – various presents, and I sent them a present of rifles – seven rifles for seven chiefs.[61]

Éamon de Valera's fortieth birthday fell on Saturday, 14 October 1922. He can scarcely have 'celebrated' it, because on that day the Irish gov-

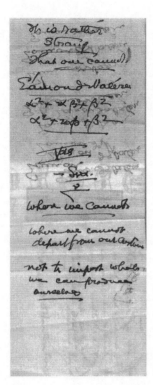
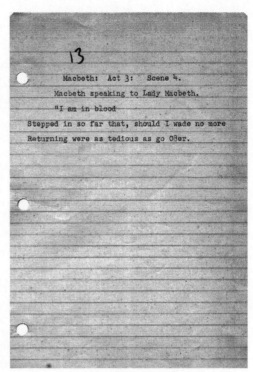

Left: This page in one of his private notebooks (from the late 1940s) contains a draft of a sentence in separated fragments, perhaps for a speech, stating 'It is rather strange. That one cannot. Where we cannot. Where one cannot depart from our [custom?] ... not to import what we can produce ourselves.' There is also, as elsewhere within his notebooks, his signature. He sometimes varied the way in which he spelt his name (see above pp.180-181), in this case placing a *fada* (long accent) on the letter 'a' in his first name rather than as usual on the initial upper-case letter 'e', and another fada in his surname on the letter 'e' where he more usually left the surname without a fada. And then there is the mathematical scribble where he reproduces algebraic factors and a product, similar to that which he got wrong when orally examined by a teacher on applying in 1896 to enter the Christian Brothers' school in Charleville, Co. Cork (see above p. 119). The contents of some pages in his notebooks seem quite random. Courtesy UCD Archives P150/3701.

Right: One of two quotations from Shakespeare's *Macbeth* in a notebook that includes a range of other quotations from writers including Horace, St Luke, Thomas Davis and Cardinal Mercier. Courtesy UCD Archives P150/3704.

ernment released transcripts of captured correspondence that revealed de Valera's desperation. The Civil War was grinding on and he found himself sidelined even by the anti-Treaty IRA, of which he was not only a member but also the ostensible political leader. Newspapers that same weekend reported attacks on Free State forces in Cork, Kerry, Limerick and Drogheda. Anti-Treaty raiders burnt down Blessington and Kilbride courthouses. But his side had already lost the battle for minds. In one of the disclosed letters, written on 13 September just three weeks after the killing of Michael Collins, he had referred to 'Rory O'Connor's unfortunate repudiation of the Dáil, which I was so foolish as to defend even to a straining of my own views to avoid the appearance of a split' and he had identified that repudiation as being 'now the greatest barrier that we have'. O'Connor is described in the *Dictionary of Irish Biography* as 'the chief catalyst in the group of senior IRA officers that opposed the Anglo–Irish treaty' and he was a senior commander in the occupied Four Courts in Dublin from April 1922. De Valera, in that same leaked letter, confessed that:

> even if we had the allegiance, we have not the military strength to make our will effective, and we cannot, as in the time of the war with the British, point to authority derived from the vote of the majority of the people. We will be turned down definitely by the electorate in a few months' time, in any case.[62]

It looked like another of de Valera's ambitions had been permanently extinguished, that his aspiration to be the symbol of a new Irish state had come to nothing. Yet he was to spend less than a year in jail at the end of the Civil War and was to emerge free to found a new political party of his own. He had been relatively lucky when it came to jail. After Easter 1916 he thought he might have had to serve his full sentence of penal servitude for life, but after just thirteen months the British released him and other rebels under a general amnesty. While interned with others in England in 1918, he was sprung by Collins and Boland. For most of the War of Independence he was lodged in the Waldorf Hotel in New York, and when he returned to Ireland was left free for the first six months of 1921 (apart from one very brief detention) while Griffith and others languished in prison. And, notwithstanding his central role in support of anti-Treaty insurgents during the Civil War of 1921–22, for which in other circumstances or in other countries he might have been locked up for years or shot, de Valera benefited from the general release of combatants eleven months after his arrest in that war.

FIANNA FÁIL FOUNDED

After his release from Irish Free State custody in 1924, de Valera decided that continued armed militancy served no useful purpose and that he needed to go in a new direction.[63] He broke away from what remained of the old Sinn Féin and brought with him many of its former members who had not already lent their support to the pro-Treaty side. In March 1926 Sinéad wrote to a friend, 'He is in very good spirits and is hopeful that he will yet be able to rally much of what is best in the county.' During April and May 1926 he founded his own political party.[64]

De Valera chose for his new party the name 'Fianna Fáil'. The mythology of the Fianna as a noble, truthful and heroic standing army was familiar to adults and children across Ireland down the centuries. The Fianna had been Gaelic warriors and '*Fál*' (genitive: *Fáil*) is one of the old alternative names for Ireland. At Tara Hill, seat of the old high kings of Ireland, there stands an ancient monument called the '*Lia Fáil*', although commonly known in English as the 'Stone of Destiny' rather than 'Stone of Ireland'. Dinneen described it as 'the chief fetish' of the old Irish capital. About two metres long, it 'was supposed to shriek on the inauguration of the rightful monarch of all Ireland'.[65]

The name 'Fianna Fáil' already sounded familiar to many of de Valera's contemporaries for it occurred in the first three words of a rousing call to arms. Sometime in or before 1910 Peadar Kearney of the IRB wrote 'A Soldier's Song', frequently sung thereafter by the Irish Volunteers. Between 1916 and 1923 Kearney's song was translated into Irish, being given the title '*Amhrán na bhFiann*' ('Song of the Fianna') and the opening words of its chrous translated as 'Sinne Fianna Fáil' (meaning 'We are the Fianna of Destiny' but found less romantically in the English version as 'Solders are we'). The air was used, first informally, as a national anthem for the new Irish Free State. De Valera harnessed its emotive energy. Nevertheless, in July 1926 the air along with the Irish-language chorus were formally adopted as the Irish national anthem by the Free State government. Anyone who now sang the national anthem would unavoidably invoke the militant name of de Valera's political party and reinforce its association with a patriotic tradition. Later proposals to change the opening words came to nothing.[66]

As both an evocative name for his new organisation and an expression of his own self-image as symbol of an Irish republic, de Valera's choice was inspired. He had, as it were, fulfilled his own destiny and thereby promised to fulfil that of republicans who supported him. Whelan has suggested that the 'Soldiers of Destiny' tag was employed 'usually derisively', but one assumes that this was only so among those who did not support Fianna Fáil.[67] The subsequent role of de Valera in the evolution of Fianna Fail, from its revolutionary origins through extended periods in office has been considered elsewhere by others.[68]

After 1924 de Valera went on to become the foremost political leader in Ireland. The frustration of his earlier ambitions to become either a priest or a professor had propelled him via rebellion into politics. His fate in becoming the most prominent Irish statesman of the twentieth century was due as much to his ability and determination as it was to chance. He learnt from his childhood and youth to take nothing for granted. Founding Fianna Fáil in 1926, he took charge of his future. If he aptly quoted Shakespeare's *Macbeth* on the bloody path of history that he trod, he might also quote Shakespeare's *Julius Caesar* on how he found his ultimate destiny: 'Men at some time are masters of their fates: The fault, dear Brutus, is not in our stars.'

The harsh circumstances of his birth, the poverty of his childhood, his individual struggle to be educated to a high level were all factors in his emergence from challenging social and economic circumstances to become a man to be reckoned with. It was never easy for him when he was young. The labouring son of a single female emigrant/immigrant, he was determined to succeed, first for himself and then for his ideal Irish republic. His aspirations set him on twisting paths that led eventually to his personal success and security. Whether or not his ambition had dangerous and damaging consequences for the state that he came to lead is still debated.

- POSTSCRIPT -

THE ABSENT DE VALERA

What pieces are missing from the jigsaw of de Valera's life before he founded Fianna Fáil in 1926? What do we *not* know because revealing documents never existed or have been destroyed or lost?

All historians depend heavily on paper trails. Many have had the experience of stumbling on a new source that radically changed their view of an individual or of an event. Just a single document may make a big difference to how we understand the past. We know too well that women in general or members of national and social minorities or of the lowest social classes have not been heard simply because what they thought or said was not recorded at the time.

We know too that Éamon de Valera carefully guarded his reputation and that, in his case, letters and other material that would throw more light on his character and actions, on his personal and political relations, have disappeared. A number of instances of 'known unknowns' are mentioned in the narrative above, where quite extensive correspondence between himself and his mother or his wife or others is known to have once existed but is not found today among his papers.

Other absences are frustrating but cannot be said for certain to involve lost documents. These are the 'unknown unknowns'. There is, for example, little or nothing in his papers that throws light on his relationships with Arthur Griffith or Patrick Pearse or Michael Collins. And what of the lack of more detailed information or correspondence about the events of Easter Week 1916, or the dealings between himself and the team sent to London for treaty negotiations in 1921. He later worked up with Frank Pakenham a version of what happened that year for the latter's misleading account in *Peace by Ordeal*. If such papers existed might they radically change our opinion of him and of events when read now? How do we deal with the dynamics of such interpersonal political encounters if few relevant letters or journals can be found?

Historians are fully aware of the danger of depending entirely on whatever written evidence they can uncover to construct a picture of the past. People may destroy papers for understandable reasons, particularly to avoid their capture by enemies. Arthur Griffith and his wife did so, and Mrs Griffith also later destroyed some personal letters because she did not want others reading details of their private life and relationship. Where Griffith died suddenly, de Valera lived long and took his time to shape his personal profile. This makes any loss of his potentially revealing papers all the more unfortunate. A writer who falls back credulously on making do with extant materials can be posthumously manipulated by those in the past who have destroyed or altered records.

One response to the challenge of inadequate or incomplete sources is 'faction', a mixture of imagination and archival research that may be quite persuasive or stimulating when the pen is in the hand of a Colm Tóibín or Hilary Mantel or Robert Harris but which is ultimately unsuccessful if the objective is the writing of 'pure history'. The latter objective faces enough obstacles in the form of bias and error and deception in respect to both author and sources without complicating the task by weaving fact and fiction into an ostensibly seamless garment. W.G. Sebald does this in a fascinating way, for example in his *Austerlitz*, but a historian finds in Sebald's *The Rings of Saturn* references to Roger Casement that undermine its publisher's claims for the work. Sebald incorrectly writes that Casement had no legal representation at his trial in London. And if Casement 'could not rid his thoughts of the fact that almost half the population of Ireland had been murdered by Cromwell's soldiers', Sebald might have checked that quantitative 'fact' with contemporary historians. War in the Cromwellian period had a catastrophic impact on Ireland, but accuracy matters in history if not in fiction. Similarly, the life of Michael Collins provided ample drama for a gripping and popular film by Neil Jordan about the Irish rebel leader, but certain factual errors in that work of 1996 raise a question about the ultimate value of creative or 'poetic' license in the context of history.

Yet imagination may play a role is whetting one's appetite for further research and exploration, and in stimulating further analysis. The present author at one point intended to include in the narrative above a number of imagined scenes and monologues where the lack of more complete information is otherwise frustrating. On reflection, the author excluded these from the main text. Nevertheless, a challenge remains for some skilled novelist to draw together what we know of de Valera's childhood and relationship with members of his family as well as his interaction with figures such as Griffith, Pearse and Collins and, by artfully imagining what we do not know, to weave an engaging story of de Valera's home and public life that would represent a more complete picture of his wife Sinéad's role in particular and of his own actual participation in the fighting of 1916, in the conduct of Treaty talks and in the waging of a civil war that he might have done more to prevent. For while the archives are extensive, there remain too many gaps in what they tell us about 'the Chief'.

PAPERS 'HAVE HAD TO BE DESTROYED'

In 1922 De Valera was 'very anxious' that a certain Franciscan priest be aware of his wishes 'in case of my death, imprisonment etc.' He took steps to preserve some of his papers. However, he also mentioned that 'very many of the papers – important links in the chain – have had to be destroyed'.[1]

While the surviving de Valera papers in the UCD Archives are helpful to researchers, and the opportunity to transcribe his early letters has been especially useful when writing the present book, researchers must always bear in mind that he himself said that some of his sensitive papers had been destroyed by 1922. These are not the only relevant documents no longer available. Some missing material is identified in UCD's own useful online guide to the de Valera papers and, as one reads through particular papers it is clear from references within them that other documents then extant are also now absent. For example, certain letters referenced in extant letters are not themselves in the UCD Archives. It is intriguing to find scribbled on one of de Valera's surviving notebooks in UCD the instruction 'Look thro' to destroy' (a notebook from long after 1922).[2] Evidence of other letters surfaced at the end of the twentieth century, although the author cannot now locate these letters themselves.

Around 1972 a journalist named Liam Robinson rejoined the *Irish Press* after a spell with Express Newspapers in England. It is understood that during the time he worked in England he was offered some de Valera papers and may have informed Vivion de Valera, by then the controlling director of the *Irish Press*, of this fact. It is not known if any such papers were ever retrieved from England or what they were exactly, or even if they included letters later put on sale at Mealy's in the year 2000.

Tim Pat Coogan, a former editor of the *Irish Press*, included in his 1993 biography of de Valera long extracts from a couple of early letters from de Valera to his wife. He wrote that 'an anonymous benefactor' had sent him copies of the letters, and Coogan has told this author he subsequently gave all copies he had to a member of the de Valera family.[3] Then in 2000 a cache of letters from de Valera to his wife, initially reported to number seventeen or eighteen, was advertised for auction in Dublin by Mealy's of Castlecomer who expected the seller to get £15–20,000 for the lot. Some were partly quoted and even reproduced in newspapers. Gardaí stopped the sale because the letters had ostensibly been among papers belonging to Sinéad de Valera that were stolen from an outhouse at her and her husband's Blackrock home, 'Herberton'. It was reported that, '[Mealy's] understand the letters turned up in England, and have passed through several hands; beyond that, the provenance is unexplained. However, there is no possible doubt about their authenticity. The handwriting is immediately recognizable, and the circumstantial detail is more than sufficient to preclude any doubt.'[4] The letter from Lewes Jail which was one of those of which Coogan says he received a copy was not the single letter from Lewes reportedly due for auction at Mealy's in 2001.

In November 2001 a detective-sergeant reportedly told Dún Laoghaire District Court that he subsequently travelled to England and received another seven letters from the attempted seller. It was stated that gardaí had returned all the seized letters to the de Valera family.[5] These letters do not appear to have been added to the UCD Archives and the present author has not found them. From what we do know of them they paint a picture of Sinéad as young and potent and influential in the direction de Valera took in life, where she is so often remembered simply as an uncomplicated grandmother figure.

As has been noted above, a parcel of letters from de Valera as a boy to his Uncle Ed in Connecticut – letters said to have been sent regularly to that uncle who first brought him to Ireland – was reported by one of Uncle Ed's daughters to have been given directly to de Valera on one occasion when he visited America as an adult. What happened to them? Why keep some contemporary papers so carefully, and not others if they existed?

Such letters or other papers could throw more light on, for example, what Eddie felt and thought when he found himself growing up without parents or siblings in Bruree, being reared by an unmarried uncle and a grandmother. They also allow glimpses of sexual pleasures and abuses that were too often passed over in silence in 'de Valera's Ireland' in the twentieth century. What mysteries remain to be solved? What, for example, was de Valera doing in Dublin on the lost weekend of 26th to 29th May 1905? 'What for?' he asked himself in one of two notes that he made in later life indicating puzzlement at being unable to recall why he spent the weekend up in the city, where Arthur Griffith was then publishing his exciting polemic *The Resurrection of Hungary* in his *United Irishman* paper and where James Joyce set his novel *Ulysses*.[5] Or how often during the Civil War did de Valera actually fire a shot? He certainly played a part on the ground in organizing others to fight, but his principal role appears to have been as a propagandist whose willingness ultimately to compromise meant that he was not fully trusted by the militant leadership of the anti-Treaty IRA. Further evidence of his actions and attitude could colour our view of history.

ACKNOWLEDGEMENTS

This study of Eddie/Éamon de Valera's early life owes much to the assistance of others. In particular I wish to thank the archivists and librarians of Blackrock College Dublin, Bray Public Library, Dublin City University, King's Inns, the Library of Congress, National Library of Ireland, New York–Presbyterian Weill Cornell Medical Center Archives, New York Public Library's General Research Division, RTÉ Archives, Royal Irish Academy, Trinity College Dublin, University College Cork, University College Dublin, University of Manchester.

The UCD Archives constitute the principal repository of de Valera's known surviving papers. From as early as 1922 de Valera himself secretly took steps to arrange and safeguard some of his papers. De Valera survived the Civil War and only died in 1975. Papers of his that were subsequently deposited in the Franciscan Library in Killiney, Co. Dublin, were later transferred to UCD under the terms of a UCD-OFM Partnership. The copyright in the papers is the property of the Irish Province of the Order of Friars Minor and is administered by UCD Archives who have kindly granted the author permission to quote them and to reproduce relevant photographs. The extent to which the private life of individuals is relevant to an historical assessment of their motivations or public actions is a matter of debate, and nobody is obliged to make available to posterity a family's personal correspondence and papers. However, insofar as it may be possible to complement the papers already in the UCD Archives by the addition of further extant material relevant to the life and personality of Éamon de Valera, one hopes that our record of this important architect of Ireland in the twentieth century may be as complete as possible.

I am grateful to Ann Gallagher – the copyright holder of the late Frank Gallagher's papers in Trinity College Dublin – for permission to quote from those papers; to Pól Ó Murchú, solicitor for his encouragement; to Éamon Ó Cuív TD for a discussion about his grandfather Éamon de Valera, some of whose papers are now in UCD Archives; to Oliver Murphy for a maths grind; also to those authors who have written significant biographies of de Valera's long life. Readers who wish to know more about Dev, particularly after 1926, are referred to their works and to the substantial bibliographies therein. The present volume by this author is intended to complement their research by concentrating on the earlier period of de Valera's life and by focussing on particular aspects of it that formed or illustrate his character before 1926 and thus, hopefully, by providing new insights. The sources of my own research are clearly identified in endnotes below.

I express gratitude once more to my wife Catherine Curran, who is a constant support and encouragement, and to my sons Oisín, Conor and Sam, who keep me on my toes.

I recall my late mother Eileen speaking with respect of Éamon de Valera, even while my father Michael was more sceptical of 'the long fellow' – as Dev was widely known. One does not have to take sides to find de Valera interesting, or to try and understand what made him ultimately the man he was, a flawed human being but also a crucial political influence. Heated references to him during the recent 2024 referendums on the family and carers, in the context of 'his' Irish Constitution of 1937, have demonstrated his abiding impact to this day.

ENDNOTES

1. 'Here goes'

1 RTÉ, *Boy from Bruree* (a radio series in five parts, 1966), part 1; Donncha Ó Dulaing, *Voices of Ireland* (Dublin, 1984), p. 14; de Valera Papers, University College Dublin Archives P150 (hereafter UCD P150)/7 for de Valera's later unsuccessful efforts to have the Library of Congress and others identify the book. With minor differences his version corresponds to Ernest Griset, *The Alphabet of Animals* (London, [1880]).

2 *Freeman's Journal*, 27 Oct. 1917.

3 David Dwane, *Early Life of Eamonn* [sic] *de Valera* (Dublin and London, 1922), p. 53.

4 Diarmaid Ferriter, *Judging Dev: A Reassessment of the Life and Legacy of Éamon de Valera* (Dublin, 2007) pp. 237–41.

5 Elizabeth Coll Millson, 'My cousin Eamon de Valera', *Commonweal*, 18 Feb. 1938, pp. 455–6.

6 UCD P150/3375.

7 UCD P150/3375.

8 Seán Farragher, *Dev and His Alma Mater: Éamon de Valera's Lifelong Association with Blackrock College 1898–1975* (Dublin and London 1984), p. 58.

9 RTÉ, *Boy from Bruree*, part 5; Abbott, *History of Napoleon Bonaparte* (2 vols, New York: Harper, 1855–6), preface; Abbott, *The Life of Napoleon Bonaparte* (London: Ward, Lock [1883]).

10 'Various incidents and recollections of Bruree, dictated by Chief 4 July 1954 and 20 Aug. 1956' (UCD P150/87).

11 Thomas Bartlett, 'Was Bonaparte in the GPO? The legend of Napoleon in Irish history, 1796–1916' in *Paris – Capital of Irish Culture: France, Ireland and the Republic, 1798–1916*, ed. P. Joannon and K. Whelan (Dublin, 2017).

12 UCD P150/379.

13 Emmanuel-Auguste-Dieudonné, Count de la Case [aka Las Cases/ Casas], *Memoirs of the Life, Exile and Conversations of the Emperor Napoleon* (new ed., 4 vols, London, 1835–6. vol. 4 at 20 Nov. 1816) gives 'concerted fable', but J.C. Abbot, *Napoleon at St. Helena: or Interesting Anecdotes and Remarkable Conversations of the Emperor During the Five and a Half Years of his Captivity* (New York, 1855), pp. 497–8 has 'fable agreed' and this version is quoted here.

14   UCD P150/1569, 3662 and 3664; Nadia Clare Smith, *Dorothy Macardle: A Life* (Dublin, 2007), pp. 47, 59, 74–83; Leeann Lane, *Dorothy Macardle* (Dublin, 2019), pp. 171–5; Terry de Valera, *A Memoir* (Dublin, 2004), pp. 19–20; Eunan O'Halpin, 'Historical revisit: Dorothy Macardle, *The Irish Republic* (1937)', *IHS*, 31, no. 123 (May 1999), pp. 389–94.

15   UCD P150/25; Minutes of debates (Blackrock College Archives).

16   Abbott, *Napoleon at St. Helena*, pp. 497–8 at 20 Nov. 1816. Abbott's *History of Napoleon*, vol. 2 does not include this part of the entry.

17   Earl of Longford [Frank Pakenham] and Thomas P. O'Neill, *Eamon de Valera* [*sic*, no accent] (London, 1970), p. 1. De Valera had written to the publisher, 'I will recognise this work, if satisfactory, as my official biography and will make available to Mr O'Neill all the papers and give him all the general directions necessary for his work, and will not make these facilities available to any other biographer for a period of at least five years from the date of your agreement with him' (de Valera to Robert Lusty of Hutchinson, 30 April 1963, at UCD P150/383).

18   C. Kenny, 'Redeeming Dev, damning Griffith: Pakenham's *Peace by Ordeal*', *History Ireland*, 30, no. 4 (July/August 2022), pp. 14–15. For full analysis, see www.theirishstory.com, 'A Challenge: Rewriting Arthur Griffith's Role'.

19   Patrick Murray, 'Obsessive historian: Éamon de Valera and the policing of his reputation', *Proceedings of the Royal Irish Academy: Archaeology, Culture,*

History, Literature, 101C, no. 2 (2001), pp. 37–65.

20   Frank Gallagher Papers, NLI MS 18,375 (18), 'Notes re Dev', 6 April 1944, typed. Gallagher's Papers are held in the National Library of Ireland and Trinity College Dublin.

21   Gallagher Papers, NLI 18,375 (3).

22   Ryan, *Unique Dictator: A Study of Éamon de Valera* (London, 1936), p. 21.

23   Correspondence relating to the National Broadcasting Company's recording and production of an interview with de Valera entitled *Conversation with Éamon de Valera* (1955), (UCD P150/420). For this production see https://www.youtube.com/watch?v=QE-UjUGVZyw (8 March 2024).

24   'De Valera, Sinéad', by Frances Clarke in the RIA's *Dictionary of Irish Biography* (henceforth *DIB*); *Chicago Tribune* (Europe edition), 18 Sept. 1921, picked up by the *Roscommon Herald*, 24 Sept. 1921. See also Mark Holan at www.theirishstory.com for the suffragette's interview with Sinéad. Griffith's advanced nationalist weeklies were largely in English.

25   Margaret Ward, *Unmanageable Revolutionaries: Women and Irish Nationalism* (London, 1989), pp. 50–1; UCD P150/129–30.

26   *The Gael*, July 1902, pp. 230–1 (gives Jane O'Flanagan); UCD P150/132–3; Terry de Valera, *Memoir*, pp. 104–5. Griffith credited Butler with persuading him to adopt the name Sinn Féin.

27   UCD P150/132; Terry de Valera, 'My father Éamon de Valera: a hero to his

family as well as the nation', *Sunday Independent*, 3 Oct. 1982.

28 UCD P150/183.

29 Sinéad to Frank Hughes, 28 Dec. 1921 (Blackrock College Archives).

30 Caitlín Bean Uí Thallamhain, *Sinéad, scéal Shinéad Bean de Valera* (Dublin, 1979). Also De Valera, *Memoirs*, ch. 6.

31 De Valera, 'The Boyhood of Great Men' in undated exercise book with petrol-blue cover (Blackrock College Archives).

32 Dwane and de Valera went to different national or primary schools but both attended the Christian Brothers' school in Charleville. Dwane's native townland was Clogher, adjacent to Knockmore townland where de Valera lived with his Uncle Pat. Dwane knew Pat and spoke to him for the book. De Valera looked over Dwane's version before publication and found 'several inaccuracies'. In 1959, he also told Dwane there were 'several mistakes in the information you gathered from the neighbours' but did not list these. See UCD P150/82, 214, 1609 for correspondence with Sealy, Bryers and Walker (2 June 1922), Lizzie Coll Meagher, Knockmore (10 Aug. 1944), Dwane (1959); *Evening Herald*, 15 July 1922; *Cork Examiner*, 28 Dec. 1960; Mannix Joyce [= Seoighe], 'Éamon de Valera – Bruree man', *Capuchin Annual* 1963: pp. 240–58 at p. 255.

33 De Valera to Marie O'Kelly, 15/2/1962 (UCD P150/445).

34 'The Volunteers', 22 Feb. 1950 (P150/447).

35 'De Valera, Éamon ('Dev')', by Ronan Fanning in *DIB*; John A. Murphy,

'The achievement of Éamon de Valera' in J.P. O'Carroll and J.A. Murphy (eds), *De Valera and His Times* (2nd ed., Cork, 1986), pp. 1–2.

2. A Man from Manhattan

1 Reminiscences by de Valera, noted in the hand of Dorothy Macardle, apparently at Government Buildings in Dublin on 30 July 1934 (UCD P150/3662), include Crusoe references.

2 See https://www.britannica.com/topic/Robinson-Crusoe-novel (20 June 2024).

3 David Macaree, 'Daniel Defoe, "The True-Born Englishman", and Irish affairs', *Canadian Journal of Irish Studies*, 8, no. 1(1982), pp. 16–24.

4 Dictated by Chief, 5/8/1955 (UCD P150/435).

5 De Valera to his mother, 21 Dec. 1905 (UCD P150/170).

6 Gallagher Papers, TCD MS 10065/125 and 128 (1 April 1927 and 25 Dec. 1927). Gallagher made sequential diary notes during his visits with de Valera to the USA in 1927–28, mailing them regularly to his wife in Ireland. They are intermingled with other material within the Gallagher Papers at TCD MSS 10065 (begun as 'The Great Adventure' at MS 10065/115).

7 Reminiscences noted by Macardle (UCD P150/3662).

8 *New York Times*, 10 Jan. 1882.

9 For Wilde's visit to America see https://www.oscarwildeinamerica.org/ (20 June 2024)

10 'Valéra family – my father's people' ('I was told the following by my mother who in turn had heard it from my father'), undated (UCD P150/228).

11 Speranza, 'The stricken land', *The Nation*, 23 Jan. 1847.

12 *Daily Globe* (St Paul), 18 March 1882.

13 'Country life in Bruree' (UCD P150/87); 'Valéra family' and other related notes (UCD P150/228); For the SS *Nevada* passenger list with 'Kate Coll' see US National Archives free online (Reel 0420, New York 15 Sept.–5 Nov. 1879) at https://archive.org/details/passengerlistsof0420unit/page/n423/mode/2up (15 April 2024).

14 Notes made in August, 1955 (UCD P150/228).

15 Edward Le Roy Rice, *Monarchs of Minstrelsy* (New York, 1911), pp. 73, 140–2 for a brief biography and photo of Girard. For poster see https://hdl.huntington.org/digital/collection/p16003coll4/id/2662/rec/1 (20 June 2024).

16 'Incomplete letter dated 5 April 1878, to "My Dear Uncle"', Irish Emigration Database ID 9903184 (https://www.dippam.ac.uk/ied/records/39766); Ciara Breathnach, 'Immigrant Irishwomen and maternity services in New York and Boston, 1860–1911', *Med. Hist.*, 66, no. 1 (2022): pp. 3–23.

17 Mary Francis Cusack ['The Nun of Kenmare'], *Advice to Irish Girls in America* (New York, 1872), p. 149.

18 *Annual Report* 1883; Julie Miller, 'Transatlantic anxieties: New York's nineteenth-century foundling asylums', *Annales de Démographie Historique*, 114, no. 2 (2007), pp. 37–58.

19 *Annual Report* 1883.

20 *Annual Report* 1885.

21 UCD P150/101–4.

22 *Annual Reports* 1866, 1868, 1880, 1886; Miller, 'Transatlantic anxieties' pp. 43, 46–8. See also Elaine Farrell and Leanne McCormick, *Bad Bridget: Crime, Mayhem and the Lives of Irish Emigrant Women* (Dublin, 2023) for a broad context.

23 *Annual Report* 1883; Julie Miller, *Abandoned: Foundlings in Nineteenth-Century New York City* (NYU Press, 2018), pp. 110, 112–3.

24 *New York Herald Tribune*, 13 June 1932.

25 *Annual Reports, passim.*

26 *Irish Times* and *Irish Independent*, 3 March 2021, reporting an 'RTÉ Investigates' documentary.

27 Denise Petski, 'The Gilded Age', *Deadline*, 10 Dec. 2020. At https://deadline.com/2020/12/the-gilded-age-cast-hbo-julian-fellowes-drama-1234653998/ (14 March 2024).

28 Kees Van Hoek, 'Young Dev', *Irish Times*, 14 Oct. 1950.

29 UCD P150/4 (nos 1–4) and P150/5, nos. 4–5 (Mackey's Photo Gallery, 418 Grand Street, NYC).

30 UCD P150/3662.

31 Dictabelt begun 4 July 1954 (UCD P150/87).

32 Longford and O'Neill, *de Valera*, p. 1, date this memory of his mother as being of a moment in 1885.

33 Untitled typed page (UCD P150/87).

34 M.C. Bromage, *De Valera and the March of a Nation* (London, 1956), p. 16.

35 Dwane, *de Valera*, p. 4.

36 Edward Patrick Coll, 'My cousin Ed', *The Irish Rosary*, Jan. 1960, pp. 20–2 (copy at UCD P150/210) includes his description of de Valera when they

met in 1919 as having 'an austere and almost sad countenance'.

37 US Census 1905 and 1900 at Washington, Litchfield, Connecticut; Dwane, *de Valera, passim*.

38 Coll, 'My cousin Ed', pp. 20–2.

39 E.C. Faust, 'The history of malaria in the United States', *American Scientist*, 39, no. 1 (1951), pp. 121–30, at p. 122.

40 Ann Y. Smith, *Ehrick K. Rossiter: Designs for Modern Living 1880–1930* (Roxbury CT, 2013).

41 Dwane, *de Valera*, pp. 18–19, who includes a plate of his large family in the early twentieth century (1900–10).

42 The census of 1920 gives 1883, but the 1882 register of the Nursery and Child's Hospital had his sister Kate giving his address in the USA. No record has been found corresponding to an arrival by an Edward Coll in 1880–81.

43 Coll Millson, 'My cousin Eamon de Valera', *Commonweal*, 18 Feb. 1938, pp. 455–6 (copy at UCD P150/209).

44 'Statistics concerning the transatlantic crossing', at http://www.norwayheritage.com/articles/templates/voyages.asp?articleid=37&zoneid=6 (14 March 2024).

45 William Henry Flayhart, 'The Inman Steamship Company Limited: Innovation and competition on the North Atlantic, 1850–1886', in *The Northern Mariner/Le marin du nord*, 12, No. 4 (Oct. 2002), pp. 29–46; John Warner, 'Travel journal [including SS *City of Chicago* in May 1890]' (University of Manchester Library, GB 133 Eng MS 1322).

46 Coll Millson, 'My cousin de Valera'; *Cork Examiner*, 17 April 1885; Alice E. Murray, *History of the Commercial and Financial Relations between England and Ireland from the Period of the Restoration* (London, 1903), p. 343.

47 Coll, 'My cousin Ed'.

48 *Monthly Weather Review*, 13, no. 4 (April 1885), pp. 86–7.

49 *Belfast Newsletter* and *Cork Examiner*, 8 April 1885.

50 *Belfast Newsletter* and *Cork Examiner*, 20 April 1885 for the arrival at Queenstown from New York of the *Chicago* on Saturday 18 April; Letter from Irish Shipping Ltd. to de Valera, 11 March 1955, with information from Lloyd's confirming this as the date of arrival (UCD P150/439). The vessel was back in Queenstown again on 29 April 1885, on its way from Liverpool to New York (*Cork Examiner*, 30 April 1885). De Valera himself later gave his date of arrival as 25 April 1885, according to one typescript among his papers, but omitted or deleted the day and month of 1885 on another very similar typescript among the same papers (UCD P150/1 for both typescripts). Also see http://www.norwayheritage.com/p_ship.asp?sh=cichi (20 June 2024).

51 Copies procured by the author were first reproduced in C. Kenny, 'Éamon de Valera's mother-and-baby home', *History Ireland*, 31, no. 5 (Sept./Oct. 2023), pp. 38–42.

52 The Nursery and Child's Hospital registers are now kept at the Medical Center Archives, New York-Presbyterian/Weill Cornell Medicine, which kindly furnished a photocopy of

the 1882 entry for Kate to this author. See also the copy of an affidavit of Kate [Coll] Wheelwright in 1916 (UCD P150/528).

53   NYC Municipal Archives, B–M–1882–0352241 (https://a860-historicalvitalrecords.nyc.gov/view/68888).

54   UCD Archives P150/528 for both the affidavits and the correspondence with senators and others in Washington in 1916.

55   The Church of St Agnes kindly furnished this author with a photocopy of the original entry. A scrap of paper with the name of the then rector of St Agnes, Henry C. MacDowell is also pasted onto the entry in the church register. MacDowell is said to have baptised de Valera (UCD P150/03).

56   Hand to Farragher, 10 April 1986 (Farragher Papers, Blackrock College Archives); Farragher, *Alma Mater*, p. 9; Tim Pat Coogan, 'De Valera's begrudging attitude to the "Big Fellow"', *Irish Times*, 31 Jan. 2005.

57   J.M. Silinonte, New York, *Irish Times*, 18 June 1999 (letter).

58   UCD P150/3; Éamon de Valera to Sinéad, 'Sat. Evg.' [June 1917], 'author's copy' cited in Tim Pat Coogan, *De Valera: Long Fellow, Long Shadow* (London, 1993), p. 5. This is one of the letters of which Coogan says he received a copy anonymously. Others were De Valera to Sinéad in August 1912 (from an Irish language school in Co. Galway) and de Valera to Sinéad on Easter Saturday 1917 (from Lewes Jail), for both of which see Coogan, *De Valera*, pp. 41–2, 63 and below here.

59   These, however, give his baptismal name anachronistically as 'Éamon' instead of the 'Edward' it was on the church register (UCD P150/3).

60   Gallagher Papers, NLI MS 18,375 (2), p. 1, 'Broadcast: de Valera'.

61   Memorandum by Marie O'Kelly, 8 August 1961 and 'Valéra family' (UCD P150/228).

62   Notebook of recollections by Sinéad de Valera, compiled for Terry de Valera, *Memoir*, pp. 91ff.

63   Gallagher Papers, TCD MS 10065/158 (Christmas Day 1927), ff. 5–7.

64   'Notes which I took in conversation with Mother', undated, typed (UCD P150/228); Personal dates [1826–1910], dictated by President to M. O'Kelly and checked against documents etc. (UCD P150/435). However, elsewhere de Valera says they met at Greenville village ('Valéra family', UCD P150/228).

65   UCD P150/184. This file also indicates that Kate made a will in 1928. She died in July 1932.

66   *New York Evening Journal*, 1 Aug. 1924, quoted in Terry de Valera, *Memoir*, p. 148.

67   UCD P150/187.

68   Undated 'Extracts' (UCD P150/228).

69   *New York Evening Journal*, 1 Aug. 1924, quoted in Terry de Valera, *Memoir*, p. 148.

70   Michael Böss, 'De Valera remembering', in M. Böss, W. Huber, C. Maignant, H. Schwall (eds), *Ireland: Representation and Responsibility* (Trier, 2008), pp. 111–20 for a close analysis of this first chapter. In 1964 de Valera's personal secretary informed one correspondent 'I am most interested

in anything – documents or accounts – relating to the President's ancestors as I am presently engaged in filing and indexing his papers. This work is proving of immense value to Mr. T. O'Neill who is writing an authorized life of Mr de Valera' (Letter to Miss Fern Kelly, 9 Jan. 1964 (UCD P150/188)).

71 'Appendix: de Valera'; 'Further notes'; Memo 8 Aug. 1961; 'Harnett, May 1923' (UCD P150/221-2,228).

72 'Valéra family' (P150/228) also has Éamon stating that Kate said his father 'went to Denver in fall of that year [1880]'.

73 'Valéra family' (P150/228) has Éamon stating in 1955 'It is thought that father was buried either at Denver or Minneapolis'.

74 De Valera says elsewhere 'mother's shoes used fit him (!!)' and he 'was 28 years of age at marriage' ('Valéra family', P150/228).

75 Terry de Valera, *Memoir*, p. 14 himself spelt his christening name with a letter 'h' after the letter 'b'. The words given as 'Street' and 'Dec.' above are unclear. The question marks are on the Bible. The addition of 'Denver' as his father's place of death may be in the same hand as alterations to the entry for de Valera in the baptismal records of St Agnes Church, Manhattan, but Farragher, *Alma Mater*, pp. 8–9 unfortunately makes to attempt to explain either. *Ibid.*, p. 230 states that in 1973 de Valera gifted back this Bible to Blackrock College. Blackrock College is now unable to locate it, but has a photocopy of at least some of this page – which is also partly reproduced in Farragher, pp. 8–9, 53

and which is relied upon here. Note that in Farragher, p. 9 the *in-text* quotation from de Valera's inscription is an edited version. UCD P150/228 also has a copy of this part of the tree, while UCD P150/129 includes a typescript of notes relating to Sinéad de Valera's family said to have been entered also on another fly-leaf of a Bible.

76 'Notes which I took in conversation with Mother' (UCD P150/228) specify Denver as the destination. These notes also state that Pat Regan, a brother of Kate's godmother and 'most constant friend from Ireland' Mrs Johanna Hennessy, 'was in the police force and verified father's death'; 'Valéra family' (P150/228) further indicates that Kate told her son that Frederic Hamilton was a bachelor friend of his father and lived 'somewhere in Brooklyn'.

77 Terry de Valera, *Memoir*, pp. 147, 153.

78 Miss Fern Kelly to de Valera, 2 July 1958 (UCD P150/188), includes part of an undated press cutting about the chalice. This makes no reference to Kate, and the correspondent (who says that it was a mutual friend of Kate and herself who organised the tribute) does not in her letter clearly identify her source; Thomas Wheelwright to de Valera (UCD P150/200).

79 Letters from Edward Coll, Hotel de Vargas, Santa Fé, NM, to various curators of records, 1963 (UCD P150/216).

80 De Valera to Thomas Wheelwright, 31 May 1943 (UCD P150/200).

81 UCD P150/208.

82 Thomas Wheelwright to de Valera, 12 August 1943 (UCD 83 P150/200).

83 Letter for de Valera to Ambassador Kerney, Madrid, 5 Feb. 1936 (UCD 150/228) and De Valera's Bible (Blackrock College Archives).

84 Further Notes (UCD P150/228). The verb 'come' here suggests original handwritten notes made on one of de Valera's visits to Rochester.

85 Notes, Ambassador Kerney (1936) and Harnett (1922–3) (UCD P150/228); Gallagher Papers (NLI MS 18,375 (18)), 'Notes re Dev'.

86 For example, UCD P150/171–2, 216–29, 1200, 3673.

87 Gallagher Papers, TCD MS 10065/155, f. 23 (Dec. 1927).

88 UCD P150/167–9.

89 Dictabelt begun 4 July 1954 (UCD Archives P150/87); Notes made August 1955 and 'Valéra family' and 'Notes which I took in conversation with Mother', all at UCD P150/228. The latter indicates that Doyle's maiden name was Kate Hennessy.

90 Letter, 6 March [1900] (UCD P150/170).

91 US census and birth/marriage/death data here and below accessed via the free 'Family Search' online service. Also New York City records online. In the UK census 1881 Wheelwright's age is given exceptionally as '27' and not '24', a transcription error perhaps as all other sources indicate he was born in 1855.

92 NYC Department of Records (online), 'New York City Births, 1846–1909', B-M-1889-0020528 (Annie Wheelwright) and B-M-1890-0038431 (Thomas Wheelewright [sic]). The certificates note that the 'medical attendant or other authorized person'

was Dr Reuben B. Burton of 228 East 48th Street.

93 UCD P150/170.

94 UCD P104/259 (1–9) and P150/1106; Terry de Valera, *Memoir*, pp. 147–8; De Valera, *Dáil Éireann Debates*, 2 March 1934. Dudley Edwards, *de Valera*, p. 150 cites 'private information' as his source of Blythe's description. Murray, 'Obsessive historian', pp. 37–65.

95 Appendix: De Valera (UCD P150/228).

96 Bromage, *De Valera*, p. 15; Seán Ó Faoláin, *The Life Story of Eamon de Valera* (Dublin and Cork, 1933), p. 16.

97 *Soards' New Orleans City Directory 1884*, p. 270; US Census 1895 and 1900; New Jersey Marriages, 1678–1985 database; New Jersey Births and Christenings, 1660–1980 database at their son Joseph devalera [sic], 20 Sept. 1893 in Jersey City. One Juan de Valera of Spain, aged fifty-nine, entered at New York in 1884.

98 Personal dates [1826–1910]: Dictated by President to M. O'Kelly and checked against documents, etc. (UCD P150/228 and 435).

99 Report of Leopold H. Kerney to Éamon de Valera, Madrid, 16 January 1936, with related memorandum – two copies on file, one annotated (UCD P150/ 223–6). The memo gives 'Antonio' as the brother, a naval officer, and gives the wealthy family as Armenteres, not Acosta.

100 'Valéra family' (UCD P150/228). Also P150/171, no.3; P150/220 re Lorenzo and his son Federico Coullaut-Valera, sculptors from Madrid (1961–2).

101 Extracts as recalled by the wife of Juan Vivion de Valera [i.e. Kate!]', undated, unsigned typescript (UCD P150/228).

102 Terry de Valera, *Memoir*, pp. 141–6.

103 'Appendix: De Valera' (UCD P150/228).

104 UCD P150/220, for Lawson.

105 UCD P150/220, *passim*.

3. No rural paradise

1 *Cork Examiner*, 15 April 1885; *Kerry Evening Post*, 18 April 1885.

2 My Parents, My Birth, and my Arrival in Ireland, undated (UCD P150/1). Also P150/87 and Reminiscences by de Valera (UCD P150/3662).

3 Carole Peterson, 'What is your earliest memory? It depends', *Memory* 29, no. 6 (2021), pp. 811–22.

4 Gallagher Papers, NLI MS 18,375 (18), 'Notes re Dev'.

5 The number of houses in the Dispensary or Registrar's District of Bruree declined from 1,240 in 1841 to 654 in 1881, and in Mullinahone from 1,335 in 1841 to 746 in 1881, that is by nearly one half (*Census of Ireland 1891*, pt 1, vol. 2 (Munster), pp. 546, 691).

6 R.V. Comerford, *Charles J. Kickham: A Study in Irish Nationalism and Literature* (Dublin, 1979), p. 200.

7 Chapter 4 for what he read.

8 Kevin Rockett, 'Knocknagow, the Film Company of Ireland, and other Irish historical films, 1911–1920', *Screening the Past*, 33 (April 2012), special Knocknagow issue, at http://www.screeningthepast.com/issue-33/ (20 June 2024). This site also includes a link to an online screening of the film.

9 See, for example, 'The history of labour in Limerick in the nineteenth century', UCG doctoral dissertation by Dominic Haugh, 2000, at https://aran.library.nuigalway.ie/handle/10379/16065.

10 RTÉ, *Boy from Bruree*, part 2 for Mrs Joyce of Tankardstown, 'a contemporary of young Dev at Bruree school', attesting to this name.

11 Personal Dates. Dictated by President to M. O'Kelly and checked against documents etc., 3 pages (UCD P150/435). This also gives the dates of Kate's emigrant voyage as 21 Sept. to 2 Oct. 1879

12 *Ibid.*

13 *Report of the Commissioners, Census 1841*, pp. xvi–xvii. The term 'family' was defined to include servants, resident apprentices and labourers who used the same kitchen and boarded under the same roof as a head of household who supported them. If someone lived independently under the same roof on his or her own means of support, then that person was a separate family.

14 Census 1901 for 'general labourer' and 1911 for 'general carter'.

15 F.H.A. Aalen, 'The rehousing of rural labourers in Ireland under the Labourers (Ireland) Acts, 1883–1919', *Journal of Historical Geography*, 12, no. 3 (July 1986), pp. 287–306 at p. 287; Longford and O'Neill, *de Valera*, p. 3. For more on the cottages generally see Enda McKay, 'The housing of the rural labourer, 1883–1916', *Saothar*, 17 (1992), pp. 22–38.

16 H.D. Gribbon, 'Economic and social history, 1850–1921,' Oxford *New*

History of Ireland, 6, pp. 260–356 at 276–8.

17 De Valera to 'Mr. Connelly', 9 Sept. 1968, reproduced at Mainchín Seoighe, *De Valera and Bruree* (Bruree, 1985), pp. 24–5. Chapter 3 for Mortell.

18 Gallagher Papers, NLI MS 18,375 (18), 'Notes re Dev'.

19 RTÉ, *Boy from Bruree*, part 1.

20 RTÉ, *Boy from Bruree*, part 1.

21 Reminiscences noted by Macardle (UCD P150/3662).

22 Dictabelt begun 4 July 1954, and also untitled typed page (UCD P150/87), including 'She would have been at that time I suppose, about sixteen or seventeen years of age'; RTÉ, *Boy from Bruree*, part 1, including that she was 'about fifteen years or so I suppose'. In typed-up notes de Valera is quoted as saying that his aunt Johanna or Hanna was known generally as 'Hannie' (UCD P150/1A and B), possibly an audio transcription error, for it is 'Annie' in his surviving letters to his mother and half-brother. See too UCD P150/435.

23 Longford and O'Neill, *de Valera*, p. 2.

24 Gallagher Papers, NLI MS 18,375 (18), 'Notes re Dev'.

25 The *Waterford News and Star*, 6 March 1885, thought a labourer called Horton was the first to be declared a tenant under the act, but noted that his cottage would not be ready for occupation until May; *Cork Examiner*, 10 Feb. and 19 Aug. 1885.

26 RTÉ, *Boy from Bruree*, part 1.

27 Dictabelt begun 4 July 1954 (UCD P150/87).

28 RTÉ, *Boy from Bruree*, part 1.

29 Dictabelt begun 4 July 1954 (UCD P150/87).

30 *Ibid.* See also Gallagher Papers, NLI MS 18,375 (18), 'note, 1951', where his grandmother is said to have risen at 6 o'clock daily and his Uncle Pat 'later'.

31 *Cork Examiner*, 22 and 23 Dec. 1880.

32 *Freeman's Journal*, 16 Dec. 1880; The *Nation*, 18 Dec. 1880.

33 *Cork Examiner*, 18 Dec. 1880; *The Nation*, 25 Dec. 1880. Davitt described the justice of the peace Thomas Sanders, who owned property near Charleville, Co. Cork, as 'guilty of rackrenting' and noted that Sanders was now boycotted (*Dundalk Democrat*, 11 Dec. 1880). For Bruree band see *Cork Examiner*, 25 Oct. 1880.

34 Seán T. Ó Ceallaigh, Minister for Local Government, *Dáil Éireann Debates*, 20 Nov. 1935.

35 *Belfast Newsletter*, 21 Nov. 1885.

36 J. Costello, CC, to the editor, *Cork Examiner*, 28 Feb. 1884.

37 *Cork Examiner*, 21 March 1884.

38 *The Nation*, 20 Sept. 1884.

39 *Cork Examiner*, 11 Jan. 1886.

40 *Cork Examiner*, 2 and 6 July 1886; UCD P150/87 and 3704; 'Gubbins, John Russell', by Nicholas Allen in *DIB* does not refer to the boycott.

41 Correspondence with John Ryan of Croom, 1966 (UCD P150/82; Gallagher Papers, NLI MS 18,375 (18), 'Notes re Dev', and handwritten unlined page and a note on a lined diary page dated 1954). Fedamore is about seventeen kilometres north of Bruree. See Charles Kickham. *Knocknagow OR The Homes of Tipperary* (32nd impression, Dublin, 1953), pp. 2–3, 5, 7.

42   RTÉ, *Boy from Bruree*, part 1. This significant qualifying detail is absent from the published version of this interview at Ó Dúlaing, *Voices*, p. 28.

43   National Folklore Collection, Schools, vol. 0498, p. 164 (P. Coll, Knockfenora, Co. Limerick) at https://www.duchas.ie/en/cbes/4922000/4916906/4949353 (14 March 2024). Early recollections – mainly political (UCD P150/87) states that his hunt was stopped at Rockhill on 4 Jan. 1886 and that Gubbins sold his horses at Tattersalls in London on 8 Sept. 1886; *Limerick Chronicle*, 6 Jan. 1887 for the Lyons case.

44   'Country life in Bruree' (UCD P150/87). Also P150/83.

45   Mainchín Seoighe, *The Story of Kilmallock* (2nd ed., Kilmallock, 2012), ch. 21: 'Recovery, labourers' cottages, hiring fair, rural district council', p. 238.

46   *Dundalk Democrat*, 15 Jan. 1887. Also see *Nationalist and Leinster Times*, 5 March 1887 for him in Newbridge, Co. Kildare. *Cork Examiner*, 31 March 1894; Draft i: Introduction, de Valera's talk from the former altar, Bruree, 2 Jan. 1957 (UCD P150/89).

47   Gallagher Papers, NLI MS 18,375 (18), 1 Aug. 1953.

48   Gallagher Papers, NLI MS 18,375 (11); RTÉ, *Boy from Bruree*, part 1.

49   *Cork Examiner*, 31 March 1894; Draft i (UCD P150/89).

50   'Sheehy, Eugene' and 'Sheehy, David', by Owen McGee in *DIB*; Sheehy to John Devoy from Bruree, 14 Dec. 1904 (NLI MS 18,012/4/4).

51   Draft i (UCD P150/89).

52   John Harrold, 'Fr Eugene Sheehy', *Old Limerick Journal*, 50 (2016), pp. 119–20; O'Sullivan, William Henry, by Owen McGee in *DIB*.

53   *Irish Press*, 26 May 1938. See also *Irish Press*, 25 May 1938; *Cork Examiner*, 30 Nov. 1898 and 26 May 1938; *Kerry Weekly Reporter*, 20 May 1916; *Limerick Leader*, 25 May 1938.

54   'Questions for *Living Biography*, 1966–7' (UCD P150/431); Ó Dúlaing, *Voices*, p. 22 for the Christmas fare.

55   Kees Van Hoek, 'Young Dev', *Irish Times*, 14 Oct. 1950. Ryan, born at Bruree on 13 Dec. 1890, became a senior counsel and professor of law (*Limerick Leader*, 25 Oct. 1952). His father was an uncle of Tony Ryan of Ryanair.

56   RTÉ, *Boy from Bruree*, part 5; UCD P150/6 for a lock labelled 'President de Valera's hair as a young boy'; National Library of Ireland Tuke 37 for a photo of older boys in petticoats outside a school in Connemara.

57   UCD P150/5; 'Personal dates [1826–1910]' (UCD P150/435); RTÉ, *Boy from Bruree*, part 1.

58   Dictabelt begun 4 July 954 (UCD P150/87).

59   *Ibid.*

60   *Kerry Evening Post*, 11 April 1888.

61   Richard Ellmann, *Oscar Wilde* (London, 1987), p. 171.

62   'Frances Hodgson Burnett', at https://www.newworldencyclopedia.org/entry/Frances_Hodgson_Burnett (14 March 2024).

63   K.L. Carson, '*Little Lord Fauntleroy* and the evolution of American boyhood', *Jn. of the History of Childhood*

64 *and Youth*, 3, no. 1 (2010): 39–64 at p. 41.

64 New York passenger lists 1820–91, *via* familysearch.org.

65 Coll, 'My cousin Ed'.

66 UCD P150/207; Farragher, *Alma Mater*, p. 55.

67 Reminiscences noted by Macardle (UCD P150/3662); Seoighe, *Bruree*, pp. 9, 30.

68 RTÉ, *Boy from Bruree*, part 2.

69 UCD P150/9.

70 For the neglect of the Irish language then in particular see Séamus Ó Buachalla, 'Educational policy and the role of the Irish language from 1831 to 1981' in *European Journal of Education*, 19, no. 1 (1984): 75–92 at pp. 75–9.

71 Copy of a page of the Headline copy book transcribed by de Valera in Bruree School, 11 Aug. 1891, at Seoighe, *Bruree*, p. 13.

72 UCD P150/89; *Capuchin Annual* 1963, p. 256; RTÉ, *Boy from Bruree,* part 3.

73 Draft i: (UCD P150/89).

74 UCD P150/89; Joyce, 'de Valera', p. 255; RTÉ, *Boy from Bruree*, parts 3, 5 (*edited* version at Ó Dúlaing, *Voices*, pp. 30–1). Fianna Fáil arranged De Valera's talk. For de Valera in Bruree see *Limerick Leader*, 28 June 1950 (a visit 'after an absence of thirty-three years', i.e. first since 1917) and 5 Jan. 1957. RTÉ's interviewer (Ó Dúlaing) asks 'You have visited Bruree many, many times over the years … Can you pinpoint any other occasion?' De Valera simply replies that his first visit after the Rising was on his way to the Clare election. Perhaps nostalgia set in after 1950 and he went more often.

75 Draft i (UCD P150/89).

76 Reminiscences noted by Macardle (UCD P150/3662).

77 Gallagher Papers, MS NLI 18,375/(18), handwritten unlined short page, 19 July 1952.

78 Dwane, 'Ireland growing and my adventures in Black and Tan days [draft autobiography, *c.* 1930?]', NLI MS 39,932/1-2, ch.1, p. 4. This manuscript has few references to de Valera. In it (ch. 4, p. 16) he states that the term 'IRA' was replacing 'Volunteers' in Co. Limerick from May 1918. Dwane, then postmaster in Kilmallock, provided intelligence to the IRA during the War of Independence.

79 Joyce, 'de Valera', p. 253; RTÉ, *Boy from Bruree*, part 1; David Greene, 'The founding of the Gaelic League' in *The Gaelic League Idea*, ed. Seán Ó Tuama (Cork, 1972), pp. 9–11, who cites P.J. Keenan, chief inspector of national schools, and Sir William Wilde for striking incidents.

80 *Conversation with Éamon de Valera*, NBC recording and transcript (UCD P150/420–1).

81 Dictated 29 Oct. 1956 (UCD P150/445 and 447).

82 Dwane, *de Valera*, pp. 37–8.

83 Census 1911 and 1921 online for Patrick Coll, Bruree; *Census of Population Ireland 1926*, vol. 8: Irish Language, p. 69; Brian Ó Cuív, *Irish Dialects and Irish Speaking Districts* (Dublin, 1951), pp. 36–7, 61–2, 88; *Limerick Leader*, 28 June 1950.

84 *Cork Examiner* and *Irish Press*, 29 Jan. 1946; *Waterford News and Star*, 19 June 1962; *Munster Express*, 22 June

1962; Joyce, 'de Valera', p. 241; 'Odds and ends', by 'An Mangaire Sugach' [Mannix Joyce], *Limerick Leader*, 5 Nov. 1949.

85 RTÉ, *Boy from Bruree*, part 4 for interview with John J. Savage. Also see Savage's letter at UCD P150/82.

86 Gallagher Papers, NLI MS 18,375 (2), p. 1; RTÉ, *Boy from Bruree*, part 1.

87 Dictabelt begun 4 July 1954 (UCD P150/87).

88 Dictabelt begun 4 July 1954 (UCD P150/87).

89 UCD P150/87; Gallagher Papers NLI MS 18,375 (18), handwritten unlined page numbered '3'. For St Coleman's Well (Gortroe, Co. Limerick) see National Folklore Collection, Schools, vol. 0497, pp. 370–3 at https://www.duchas.ie/en/cbes/4921998/4916656/4948819 (14 March 2014).

90 Farragher, *Alma Mater*, pp. 11–12. Farragher, 'Dev–personal memories', wrote that he 'had many interviews with Dev over a period of almost twenty years beginning in the mid 1950s', the first of which alone lasted for almost three hours (Blackrock College Archives, 2 pages).

91 Reminiscences noted by Macardle (UCD P150/3662); Longford and O'Neill, *De Valera*, p. 3.

92 School roll books (UCD P150/83); Dictabelt begun 4 July 1954 (UCD P150/87); RTÉ, *Boy from Bruree*, part 2; Longford and O'Neill, *De Valera*, p. 3, gives him enrolled aged 'six' but his sixth birthday was still five months away.

93 Reminiscences noted by Macardle (UCD P150/3662); De Valera to Commissioners, undated draft letter (UCD P150/211); 'Various incidents Bruree' (UCD P150/87); RTÉ, *Boy from Bruree*, part 3. For a description of the declining 'dairyman system' see Seoighe, *Kilmallock*, pp. 236–7.

94 'Recollections of riding horses, etc., dictated by Chief. June 1956' (UCD P150/87).

95 'Country life in Bruree' (UCD P150/87); RTÉ, *Boy from Bruree*, part 5.

96 Reminiscences noted by Macardle (UCD P150/3662). David McCullagh, *De Valera* (2 vols, Dublin, 2017), vol. 1, p. 25 reads 'played hurling but' as 'stayed larking about but'. Also see RTÉ, *Boy from Bruree*, part 4 for his *camán* (hurley stick).

97 Gallagher Papers, NLI MS 18,375 (9), 'Dev's biography'.

98 Dictabelt begun 4 July 1954 (UCD P150/87); Longford and O'Neill, *de Valera*, p. 5.

99 UCD P150/87.

100 RTÉ, *Boy from Bruree*, part 2, citing 'Mrs Joyce'.

101 RTÉ, *Boy from Bruree*, part 2.

102 RTÉ, *Boy from Bruree*, part 5. This account is absent from the published version of this interview in Ó Dúlaing, *Voices*.

103 Seán Ó Súilleabháin, *Irish Wake Amusements* (Cork, 1967), p. 66.

104 National Folklore Collection, Schools, vol. 0498, p. 041 (Rockhill School, Bruree). Writing to de Valera on 10 Aug. 1944, Lizzie Coll attributes this account to Uncle Pat (UCD P150/214). It is incomplete as transcribed at https://www.duchas.ie/en/

cbes/4921999/4916782?HighlightTex-
t=Croom&Route=stories&SearchLan-
guage=en (14 March 2024).

105 'Country life in Bruree' and 'Various
incidents Bruree' (UCD P150/87);
Margaret O'Brien, 'Pasteur and Uncle
Paddy', *Lowell Review* 2021, pp. 161–4.
Online free at https://issuu.com/
thelowellreview/docs/thelowellreview_
v13_07.04.21_issuu/189 (14 March 2024).

106 'Recollections of riding horses, etc.',
and 'Various incidents Bruree' (UCD
P150/87).

107 'Gallagher Papers, NLI MS 18,375 (18),
'Notes re Dev'; UCD P150/87, dictabelt begun 4 July 1954; *ibid.*, 'Families
in the houses on the various roads'.

108 'Country life in Bruree' (UCD
P150/87). RTÉ, *Boy from Bruree*, Radio
Éireann, 5 Aug. 1966, archived tape at
c. 40 minutes (additional material).

109 De Valera, *Dáil Éireann Debates*, 2
March 1934.

110 RTÉ, *Boy from Bruree*, part 4.

111 UCD P150/170.

112 Personal dates [1826–1910]: Dictated
by President to M. O'Kelly and
checked against documents, etc.
(UCD P150/435); Longford and
O'Neill, *De Valera*, p. 5.

113 Dictabelt begun 4 July 1954 (UCD
P150/87).

114 RTÉ, *Boy from Bruree*, part 2.

115 Dictabelt begun 4 July 1954' (UCD
P150/87); RTÉ, *Boy from Bruree*, part 3.

116 Synge, 'de Valera', p. 651.

117 Families in the houses on the various
roads (UCD P150/87); RTÉ, *Boy from
Bruree*, part 3.

118 Longford and O'Neill, *de Valera*, p.
3; Reminiscences noted by Macardle
(UCD P150/3662).

119 Dictabelt begun 4 July 1954 and
'Country life in Bruree' (UCD
P150/87). The former includes a full
description of the game of 'Duck'; Ó
Dúlaing, *Voices*, p, 17; Seoighe, *Bruree*,
pp. 30–1.

120 RTÉ, *Boy from Bruree*, part 2.

121 'Various incidents Bruree' (UCD
P150/87); *Capuchin Annual 1963*, p.
256; RTÉ, *Boy from Bruree*, part 5. See
also https://paulkirtley.co.uk/2011/
conopodium-majus-pignut-forage/ (20
June 2024).

122 'Country life in Bruree' (UCD
P150/87); Dwane, *de Valera*, pp. 25–6;
Kickham, *Knocknagow*, pp. 78–9, 89.

123 Pauric Travers, *Éamon de Valera*
(Dundalk, 1994), p. 3, citing Eoghan
Ó Súilleabháin who cited his uncle
Seán Ó Súilleabháin of the Folklore
Department in UCD who told him
that de Valera had told him the tale
about Martin Callaghan and himself
in 'quite fluent but faintly ungram-
matical Irish'. For this period see also
Joyce, 'de Valera'.

124 UCD P150/87; P150/435.

125 RTÉ, *Boy from Bruree*, part 2; Seoighe,
Bruree, pp. 31–2.

4. 'I was alone a good deal'

1 Reminiscences noted by Macardle
(UCD P150/3662).

2 Reminiscences noted by Macardle
(UCD P150/3662).

3 Gallagher Papers, NLI MS 18.375 (18),
'Notes re Dev'. Also see Gallagher
Papers, NLI MS 18,375 (9), 'De Valera
obit.', p. 2 (typescript).

4 RTÉ, *Boy from Bruree*, part 4.

5 Terry de Valera, *Memoir*, p. 141.

6   UCD P150/170 (no. 2 of 8 letters here).

7   UCD P150/170, dictated 28 Sept. 1964 by President de Valera on hearing the letter read to him by M. O'Kelly.

8   Terry de Valera, *Memoir*, p. 150.

9   'Country life in Bruree' (UCD P150/87); RTÉ, *Boy from Bruree*, part 2.

10 'Country life in Bruree' (UCD P150/87); Seoighe, *Bruree*, p. 32. For a film of raking and tumbling in Tipperary in the 1930s: https://www.youtube.com/watch?v=ppC6uQbd_ys (23 Nov. 2023).

11 *Dáil Éireann Debates*, 2 July 1943 (misattributed by some writers to the Treaty Debates of 1921–22).

12 Elizabeth ('Lizzie') Coll Meagher, Knockmore, to de Valera, 10 Aug. 1944 (UCD P150/214).

13 'Recollections of riding horses, etc.' and 'Various incidents Bruree' (UCD P150/87); RTÉ, *Boy from Bruree*, parts 3 and 4; Joyce, 'Éamon de Valera', p. 256; Longford and O'Neill, *de Valera*, p. 6; 'Gubbins, John Russell', by Nicholas Allen in *DIB* does not mention his connection with de Valera. For Gubbins' fancy marriage to Edith Legh of Cheshire see *Leinster Express*, 9 Nov. 1889.

14 RTÉ, *Boy from Bruree*, Radio Éireann, 5 Aug. 1966, Archive tape at *c.* 44 minutes (additional material).

15 'Various incidents Bruree' (UCD P150/87); RTÉ, *Boy from Bruree*, part 2.

16 De Valera to Commissioners, undated draft letter (UCD P150/211).

17 RTÉ, *Boy from Bruree*, part 3.

18 *Limerick Leader*, 28 May 1938; *Cork Examiner*, 26 May 1938.

19 De Valera to Mrs Bridget J. Farrell, 5 Jan. 1966 (UCD P150/82).

20 RTÉ, *Boy from Bruree*, parts 4 and 5 for books mentioned here; 'Recollections of riding horses, etc.' (UCD P150/87); Bromage, *de Valera*, p. 20.

21 'MacGeoghegan, James', by Turlough O'Riordan in *DIB*; Vincent Geoghegan, 'A Jacobite history: the Abbé MacGeoghegan's "History of Ireland"', *Eighteenth-Century Ireland*, 6 (1991), pp. 37–55.

22 John Bies, 'The historical novel, Scottish nationalism and the good hero: Jane Porter's *The Scottish Chiefs* as historiography', *Advances in Social Sciences Research Journal*, 8, no. 4 (2021), pp. 738–51; Graeme Morton, 'The social memory of Jane Porter and her "Scottish Chiefs"', *Scottish Historical Review*, 91, no. 232, pt.2 (2012), pp. 311–35; Thomas McLean, 'Nobody's argument: Jane Porter and the historical novel', *Journal for Early Modern Cultural Studies*, 7, no. 2 (2007), pp. 88–103; RTÉ, *Boy from Bruree*, part 5.

23 Kickham, *Knocknagow*, pp. 25, 71, 94.

24 RTÉ, *Boy from Bruree*, part 5.

25 See 'Bob Pentland, or the gauger outwitted' and 'Condy Cullen and the gauger' in Carleton, *Tales and Sketches of the Irish Peasantry* (Duffy: Dublin, 1845 edition), pp. 275–8; Brian Earls, 'A note on Seanachas Amhlaoibh Í Luínse', *Béaloideas*, 52 (1984), pp. 9–34 at 29–30.

26 Ríona Noc Congáil, '"Fictions, amusement, instruction": the Irish Fireside Club and the educational ideology of

the Gaelic League', *Éire-Ireland*, 44,
nos 1&2 (2009), pp. 90–117, at 99,
105–6; *Weekly Freeman*, 16 June 1894
etc. for 'Freeman Publications'.

27 'Scott, Sir Walter' by David Hewitt in
DNB; *Britannica.com* at 'The Waverley
novels'.

28 RTÉ, *Boy from Bruree*, part 4;
'Sullivan, Alexander Martin' by Patrick
Maume in *DIB*.

29 Note 25 above for 'Bob Pentland'.

30 Comerford, *Kickham*, p. 16 citing
Kickham, 'Young Ireland', 24 Sept.
1881.

31 For Uncle Pat reading O'Growney's
first Irish lesson in the *Freeman's
Journal*, for example, see UCD
P150/445 and 447.

32 Gallagher Papers, NLI MS 18,375
(9), 'Dev's biography' for de Valera's
referring to the cartoon with the
shamrock (and also to a cartoon of
Lord Salisbury and Tim Harrington
relating to 'party funds'). Most cartoon
sheets were about 28 x 44 cm (11 x 17
inches) but some, including that about
the shamrock, were 40 x 57 cm (16 x 22
inches). I am grateful to the librarian
of King's Inns for access to its bound
collection of cartoons. Also see Felix
Larkin, 'Icons of freedom', *Irish Arts
Review*, 39, no. 2 (Summer, 2022), pp.
106–9.

33 Desmond Ryan, *Unique Dictator: A
Study of Eamon de Valera* (London,
1936), p. 22.

34 RTÉ, *Boy from Bruree*, part 5; Russell
Mitford attended school in Hans
Place, London – where Irish negotiators were to lodge in a house during
treaty talks in 1921.

35 Katie Trumpener, *Bardic Nationalism:
The Romantic Novel and the British
Empire* (Princeton, 1997), pp. 256–7.

36 Joyce, 'de Valera', p. 257; 'Séadna',
Gaelic Journal, nos 56–84 (1894–97),
with a second part published by the
Gaelic League in 1898 (copy at NLI IR
89162 (O) L1/2–3).

37 Personal Dates, 1826–1901 (UCD
P150/435).

38 Gallagher Papers, NLI MS 18,375
(18), 'Notes re Dev', and handwritten
unlined page numbered '1'.

39 The *OED* defines 'exhibition' as
(among other things) 'a fixed sum
given for a term of years from the
funds of a school, college, or university, generally upon the result of a
competitive examination'.

40 Douglas Kanter, 'Post-famine politics,
1850–1879', in Cambridge *History
of Ireland*, vol. 3, pp. 677–715 at
714; D.H. Atkinson, 'Pre-university
education, 1870–1921', *Oxford New
History of Ireland*, vol. 6, pp. 523–38 at
523–4. UCD and the Queen's Colleges
of Cork and Galway were from 1908
absorbed into the framework of the
new NUI that, along with Queen's
University Belfast (formerly Queen's
College Belfast), replaced the Royal
University of Ireland. The NUI and
Queen's College Belfast were nomi-
nally non-denominational 'but each
with its own particular atmosphere'
(Susan M. Parkes, 'Higher education,
1793–1908', *Oxford New History of
Ireland*, 6, pp. 539–70 at 539).

41 Arnold F. Graves, 'On the reor-
ganization of Irish education
departments and the appointment
of a minister of education', in

Journal of the Statistical and Social Inquiry Society of Ireland, 8, part 60 (1881/1882), pp. 350–9 at 351.

42   Irish Universities Bill, *Hansard*, HL Deb. 27 July 1908, vol. 193, *c.* 765. Browne later sat in the senate of the Irish Free State.

43   Mainchín Seoighe *De Valera and Bruree* (Bruree: De Valera Museum Publications, 1985), p. 10. What 'otherwise' signifies here is unclear.

44   UCD P150/13 and 13A, typescript of dictabelt recorded 6 Aug. 1955.

45   UCD P150/13; RTÉ, *Boy from Bruree*, part 4 for interview with Shea.

46   Maurice C. Hime, *An Introduction to the Greek Language*, 'comprising Accidence and Syntax, Exercises and Vocabularies, together with hundreds of original Examination Questions on the text, besides tabulated lists of the questions on Greek Grammar set at the Intermediate Examinations 1879 to 1890' (London and Dublin, 1891).

47   UCD P150/13. See also Personal Dates, 1826–1901 (UCD P150/435); RTÉ, *Boy from Bruree*, part 4, Shea interview and de Valera saying Prendiville was the only Christian Brother in the school.

48   Reminiscences noted by Macardle (UCD P150/3662).

49   UCD P150/13 and 13A.

50   Gallagher, 'The Great Adventure', at Gallagher Papers, TCD MS 10065/115, f. 11 (Feb. 1927).

51   'Incident, etc.' (UCD P150/87).

52   Gallagher Papers, NLI MS 18,375 (18), 'Notes re Dev', handwritten unlined page numbered '1'.

53   RTÉ, *Boy from Bruree*, part 3.

54   Farragher, 'Dev–personal memories' (Blackrock College Archives). The abbreviation 'bl' might stand for 'bloody' or 'blooming'.

55   Note dated 30 July 1936 at Government Buildings (UCD P150/3662).

56   Joyce, 'de Valera', p. 258; RTÉ, *Boy from Bruree*, part 2.

57   M.E. Daly, *Dublin the Deposed Capital: A Social and Economic History 1860–1914* (Cork, 1984), p. 48; Brian Griffin, *Cycling in Victorian Ireland* (Dublin, 2006), pp. 40–101. Commercial production of bikes fitted with Dunlop's pneumatic tyre began in 1890. For political cartoons featuring such bicycles see for example *Weekly Freeman* 13 May 1893 and 18 May 1896.

58   UCD P150/11, 12, 14, 20 for his Junior Grade Exhibition won in 1898 while at CBS Charleville, and for his Middle Grade Exhibition results at Blackrock.

59   Reminiscences noted by Macardle (UCD P150/3662).

60   UCD P150/12 front and back of photo. See also de Valera to Seán Úa Laoghaire, Sept. 1957 (UCD P150/82) for correction to names on the list at P150/12.

61   Reminiscences noted by Macardle (UCD P150/3662); Dictated by Chief 13 Sept. 1956 (UCD P150/8 and 87).

62   UCD P150/22, dictated 24 April 1956.

63   UCD P150/87.

64   'Massachusetts Deaths, 1841–1915, 1921–1924', via familysearch.org.

65   De Valera to Gerald Kelly, Massachusetts, 14 June 1956 (UCD P150/197). Kelly had been researching the Wheelwright family but de Valera told him 'When I went to America it was on official business which engaged my attention

practically the whole of the time. I know very little therefore of my mother's second husband Charles Wheelwright or of his forebears.' In the same UCD file (P150/197) is a short note from Annie Wheelwright to her parents wishing them a happy Christmas in 1896. It is without a sender's address but includes the sentence 'We are praying that the Infant Jesus will come and bless our homes' that may indicate she is in an institution of some kind.

66 UCD P150/170 (no. 3 of 7).

67 CBS copy-book of de Valera (UCD P150/12).

68 In de Valera's copy-book, 'Christian Schools (English, Classical and Mathematical) Charleville: Inter' (UCD P150/12).

5. A Holy Ghost Transition

1 'My going to Blackrock College, dictated 24 April 1956' (P150/22). Similar at Gallagher Papers, NLI MS 18,375 (18), 'Notes re Dev', handwritten unlined page numbered '1'.

2 'My Going to Blackrock' (UCD P150/22); 'John Francis D'Alton', by Diarmaid Ferriter in *DIB*.

3 Farragher, *Alma Mater*.

4 Gallagher Papers, NLI MS 18,375 (18), 'Notes re Dev', handwritten unlined page numbered '1'.

5 Healy, 'Mr. Mahaffy on Irish Intermediate education', *Irish Ecclesiastical Record*, vol. 4 (July to Dec. 1898), pp. 540–60.

6 UCD P150/13, dictabelt recorded 6 Aug. 1955.

7 UCD P150/22, dictated 24 April 1956; Farragher, *Dev*, pp. 13–14.

8 UCD P150/22, dictated 24 April 1956.

9 See, for example, UCD P150/13; Seán Farragher, *The French College Blackrock 1860–1896* (Dublin, 2011).

10 *Freeman's Journal*, 21 March 1868.

11 *Freeman's Journal*, 7 June 1911.

12 Reminiscences noted by Macardle (P150/3662).

13 Longford and O'Neill, *de Valera*, p. 7; Frank Gallagher Papers, NLI MS 18,375 (18); 'My going to Blackrock' (UCD P150/22).

14 Farragher, *Alma Mater*, pp. 15–17 for more on his first year there.

15 Blackrock College Archives for the books.

16 Typed note pasted on his copy now in the Blackrock College Archives. The note is similar in form to a typed note by his secretary Marie O'Kelly, ostensibly dated 4 June 1955, that refers to the Child of Mary medal but is possibly later, given O'Kelly's reference in it to his 'declining years'. On some Christmas cards his signature has no fada. Yet one in 1955 has a fada on the letter 'e' or 'a' in 'Eamon' and one on the letter 'e' in Valera.

17 UCD Archives P150/170 (no. 3); De Valera to Frank Hughes, 'Xmas Eve' [year absent] (Blackrock College Archives); Farragher, *Alma Mater*, pp. 19, 30–1.

18 UCD P150/200, no. 1. Tom's letter and the Christmas card to him were not found in the UCD archive. RTÉ, *Boy from Bruree*, part 4 where his cousin Lizzie recalls him in later years at Christmas bringing gifts to Bruree for her and her siblings, including 'mechanical toys for her brother that were unheard of in the area then'.

19 UCD P150/200, no. 1.

20 Farragher, *Alma Mater*, pp. 23–4.

21 UCD P150/170 (no. 4 of 8 letters here), from Blackrock College, 6 March (year illegible, but from contents *c.* Easter 1900).

22 The prayer book with an explanatory typed note by his secretary is in Blackrock College Archives; Longford and O'Neill, *de Valera*, p. 8; Farragher, *Alma Mater*, pp. 28–9.

23 Longford and O'Neill, *de Valera*, pp. 7–8.

24 Blackrock Archives, de Valera papers. In what seems to be the same hand as these ostensible corrections by a teacher is this enigmatic observation: 'E. De Valera a K.B. = new prefect in large study (at least he gives baths) – won't be allowed to pass any more billets.'

25 RTÉ, *Boy from Bruree*, part 5.

26 Healy, 'Mahaffy', p. 556. For a cartoon about the continuing inferior position of the Irish language in the Intermediate Examination system see *Weekly Freeman*, 13 July 1901.

27 http://www.census.nationalarchives.ie/reels/nai003735932/

28 Longford and O'Neill, *De Valera*, p. 9.

29 RTÉ, *Boy from Bruree*, part 4.

30 Farragher, *Alma Mater*, p. 55; Hand to Farragher, 10 April 1986 (Blackrock College Archives).

31 Farragher, *Dev and his Alma Mater*, p. 24.

32 Sports Day Programme (Blackrock College Archives).

33 Longford and O'Neill, *de Valera*, pp. 9–10.

34 See, for example, Gallagher Papers, NLI MS 18,375 (9) and NLI MS

21,273, 'de Valera', p. 2. Three letters on the latter file show that the enclosed draft pamphlet of 36 pages, written and typed up by Gallagher with a view to it being circulated widely by Fianna Fáil in support of de Valera's presidential candidature in 1959, was not printed because (Fianna Fáil said) it did not conform to the physical dimensions of free postage available to candidates.

35 UCD P155/86; Edward Patrick Coll, 'My cousin Ed', *The Rosary Magazine*, Jan. 1960, pp. 20–2; Farragher, *Alma Mater*, pp. 18,. 30; Gallagher Papers, TCD MS 10065/115, f. 4 (25 Feb. 1927): 'I made D. take a little food – sandwiches – and then some brandy.' See also Gallagher, MS 10065/128 (1927), p. 2 for 'I wanted to bring D. out and give him a bottle of claret.'; Joyce, 'de Valera', p. 245.

36 Deirdre McMahon, *Republicans and Imperialists: Anglo-Irish Relations in the 1930s* (Yale, 1984), p. 42, citing National Archives Washington, State Department Records RG59/84ID.001/3 and.00/1125.

37 Census 1901 sub Patrick Coll of Knockmore, Co. Limerick. For some tales of 'drinks and jinks' on the avenue, and two photographs of it see Farragher, *Alma Mater*, pp. 41–6, 65.

38 UCD P150/26 and 3561; Farragher, *Alma Mater*, pp. 39, 47–8.

39 UCD P150/170, from 'University Coll., Blackrock', 2 March 1901.

40 Farragher, *Alma Mater*, p. 39.

41 Farragher, *Alma Mater*, pp. 52–3 includes a photograph of the presentation inscription to 'Edward de Valera' by Fr John T. Murphy,

college president, 'Xmas, 1902'. I am grateful to the present Blackrock College archivist for her efforts to find the Bible.

42 De Valera to Dr Paddy Heffernan (UCD P150/26); 'Some recollections of the castle, Blackrock', dictabelt recorded 30 June 1956 (UCD P150/23); Farragher, *Alma Mater*, p. 65.

43 Farragher, *Alma Mater*, p. 33.

44 UCD P150/25; Minutes of debates (Blackrock College Archives); *Sunday Independent*, 19 March and *Cork Examiner*, 20 March 1922.

45 Farragher, *Alma Mater*, p. 58.

46 UCD P150/25; Blackrock College Archives; Above p. 000 for him on Napoleon.

47 UCD P150/49. On the UCD manuscript guide (p. 13) there is immediately above the description of this item a heading '*c*. Post-Rockwell College'. However, de Valera was paid as a teacher at Rockwell from September 1903 until June 1905 (UCD P150/41) and this paper was written while still at the Castle in 1903. For a discussion of some aspects of it see Farragher, *Alma Mater*, pp. 58–63.

48 Minute of meeting of 18 Feb. [1903] (Blackrock College Archives).

49 Some recollections of the Castle, Blackrock, dictabelt recorded 30 June 1956 (UCD P150/23).

50 UCD P150/23, 'dictated by Chief 27 April 1956'.

51 Farragher, *Alma Mater*, p. 54.

52 UCD P150/ 200, 'University College, Blackrock', 6 Oct. 1902.

53 Farragher, *Alma Mater*, pp. 55, 57, 89; UCD P150/23 refers to 'going over to Keegans'.

54 Farragher, *Alma Mater*, pp. 30, 41–5, 64.

55 Farragher, *Alma Mater*, pp. 81, 105; *ibid.*, p. 18 for a photograph of eighteen boarders at Blackrock in 1898, all but two of whom wear various kinds of flat cap. One of the two bareheaded ones on that occasion is de Valera.

56 De Valera to St Wilfrid's, 13 June 1903 (UCD P150/49). He states that along with mathematics (pure) and maths physics at the RUI he is studying Latin, Greek and French but that he is best qualified to teach maths. Now closed, St Wilfrid's was also known as Cotton College.

57 Farragher, *Alma Mater*, pp. 65–71.

58 R.F. Walker, 'The hundred years', *Rockwell College Annual 1964*, pp. 6–51; Farragher, *Alma Mater*, p. 71.

59 UCD 150/40 and 435.

60 Gallagher Papers, TCD MS 10065/115, f. 11.

61 *Freeman's Journal*, 7 June 1911; Farragher, *Alma Mater*, pp. 72–3. The other lay teachers were Jack Barrett, Tom O'Donnell and Patrick T. Cremer. O'Donnell claimed to be first to call him 'Dev'.

62 Reminiscences noted by Macardle (UCD P150/3662, with 'Rock field' for Rockwell in error); Partial scheme for an autobiography *c.* 1949 (Kathleen O'Connell Papers, UCD P155/86).

63 UCD P150/13, dictated 30 June 1956 (2nd half).

64 Patrick Ryan to de Valera 30 Jan. 1965
    and de Valera to Ryan, New York, 6
    Feb. 1965 (UCD P150/44).

65 'Recollections of riding horses, etc.'
    (UCD P150/87); 'Country life in
    Bruree' (UCD P150/87); Photo and
    gun licence (UCD 150/40–4).

66 Dwane, *de Valera*, pp. 26–7.

67 De Valera to Patrick Ryan, New York,
    6 Feb. 1965 (UCD P150/44).

68 UCD P150/3375; Farragher, *Alma
    Mater*, p. 77.

69 'Joining Gaelic League and later the
    Volunteers: Dictated by Chief 29th
    Oct. 1956' (UCD P150/445).

70 Gallagher Papers, TCD MS 10065/115,
    ff. 11–12 (1927).

71 Farragher, *Alma Mater*, pp. 77–8.

72 Letters to de Valera in Rockwell
    College from Louis C. Purser, junior
    bursar and other members of the
    academic and administrative staff in
    Trinity College Dublin in answer to his
    queries about applying for a sizarship
    or scholarship to the college, and about
    entrance fees and various chemistry,
    physics, mathematics and experimental
    science lectures, 15 Aug. 1902–7 Sept.
    1905 (UCD P150/42); Reminiscences
    noted by Macardle (UCD P150/3662).

73 Outline of a biography (UCD
    P150/380); Partial scheme for an
    autobiography *c.* 1949 (Kathleen
    O'Connell Papers, UCD Archives
    P155/86).

74 *Rockwell College Annual 1964*, p. 147.

75 Gallagher Papers, NLI MS 18,375/2,
    'Broadcast. De Valera', pp. 3, 17.

76 Farragher, *Alma Mater*, p. 19.

77 Farragher, *Alma Mater*, pp. 19–20; Dr
    Paddy Heffernan to de Valera, 8 Aug.
    1964 (UCD P150/26).

78 UCD P150/23, 'dictated by Chief,
    27 April 1956', includes 'Clontarf
    match – Stewart's foul tackle, my
    reaction. Harry Boland's later
    comment'; Farragher, *Alma Mater*,
    pp. 25–6 and 49 for a photograph
    of the 1902 ticket. A postcard in
    the Blackrock Archives has Michael
    Smithwick dropping a line to
    'E.J. de Valera Esq., Hon. Sec.
    B.C.F.C.' to explain he 'cannot
    possibly play tomorrow'.

79 De Valera to Patrick Ryan in New
    York, 6 Feb. 1965 (UCD P150/44).

80 James Mellett, *If Any Man Dare*
    (Dublin, 1963), pp. 2–3.

81 *Ibid.*

82 *Nationalist*, 12, 23 and 30 March
    1904, as transcribed at UCD P150/47;
    Rockwell College Annual 1964, p. 34.

83 *Cork Examiner,* 31 March 1904.

84 *Cork Examiner,* 5 April 1904.

85 'Teachers, dictated by Chief 13
    Sept. 1956' (UCD P150/8); *Cork
    Examiner* and *Limerick Leader*, 13
    March 1905 (cutting of the latter at
    UCD P150/40); *Cork Examiner*, 2 Feb.
    1905 for his converting Rockwell's
    sole try in a match against Queen's
    College.

86 Gallagher Papers, NLI MS 18,375 (15
    and 20). Cusack was not a pupil at
    Blackrock College but taught there in
    1874–5.

87 Mellett, *If Any Man Dare*, p. 3.

88 *Cork Examiner,* 11 April 1905.

89 *Cork Examiner,* 5 April 1905.

90 *Cork Examiner,* 27 March, 5 and 11
    April 1905.

91 Farragher, *Alma Mater*, pp. 88–9, 91.

92 *Freeman's Journal*, 13 Nov. 1905 and 12
    March 1906 and 2 Dec. 1907; *Sunday*

Independent, 20 Jan. 1907; *Evening Herald*, 29 and 30 Nov. 1907.

93 Farragher, *Alma Mater*, p. 91; *Evening Herald*, 21 March 1908.

94 *Evening Herald*, 21 Feb. 1908 and 13 Nov. 1909; *Irish Independent,* 7 March 1908.

95 Dr J.P. Brennan to de Valera, 8 Jan. 1960 and de Valera to Brennan, 27 Jan. 1960 (UCD P150/44).

96 Dr J.P. Brennan to de Valera, 22 July 1962 (UCD P150/44).

97 Gallagher Papers, NLI MS 18,375 (9), page torn from small diary dated Wed., 26 February, with '1945' added in hand.

98 Gallagher Papers, NLI MS 18,375 (15 and 20).

99 *Rockwell College Annual* 1964, p. 24. For hurling and other sports in Bruree see National Folklore Collection, Schools, vol. 0498, pp. 129–30.

6. Getting On

1 UCD P150/87.

2 UCD P150/52; Farragher, *Alma Mater*, pp. 87–8; *Irish Times*, 4 Sept. 1963 and 29 Nov. 1905; *Freeman's Journal*, 29 Nov. 1906; Playbill at https://catalogue.nli.ie/Record/vtls000662183; UCD P150/201 for a postcard from his half-brother, redirected to him at Belvedere College on 10 Sept. 1905 from Rockwell College to which Thomas had mailed it.

3 UCD P150/170.

4 UCD P150/87.

5 UCD P150/36; Letter from de Valera to the Registrar, UCG, 20 April 1912 (UCD P150/58).

6 *Dáil Éireann Debates*, 2 March 1934; UCD P150/1106.

7 Places he stayed etc. (UCD P150/437–8); Personal dates [1826–1910] (UCD P150/435).

8 Deed of employment (UCD P150/53); Seán O'Faoláin, *De Valera* (Harmondsworth, UK, 1939), p. 10. Ronan Fanning describes the title as 'grandiloquent' (*DIB* at de Valera).

9 File relating to de Valera's time at Carysfort (UCD P150/53–4); Farragher, *Alma Mater*, p. 89; *DIB* for Alice and Patrick Keenan.

10 Places he stayed etc. (UCD P150/437–8). Barrett was one of those to whom de Valera drafted a farewell message in 1916 (UCD P150/539).

11 UCD P150/170 (no. 7 of 7 letters).

12 Tom to 'Mr. E. De Valera, Blackrock University', June 1907 (UCD P150/201).

13 Personal dates (UCD P150/435); Farragher, *Alma Mater*, pp. 90–1, 95–6.

14 UCD P150/200 and P150/207 (photo said to be of Eddie and Tom, half-brothers, at Lisdoonvarna in an unidentified crowd).

15 Terry de Valera, *Memoir*, p. 150; J. Doran O'Reolly, 'The boyhood of de Valera', *Irish Digest*, Apr. 1974, pp. 13–16 (copy at UCD P150/88).

16 Charles Russell (secretary and manager of the National Maternity Hospital), 5, Eaton Sq., Monkstown, to de Valera, 1971 (UCD P150/438, last item). Places he stayed etc. (UCD P150/437–8).

17 *Ibid*. The marriage register entry of 1910 may be seen free online at civil-records.irishgenealogy.ie, along with a certified 'true copy' of 1911. On the

former his father in given as 'Vivian de Valleer [*sic*]', clearly an error that de Valera himself would not have made and a reminder of the unreliability of details in some official records. It is 'Vivian de Valera' in the 1911 copy. His father's 'rank or profession' is given in each as 'professor'.

18 Farragher, *Alma Mater*, p. 105.

19 Dictated 29 Oct. 1956 (UCD P150/445). This source also gives 'Next step in my public career was the foundation of the Volunteers on the 25th of November, 1913'; Longford and O'Neill, *de Valera*, p. 15.

20 Dictated 29 Oct. 1956 (UCD P150/445) and similar recollections at UCD P150/87.

21 'Ó Conaire, Pádraic', by Lesa Ní Mhunghaile in *DIB*. The original statue is protected in Galway City Museum, with a bronze replica in Eyre Square.

22 'O'Rahilly, Thomas Francis ("T.F.")', by Diarmuid Ó Sé in *DIB*.

23 Dictated 29 Oct. 1956 (UCD P150/445).

24 Farragher, *Alma Mater*, p. 21

25 Dictated 29 Oct. 1956 (UCD P150/445).

26 'Joining Gaelic League and later the Volunteers, dictated 29 Oct. 1956' (UCD P150/445); Farragher, *Alma Mater*, p. 21. Brian Ó Cuív, 'Irish language and literature, 1845–1921', *Oxford New History of Ireland*, 6, pp. 385–432 at p. 407 notes that 'In 1890 only eighteen out of 230 boys who sat for the Senior Grade Intermediate Examination (that is, 7.8 per cent) took Irish.'

27 RTÉ, *Boy from Bruree*, part 3.

28 Brendan Walsh, '"Frankly and Robustly National": Padraig Pearse, the Gaelic League and the campaign for Irish at the National University', *Studies*, 103, no. 141 (2014), pp. 318–330 at p. 324; Ó Cuív, 'Irish language and literature', pp. 407–8.

29 *Conversation with Éamon de Valera*, NBC recording and transcript (UCD Archives P150/420–1). The interviewer appears to have been Prof. Curtis Baker Bradford of Grinnell College, Iowa and visiting professor in American Literature at Trinity College Dublin. On YouTube the programme appears to be dated wrongly as 1955, because its copyright credit gives 1958.

30 *An Claidheamh Soluis*, 31 Oct. 1908 for 'Micheal Smidic'.

31 For some instances see, for example, UCD P150/3685 (p. 771), 3678, 3700 and 3701. For the circumflex see Ó Faoláin, *de Valera* (1933), frontispiece. Also see a memorial of 3 June 1940 at the Registry of Deeds, Dublin, signed 'Eámon de Valéra [*sic*]' at https://www.tailte.ie/en/blog/education-presentation-rebranded-august-2023.pdf (20 March 2024). The approved biography by Longford and O'Neill, published in England, omits any accent on his first name. This may be a reflection of the cultural or technical limitations of some British publishers when it comes to rendering Irish words and phrases in print.

32 Recollections (UCD P150/87).

33 Gallagher Papers, MS NLI 18,375 (18), 'note, 25 Sept. 1954'. All accents/fadas added here. 'Ó Murthuile, Seán', by Patrick Long in *DIB* does not mention Sinn Féin.

34 Dictated 29 Oct. 1956 (UCD P150/445).

35 Kate to Tom Wheelwright, 23 June 1916 (UCD P150/201).

36 For example, National Library of Ireland POOLEWP2752-3 (c. 1918), NPA DEV27, 32–33, 40 and OKE/28 (c. 1920).

37 *Dáil Éireann Debates*, 14 Dec. 1921.

38 McCullagh, *De Valera*, vol. 1, 45; Examination results (UCD P150/25 and 35).

39 Farragher, *Alma Mater*, p. 39.

40 Synge, 'de Valera', p. 19; UCD P150/3334.

41 Reminiscences noted by Macardle (P150/3662).

42 Synge, 'de Valera', pp. 18–23.

43 David Fitzpatrick, 'Éamon de Valera at Trinity College', *Hermathena*, 133 (Winter, 1982), pp. 7–14; Letters from TCD to de Valera, Aug. 1902–Sept. 1905 (UCD P150/42); Correspondence between de Valera and Lady Whittaker (UCD P150/57); *Irish Independent*, 5 July 1906 for 'Edward de Valera'.

44 UCD P150/54 for the printed booklet.

45 Gallagher Papers, TCD MS 10065/115, f. 12. It is unclear exactly what 'propaganda' he had in mind.

46 Gallagher Papers, TCD MS 10065/163 f. 2v (9 Jan. 1928).

47 UCD P150/36 and 58.

48 UCD P150/58.

49 UCD P150/57; *ibid.*, P150/2609 re Whittaker and the DIAS.

50 UCD P150/58.

51 Partial scheme for an autobiography c. 1949 (Kathleen O'Connell Papers, UCD Archives P155/86).

52 UCD P150/75; Places where I lived apart from colleges and 'Digs' (UCD P150/438); *An Claidheamh Soluis*, 12 Aug. 1911 and 26 July 1913, advertisements.

53 See Donal McCartney, *The National University of Ireland and Éamon de Valera* (Dublin, 1983), pp. 19–20; E. Brian Titley, 'Rejecting the modern world: the educational ideas of Timothy Corcoran', *Oxford Review of Education*, 9, no. 2 (1983), pp. 137–45.

54 UCD P150/200.

55 UCD P150/58.

56 Ryan, *Unique Dictator*, p. 26.

57 UCD P150/58 includes the drafts.

58 UCD P150/64–6, 2902, 2909, 2913; 'De Brún Padraig (Patrick Browne)' by L.W. White in *DIB*. About this time Mannix, born in Charleville, was consecrated coadjutor-archbishop of Melbourne. He became archbishop there in 1917.

59 UCD P150/65.

60 Dwane, *de Valera*, p. 41.

61 John J. Horgan, *Parnell to Pearse: Some Recollections and Reflections* (Dublin, 1948), pp. 242–6.

62 UCD P150/65.

63 McCartney, *NUI and de Valera*, pp. 20–4 citing minutes of the UCC governing body (13 June 1913), minutes of the NUI senate, iii, 140 (4 July 1913) and the registrar's minute book.

64 Horgan, *Parnell to Pearse*, pp. 246–7 (also quoted at McCartney, *NUI and de Valera*, pp. 21–2).

65 UCD P150/65–6.

66 See McCartney, *NUI and de Valera*, p. 18; Correspondence from the NUI (UCD P150/34–35, 60–2, 67). These papers show that in May 1910, on his application pursuant to the Irish Universities Act 1908, de Valera who

had a BA from the Royal University was 'registered as a graduate, with the corresponding degree, viz.: Bachelor of Arts of the National University of Ireland'. On 1 May 1914 he received a certificate for the degree of Bachelor of Science from the NUI (P150/67).

67 UCD 150/58 for Conway's testimonial of 1912; McCartney, *NUI and de Valera*, p. 18.

68 P150/22, dictated 24 April 1956.

69 UCD P150/98 press cutting, and /2510 MacDonald to de Valera (April 1938); R.P. Graves, *Life of Sir William Rowan Hamilton* (3 vols, Dublin and London, 1882–9) vol. 2, pp. 434–5.

70 UCD P150/3334, with text reproduced at J.L. Synge, 'Éamon de Valera 14 October 1882–29 August 1975, Elected F.R.S. 1968', *Biographical Memoirs of Fellows of the Royal Society*, 22 (Nov. 1976), pp. 634–53.

71 Fitzpatrick, 'de Valera at Trinity', gives his marks examination by examination.

72 Terry de Valera, 'My father Éamon de Valera'.

73 'Ireland: The Old Country', *Time*, 29 June 1959.

74 Maureen M. Julian, 'Éamon de Valera, Erwin Schrödinger, and the Dublin Institute for Advanced Studies', *Journal of Chemical Education*, 60, no. 3 (March 1983), pp. 199–200.

75 *Dáil Éireann Debates*, 10 and 25 April 1940.

76 Alexis Fitzgerald, 'Éamon de Valera', *Studies*, 64, no 255 (Autumn, 1975), pp. 207–14 at 213.

77 IAS at https://www.ias.edu/about/mission-history (20 March 2024). See also Flexner, 'The usefulness of useless

knowledge', *Harpers*, 179 (July/Nov. 1939), pp. 544–52.

78 Synge, 'de Valera', p. 649.

79 *Éamon de Valera Centenary* (Institiúid ArdLéinn, Bhaile Átha Cliath, 1982), 42 pages.

80 Synge, 'de Valera', p. 638.

81 Kathleen O'Sullivan, 'Mathematics in the life of Éamon de Valera', UCC doctoral dissertation, 2009.

82 Gallager Papers, NLI MS 18,375.

83 UCD P150/13 and 13A, dictabelt recorded 6 Aug. 1955.

84 RTÉ, *Boy from Bruree*, part 4.

85 Gallagher Papers, NLI MS 18,375 (18), 'Notes re Dev', handwritten unlined page numbered 1.

86 Longford and O'Neill, *de Valera*, p. 7; UCD P150/87.

87 Farragher, *Alma Mater*, p. 84.

88 *Ibid.*, p. 34.

89 *Ibid.*, p. 39.

90 UCD P150/170 (no. 5 of 8 letters).

91 De Valera to St Wilfrid's, 13 June 1903 (UCD P150/49).

92 Farragher, *Alma Mater*, p. 83.

93 Keogh to de Valera, 1 Oct. 1905 (UCD P150/50).

94 Coogan, *De Valera*, pp. 37–8, citing 'President's Diary', Dublin Archdiocesan Archives, Clonliffe College.

95 Eddie to Kate, 21 Dec. 1905 (UCD P150/170, no. 6 of 7 letters. Full text above at p. 000).

96 Keogh to 'Michael', Sept. 1906 (UCD P150/50).

97 UCD P150/172, with undated notes sent from de Valera in Dartmoor for Sinéad to forward to Kate. Thomas Wheelwright was ordained 7 June 1916, first Mass 11 June 1916

(Souvenir of my ordination, UCD P150/203).

98 De Valera to Kate, Arbour Hill, Easter Sunday, 20 April 1924 (UCD P150/178).

99 UCD P150/657, Sept. 1923. His underlining.

100 Letter from de Valera to an unnamed correspondent (Blackrock College Archives); Alfred Isacsson, 'Irish in his life: Donal O'Callaghan, O. Carm.', *NYIHR*, 24 (2010), pp. 13–20; Smith, *Macardle*, pp. 136–7.

101 Farragher, *Alma Mater*, pp. 30, 41–5, 64.

102 UCD P150/87 and 129; Recollections, cited at Terry de Valera, *Memoir*, p. 107.

103 Her birth certificate may be viewed at Irish genealogy.ie and is consistent with the census for 1901 and 1911. In an ostensible error her date of birth appears as 1875 in *DIB*.

104 Census 1901, 1911; Blackrock College Archives for Jane (Sinéad) to Olivia (19 Aug. 1961); Griffith's *United Irishman*, 23 Dec. 1899 lists 'J. Flanagan; L. Flanagan' among donors, both moderate and 'advanced' nationalist, who each contributed half a crown to the Irish Transvaal Ambulance Corps Fund.

105 Inghinidhe na h–Éireann, *First Annual Report, Session 1900–1901*; Colum Kenny, *The Enigma of Arthur Griffith: Father of Us All* (Newbridge, 2020), p. 86; Mary Trotter, *Ireland's National Theatres: Political Performance and the Origins of the Irish Dramatic Movement* (Syracuse, NY, 2001), pp. 82–6.

106 *An Claidheamh Soluis*, 27 Dec. 1902.

107 *Conversation with Éamon de Valera*, NBC recording and transcript (UCD P150/420–1); *An Claidheamh Soluis*, 29 Sept., 3, 6 and 20 Oct. 1906, gives the league's first registrar as Eamonn Ceannt, with Patrick Pearse presiding at a meeting of its committee. Douglas Hyde and the Archbishop of Dublin also supported it; *Drogheda Independent*, 22 June 1907; *Nationalist and Leinster Times*, 20 Oct. 1906.

108 UCD P150/87; Personal dates [1826–1910] (UCD P150/425) has '1909: Met Sinead at Leinster College'.

109 O'Toole to Thomas St John Gaffney, 3 Aug. 1917 (NLI MS 13,085/1vii/9). 'Colmcille' ostensibly a slip for 'Celtic'.

110 UCD P150/171 (no. 1 of 3 letters).

111 Dublin North 2087831 (8 Jan. 1910): https://civilrecords.irish-genealogy.ie/churchrecords/images/marriage_returns/marriages_1910/09975/5626921a.pdf

112 UCD P150/87; Personal dates [1826–1910] (UCD P150/425) has '1909'.

113 Gallagher Papers, NLI MS 18,375 (9) no. 8, page torn from small diary, printed date 28 Feb., with 1945 added in hand.

114 UCD P150/3704.

115 Letters, Kathleen O'Connell Papers (UCD P155/4); McCullagh, *De Valera*, vol. 1, pp. 183–4.

116 Kim Bielenberg, 'De Valera in love', *Irish Independent*, 16 Dec. 2000.

117 De Valera signs as 'Edward de Valera' the 1911 census form, on which his son's name is spelt 'Vivian'. The latter's birth on 13 December 1910 had also been registered then as 'Vivian' (Bhibhian de Bhailéara). On the 1911

census return Dev's 'rank, profession or occupation' is 'BA, Dip. in Educ. Math Professor'.

118 Postcard (UCD P150/201).

119 *Irish Times*, 25 Nov. 2000, includes part of this letter put up for auction but now missing.

120 'Author's copy' of this letter, translated by Micheal O'Siadhail, quoted at some length at Coogan, *De Valera*, pp. 41–2. The letter does not appear to be among the de Valera papers in UCD. No date in August is given. The Irish word *spéirbhean* means 'a beautiful woman' but perhaps in this context the 'ideal woman'. See also Sinéad de Valera, *An Spéir-bhean ina Suan* (Dublin, 1958).

121 She places no accent on the name throughout.

122 Vivion de Valera, born 13 Dec. 1910 (*DIB*), was Éamon and Sinéad de Valera's eldest child.

123 Máirín de Valera, born 12 April 1912 (*DIB*).

124 Letter dated 12 Dec., postmarked Rochester 14 Dec. 1912 (UCD P150/171).

125 UCD P150/183. Pages of this letter missing.

126 Sinéad to Hughes, 6 May 1917 (Blackrock College Archives); Places of Residence, various documents (UCD P150/437–8); Farragher, *Alma Mater*, p. 55. Their first five children were born on 13 Dec. 1910, 12 Apr. 1912, 11 Oct. 1913, 25 July 1915, 3 Nov. 1916.

127 Cited at Brian Hanley, Historian-in-Residence at Dublin City Library and Archive, 'Sinéad de Valera' (2017), at https://www.dublincity.ie/library/blog/sinead-de-valera.

128 UCD P150/129; Places of Residence, various documents (UCD P150/437–8) indicting that some months after the birth of their last child (Terry) they moved from Greystones to 18 Claremont Road in Sandymount and then, in 1924 or 1925 to nearby Elm Villa which was said to be haunted. Then came Springville, Cross Avenue (March 1930), Bellevue, Cross Ave. (Sept 1933), Teach Cuillin, Cross Ave. (1936) and Herberton – 'formerly owned by Judge Greene' – in July 1940; Terry de Valera, *Memoir*, pp. 14, 1–22, 25–9.

129 Sinéad to Hughes, 11 July [1916] (Blackrock College Archives); Recollections, quoted at Terry de Valera, *Memoir*, p. 113; Longford and O'Neill, *de Valera*, p. 68.

130 Ó Cuív, 'Irish language and literature', p. 411.

131 J.C. Beckett, *The Making of Modern Ireland* (2nd ed., London, 1981), p. 435.

132 Gallagher Papers, TCD MS 10065/163, f. 3 (10 Jan. 1928).

133 Horgan, *Parnell to Pearse*, p. 244.

134 Augustine Martin, 'To make a right rose tree. Reflections on the poetry of 1916', *Studies*, 1966 (Spring), pp. 38–50 at p. 41. See also *Studies*, 2016 (Spring), for a number of articles relevant in this context, including notably Séamus Murphy, 'Dark liturgy, bloody praxis: the 1916 Rising'.

135 Blackrock College Archives (1 July 1915). See also ch. 4 at note 55.

136 UCD P150/3704.

137 Dictated by President de Valera to Marie O'Kelly, 1962 (UCD P150/445).

138 Dictated 29 Oct. 1956 (UCD P150/445). Also 'The Volunteers, dictated 1950' (UCD P150/447).

139 'The Volunteers' (UCD P150/447–9, including his draft of a letter to the *Evening Telegraph* about the Volunteers of Donnybrook – said to be his first letter to a newspaper).

140 Gallagher Papers, NLI MS 18,375 (2), 'Broadcast: de Valera', p. 5.

141 UCD P150/449; Denis Gwynn, *De Valera* (London, 1933), pp. 11, 25.

142 'Dictated 29 Oct. 1956' (UCD P150/445).

143 David Fitzpatrick, 'de Valera in 1917: the Undoing of the Easter Rising' in O'Carroll and Murphy (eds), *De Valera and His Times*, p. 103.

144 UCD P150/445, dictated 29 Oct. 1955.

145 P.S. O'Hegarty, *The Victory of Sinn Féin* (Dublin and London, 1924), pp. 14, 18.

146 Gallagher Papers, NLI MS 18,375 (18).

147 Maciej Ruczaj, '"Daringly, yet with reverence": Pearse, Mickiewicz and the theology of national messianism,' *Études Irlandaises*, 39, no. 1 (2014), pp. 57–71.

148 Gallagher Papers, TCD MS 10065/163, f. 3 (10 Jan. 1928); Ryan, *Unique Dictator*, p. 66.

149 Recollections, cited at Terry de Valera, *Memoir*, p. 110.

150 Letter, 11 March 1915, at *The Letters of P.H. Pearse*, ed. Séamas Ó Buachalla (Gerrards Cross, 1980), p. 340; Gallagher Papers, NLI MS 18,375 (2), 'Broadcast: de Valera', p. 8.

151 'Easter Week 1916, Mount Street Bridge by Simon Donnelly' and related papers (UCD P150/504, 506–7);

Charles Townshend, *Easter 1916: The Irish Rebellion* (London, 2006), pp. 175–8, 199–201.Max Caulfield, *The Easter Rebellion* (New York, 1963 and London, 1963/4); Coogan, *De Valera*, pp. 66–74; McCullagh, *De Valera*, vol. 1, pp. 84–96.

7. Destiny

1 UCD P150/131 for this undated holograph note from de Valera to his wife, presumably composed in April 1916 – although this may be a later copy or recollection.

2 Gallagher Papers, NLI MS 21,273, p. 3.

3 Síobhra Aiken, *Spiritual Wounds: Trauma, Testimony & the Irish Civil War* (Newbridge, 2022).

4 Coogan, *De Valera*, p. 63.

5 *Irish Times*, 25 Nov. 2000, including an image of this letter for sale at Mealy's. The letter itself has not been found.

6 Biographical account of Sinéad de Valera (UCD P150/129).

7 Sinéad to Hughes, May 1916 (with note by Hughes) and 26 Jan. 1917 (Blackrock College Archives); *Irish Times*, 25 Nov. 2000, for the text and a partial image of one of the letters.

8 Copy of letter sent anonymously to Coogan.

9 Blackrock College Archives (6 May 1917).

10 Sinéad to Frank Hughes, May 1916 (Blackrock College Archives); Transcript at Coogan, *De Valera*, p. 63 who cites de Valera to Sinéad, Lewes Jail, Easter Saturday 1917 ('author's copy').

11 *Irish Times*, 25 Nov. 2000, being one of the stolen letters.

12 Whether or not he was the most senior commandant to survive is contested. See, for example, 'Whitmore, W.J. Brennan-' by Patrick Long in *DIB*, and John Gibney's article (2022) at https://www.theirishstory.com/2022/04/28/the-last-commandant-general-of-1916-sean-mcloughlins-easter-rising/ (20 March 2024).

13 Sinéad to Frank Hughes, 11 July [1916] (Blackrock College Archives); UCD P150/3375; Robert Schmuhl, *Ireland's Exiled Children: America and the Easter Rising* (New York, 2016), pp. 119–48 ('Éamon de Valera: The Myth of Exile'); Gallagher Papers, NLI MS 18,375 (19), Memorandum of Michael Rynne (civil servant and lawyer) regarding the Taoiseach's American citizenship, 25 April 1946.

14 Gallagher Papers, TCD MS 10065/115, f. 3 (25 Feb. 1927).

15 UCD P150/172.

16 UCD P150/203.

17 UCD P150/171 (no. 3 of 3 letters at this reference number). The preceding letter at UCD P150/171 (no. 2) indicates that Kate and her husband left South Goodman Street during 1912.

18 Gerald Griffin, *The Collegian or The Colleen Bawn: A Tale of Garryowen*. First published 1829, and adapted for the stage by Dion Boucicault. Griffin was a Limerickman and Garryowen is in the neighbourhood of Limerick City.

19 UCD P150/187.

20 David Fitzpatrick, 'Decidedly a personality: de Valera's performance as a convict, 1916–17', *History Ireland*, 10, no. 2 (Summer 2002), pp. 40–6.

21 *Freeman's Journal*, 27 Oct. 1917; Roisín Higgins and Regina Uí Chollatin (eds), *The Life and After-Life of P.H. Pearse: Pádraic Mac Piarais: Saol agus Oidhreacht* (Dublin, 2009), *passim*.

22 *Cork Examiner* and *Freeman's Journal*, 27 Oct. 1917; *Sacred Heart Review*, 53, no. 8 (6 Feb. 1915), pp. 118–22); 'The martyrdom of Belgium', *Nationalist and Leinster Times*, 16 Jan. 1915 (pastoral published at the behest of the bishop of Kildare and Leighlin); *Meath Chronicle*, 23 Jan. 1915; *Drogheda Independent*, 30 Jan. 1915.

23 Dwane, *de Valera*, p. 53; C. Kenny, '"As if by magic"?: Arthur Griffith's "surrender" of the presidency of Sinn Féin to Éamon de Valera in 1917', *Éire-Ireland*, 52, nos 3&4 (2017), pp. 190–211.

24 Michael Laffan, *The Resurrection of Ireland: the Sinn Féin Party 1916–1923* (Cambridge, 1999), pp. 107–8, 122–8.

25 See, for example, Eamonn [*sic*] de Valera, *Ireland's Case Against Subscription* (Dublin and London, 1918), his pamphlet based on a speech of his own.

26 UCD P150/173, dated 2 July (year not given but he was in jail from May 1918 until February 1919).

27 UCD P150/173.

28 Gallagher Papers, NLI MS 18,375 (18), typed; Schmuhl, *Ireland's Exiled Children*, p. 129.

29 Colum Kenny, 'Arthur Griffith: President of the Revolutionary Dáil Éireann (Irish Parliament), and Father of the Irish State' in Maria Betlem, Castella Pujols et al. (eds), *Presidencies of Parliamentary and Representative Institutions, 1500–2000*, (Madrid, 2024), pp. 307–31.

30 F.M. Carroll, 'De Valera and the Americans: the early years, 1916–1923', *Canadian Journal of Irish Studies*, 8, no. 1 (1982), pp. 38–44.

31 *Rosary Magazine*, Jan. 1960, pp. 20–2 at 21.

32 Letter from Tom to Kathleen O'Connell, 17 July 1920 (UCD P155/3); *New York Times*, 23 July 1946.

33 Ó Faoláin, *de Valera* (1933), pp. 74–5.

34 McCullagh, *De Valera*, vol. 1, pp. 183–4.

35 Gallagher Papers TCD MS 10065/128, p. 3.

36 Gallagher Papers, TCD MS 10065/126 for the actual card he sent his wife.

37 UCD P150/191, postcard of her 'listening to phonograph record recently made by her distinguished son. This record is an impassioned appeal to the American people to aid Ireland in her struggle for independence'; *ibid.*, 150/192, de Valera and his mother 1919/20; *New York Herald Tribune*, 13 June 1932 (p. 15).

38 *New York Times*, 23 July 1946; UCD P150/204.

39 Circular by Harry Boland, 16 Oct. 1919 (UCD P150/869).

40 Letter to Boland from the Hotel Savery, Des Moines, Iowa, 14 Oct. 1919 (UCD P150/870).

41 C.S. Andrews, *Dublin Made Me* (Dublin, 1979), p. 307. Dorothy Macardle to de Valera, 21 Aug. 1936 (UCD P150/3662).

42 *Irish World and American Industrial Liberator*, 25 Oct. 1919. Transcript at http://historyhub.ie/wp-content/files_mf/1370809868EamondeValeraTheChief.pdf (20 March 2024). Perhaps most extensively extracted by

the *Limerick Leader*, 14 Nov. 1919. Also see *Irish Independent*, 11 Nov. 1919 and *Nenagh Guardian*, 15 Nov. 1915.

43 'Draft Interview (Broadcast Recording) with Miss Joan Hickey, Wisconsin, U.S., Oct. 8th 1955' re de Valera's tour of the USA 1919–20, 'with special reference to the Chippewa Indians and the current problem of partition' (UCD P150/1111).

44 Tadeusz Lewandowski, *Ojibwe, Activist, Priest: The Life of Father Philip Bergin Gordon, Tibishkogijik* (Wisconsin, 2019). The author states (p. 176) that de Valera later welcomed Gordon to Ireland; Paula Delfield, *The Indian Priest: Philip B. Gordon, 1885–1948* (Franciscan Herald Press, 1977).

45 Note 000 above.

46 Reminiscences noted by Macardle (UCD P150/3662).

47 Terry de Valera, *Memoir*, p. 16.

48 Owen Dudley Edwards, *Éamon de Valera* (Cardiff, 1987), p. 15, who cites no source. The anecdote is not found in Kevin McCarthy, 'Éamon de Valera's relationship with Robert Briscoe: a reappraisal', *Irish Studies in International Affairs*, 25 (2014), pp. 165–86.

49 Gordon to Kennedy Brothers, Minneapolis, 16 Nov. 1919 (UCD P150/871).

50 Note 000 above.

51 Reminiscences noted by Macardle (UCD P150/3662).

52 *Macbeth*, Act 3, sc. 4, lines copied into a ringbinder of de Valera's notes thought to be late 1940s (UCD P150/3704). The same ringbinder has a wide range of political, historical, literary and mathematical jottings.

53 UCD P150/657.

54 Gallagher Papers, NLI MS 18,375 (15), 2 Dec. 1944.

55 *Dáil Éireann Debates*, 14 Sept. 1921.

56 O'Faoláin, *de Valera* (1933), p. 10; UCD P150/382 referencing SPO 4043/1918.

57 M.J. MacManus, *Eamon de Valera: A Biography* (Dublin, 194), p. 9, quoting the classic 1847 English translation by James Clarence Mangan of a much older version in Irish.

58 León Ó Broin, *In Great Haste: The Letters of Michael Collins and Kitty Kiernan*, revised and extended by Cian Ó hÉigeartaigh (New York, 1996), pp. 114–15 for this letter.

59 *Irish Independent*, 18 and 20 March 1922; *Nationalist* and *Freeman's Journal*, 20 March 1922.

60 Bowman, 'Éamon de Valera, seven lives' in O'Carroll and Murphy (eds), *De Valera and His Times*, p. 191; 'de Valera, Éamon' by Ronan Fanning in *DIB*.

61 Reminiscences noted by Macardle (P150/3662).

62 *Evening Herald*, 14 Oct. 1922; *Cork Examiner*, 16 Oct. 1922. The letter was written to Cathal Ó Murchadha (Charles Murphy, ex TD, had served under de Valera in 1916).

63 Richard Dunphy, *The Making of Fianna Fáil Power in Ireland 1923–1948* (Oxford, 1995), pp. 63–73.

64 Sinéad de Valera to an unnamed priest, 12 March 1926 (Blackrock College Archives); *Cork Examiner*, 15 April 1926; *Irish Times* 17 May 1926.

65 P.S. Dinneen, *Foclóir Gaedhilge agus Bearla* (Dublin, 1934 edition), at 'fál'.

66 Ruth Sherry, 'The story of the national anthem', *History Ireland*, 1, no. 4 (Spring 1966); *Dáil Éireann Debates*, 31 Jan. 2012, question to Fine Gael minister Michael Noonan.

67 Noel Whelan, *Fianna Fáil: A Biography of the Party* (Dublin, 2011), pp. 17–18.

68 See, for example, Donnacha Ó Beacháin, *The Destiny of the Soldiers: Fianna Fáil, Irish Republicanism and the IRA, 1926–1973* (Dublin, 2010) and Sean McGraw and Eoin O'Malley (eds) *One Party Dominance: Fianna Fáil and Irish Politics 1926–2016*, (Abingdon, 2018).

Postscript

1 UCD P150/1698.

2 UCD P150/3695, notebook *c.* 1933.

3 Coogan, *De Valera*, pp. viii, 41–2 (from Co. Galway, Aug. 1912, translated by Micheal O'Siadhail) and p. 63 (from Lewes Jail, Easter Saturday 1917).

4 *Irish Times*, 11 Dec. 2000; *Kilkenny People*, 15 Dec. 2000; *Irish Independent*, 16 Dec. 2000; Cian Ó hEigeartaigh, 'Dev's days of sensual longing', *Irish Times* 25 Nov. 2000.

5 This enigmatic entry appears in two forms in De Valera's lists of places he resided (UCD P150/438).

INDEX

Flanagan, Jane. *See* Ní Fhlannagáin
Ní Fhlannagáin, Sinéad 12–15, 177, 208–21
   and *passim*
Flexer, Abraham 200
Flint, Mary 171
Fordham University 88
Freeman's Journal 114–5, 178, 241
French College. *See* Blackrock College

GAA 168
Gaelic Football 168
Gaelic League 5, 13, 88, 177–82, 187, 195–6,
   209–10, 221, 223, 225, 228
Gallagher, Frank 10, 19, 46, 48, 53, 62, 88,
   101, 121, 160, 226, 245, 247
Galteemore 107
Galway 4, 178, 185, 189, 190, 194–5, 215
Gardaí 270
Garrouse, Bruree 73, 107, 119
Garryowen RFC 164–6
Gilmartin, Bishop Thomas 131, 155
Giraud/Girard, Frank 25–6, 49
Gogarty, Bishop H.A. of Kilimanjaro 178
Gonne, Maud 14, 210
[Mother] Gonzaga (Carysfort) 7
Gotham Theatre, Brooklyn 27
Gordon, Fr Philip 250–1
Graves, Arnold 117–8
Greenville, NJ 25, 49, 51, 59, 279
Great Famine 21, 40, 63–4, 66, 85–6
Greystones 12, 16, 214, 220, 241, 244, 254
Griffith, Arthur 7, 13, 189, 210, 221, 228,
   239, 241, 245, 253–4, 260–1, 264, 267,
   268, 271
Gwynn, Denis 227
Gubbins, John 72–75, 79, 107
Guns 156–8, 228, 246, 251, 259

Hamilton, Frederick 49, 51
Hamilton, Msgr James A. 49
Hamilton, Sir William Rowan 197–8
Hand, Geoffrey 45

Harnett, Fr Edward 61
Harper, E.H. 195–6
Healy, Fr Larry 129–30, 132, 138, 202
Healy MP, Tim 70
Heitler, Dr W.H. 97–98
Hennessy, Johanna 51
Hennessy, John 45
Hennessy, Fr. [Patrick] 49
Hennessy, Patrick 49
Hennessy, John 45
Herlihy, Pat 25
Holy Cross College. *See* Clonliffe
Holy Ghost Order. *See* Blackrock and
   Rockwell colleges.
Home Rule 5, 195, 196, 221, 224, 226, 233,
   239
Hooley's Minstrels, Brooklyn 26
Horace 132, 224, 262
Horgan, J.J. 195–6, 223
Horse-riding 74, 91, 95, 106–8, 127
Howardstown 86, 88, 93, 104
Howth 144, 171, 176, 191, 228
Hughes, Frank 133–5, 185, 220, 224, 232
Hurling 3, 92, 97, 140, 160, 166, 168, 189,
   225
Hyde, Douglas 13, 210

Ilchester, MD 215–6
Illegitimacy 46, 31, 33
Inghinidhe na hÉireann 13–14, 209–10
Institute for Advanced Studies, NJ 199–200
Intermediate Education Act 1878 116, 129,
   174
Irish Brigade 210
Irish Fireside Club 104, 112
Irish International Exhibition 176
Irish language 3, 13, 83, 85–8, 138, 142,
   177–81, 210, 215, 221, 232, 265
Irish Republican Brotherhood (IRB) 5, 71,
   181–2, 210, 228, 264
Irish Times 241
Irish Volunteers. *See* Volunteers

BY THE SAME AUTHOR

Ireland 1970–2020 (2024)
A Bitter Winter: The Irish Civil War 1922–23 (2022)
Midnight in London: The Anglo-Irish Treaty Crisis, 1921 (2021)
Kenmare: History and Survival – Fr John O'Sullivan
and the Famine Poor (2021)
The Enigma of Arthur Griffith: 'Father of Us All' (2020)
An Irish-American Odyssey: The Remarkable Rise of
the O'Shaughnessy Brothers (2014)
The Power of Silence: Silent Communication in Daily Life (2011)
Irish Patriot, Publisher and Advertising Agent: Kevin J. Kenny (2011)
Moments That Changed Us: Ireland, 1973–2005 (2005)
Fearing Sellafield (2003)
Battle of the Books: Cultural Controversy at a Dublin Library (2002)
The Role of Believing Communities in Building Peace in Ireland (1998)
Molaise: Abbot of Leighlin and Hermit of Holy Island (1998)
Tristram Kennedy and the Revival of Irish Legal Training (1996)
Kilmainham: A Settlement Older than Dublin (1995)
Standing on Bray Head: Hoping It Might Be So (poetry) (1995)
King's Inns and the Kingdom of Ireland, 1541–1800 (1992)